# ACCOUNTS FOR SOLICITORS

Lesley King LLB, Dip Crim (Cantab), Solicitor

Published by

College of Law Publishing,
Braboeuf Manor, Portsmouth Road, St Catherines, Guildford GU3 1HA



British Library Cataloguing-in-Publication Data

A catalogue record for this book is available from the British Library.

ISBN 0 905835 86 7

Typeset by Style Photosetting Ltd, Mayfield, East Sussex

Printed in Great Britain by Antony Rowe Ltd, Chippenham

# ACCOUNTS FOR SOLICITORS

# Preface

This book is written primarily for the Legal Practice Course but it is hoped that it will be useful for others.

It is divided into two parts. The first part deals with principles of double entry bookkeeping. The second part deals with the accounts of solicitors and, in particular, the need to account for client's money.

For the sake of brevity, the masculine pronoun has been used to include the feminine.

I would like to thank my colleagues at The College of Law at Store Street for their help in the preparation of this book, and College of Law Publishing for their support during the production process.

The law is stated as at 1 May 2005.

LESLEY KING
*London*

# Contents

# Tables

## Table of Statutes



## Table of Rules and Financial Reporting Standards

# Table of Abbreviations

| | |
|---|---|
| ACT | advance corporation tax |
| ASB | Accounting Standards Board |
| FREDs | Financial Reporting Exposure Drafts |
| FRRP | Financial Reporting Review Panel |
| FRSs | Financial Reporting Standards |
| LSC | Legal Services Commission |
| pa | per annum |
| PAYE | Pay As You Earn |
| SSAP | Statement of Standard Accounting Practice |
| UTIF | Urgent Issues Task Force |
| VAT | value added tax |
| VATA 1994 | Value Added Tax Act 1994 |

# Introduction

## Why do I need to know about accounts?

The short answer is because the Law Society says that you must. However, that does give rise to a further question – 'Why does the Law Society say that?'. The answer to this question is that knowledge and understanding of accounting principles will help you enormously in your professional and personal life, in the following ways.

### To deal with the affairs of clients

A great deal of the work done by solicitors requires an understanding of accounts.

- In commercial work, you may be involved in shares or asset takeovers and will need to be able to 'read' the accounts of the company involved to understand the problems of the transaction.
- In private client work, you may be involved in the valuation of shares for taxation purposes.
- In divorce work, you may have to look critically at the accounts of a business run by a spouse when you are trying to agree the amount of a cash settlement.

### To liaise with accountants

Particularly in commercial work, you may have to work closely with accountants on certain aspects of transactions.

You will find it helpful to understand some of the concepts and jargon accountants use. Accountants have studied law and have some understanding of the solicitor's job. Therefore, as a profession, we will be at a disadvantage if we have no understanding of their job.

### To deal with your own financial affairs

It is likely that you will have money to invest, if not now then in the not too distant future. An understanding of the principles of investment is vital to your financial well-being.

### To run your own business

If you become a partner you will have to manage the financial affairs of your firm. To do so adequately you must understand profitability and solvency, and the crucial importance of cash flow.

### To comply with the Law Society's requirements as to professional conduct

The Law Society requires a solicitor who handles money belonging to clients to keep particular accounts and to record dealings with such money in a particular way. While you are unlikely to have to make the entries yourself, you will be responsible if errors are made by others.

You will frequently have to decide whether a payment which is to be made by your firm for a particular client can be made from the client bank account or must be made from the office bank account. Similarly, when money is received from a client, you will have to decide whether it should be paid into the client or office bank account.

## How to use this book

This book is not designed for passive reading. It is a work book. You will find that throughout the text there are exercises for you to do. These exercises are an integral part of the course. They are designed to develop your understanding and confidence, not merely to test you on the material you have just read. Solutions to the exercises appear at the end of the relevant chapter. It is essential that you study these solutions as you go through the text.

# Part I

# ACCOUNTING PRINCIPLES

# Chapter 1
# Basic Bookkeeping – An Introduction



## 1.1 Accounts, bookkeeping and finance

Anyone who has any money needs to keep some sort of record of what happens to that money. You probably keep pay slips, bank and building society statements and (if you have any) share certificates and dividend warrants. These documents provide a useful personal record, allowing you to calculate your financial position, and assist you in your dealings with the Inland Revenue by providing the information necessary to calculate your tax liability.

Anyone who runs a business needs similar information to keep track of the financial position of the business. However, because so many different events occur in the life of a business, it is not enough to rely on individual documents to provide the full picture. It is preferable to take the relevant information relating to a particular type of transaction from the individual documents and enter it on separate records. These records are then summaries of the individual documents and are normally referred to as 'accounts'.

While a business is small, the proprietor will probably do everything single-handed, including keeping the accounts. However, once a business expands, the proprietor will employ people to assist in particular areas. It is common to employ a bookkeeper to keep the accounts. This is because accurate day-to-day bookkeeping is vital to the success of a business, allowing the proprietor to judge whether the business is making a profit and whether or not there is sufficient cash to pay bills, but it is a fairly tedious and time-consuming process which can be handled by a relatively unskilled person. The proprietor is then free to plan the strategy for the business, improve the quality of the product and the level of customer satisfaction.

In order to plan a business strategy, it is vital that the proprietor should receive accurate, up-to-date information from the bookkeeper and be able to interpret it correctly, drawing conclusions about past performance which will enable him to make decisions as to future development. An area where correct interpretation of information provided by the bookkeeper is particularly important is the financing of a business. Should cash be contributed by the proprietors, borrowed from outsiders or, in the case of a company, raised by the issue of shares?

People whose job involves the provision of finance, for example bankers, analysts, lawyers and accountants, will probably make no bookkeeping entries themselves but will have to be able to understand the accounts presented to them so that they can correctly interpret the information the accounts contain.

## 1.2 What are accounts?

As suggested in **1.1**, accounts are simply summaries of information contained elsewhere. There will be separate accounts for every type of business transaction and all aspects of each transaction will be recorded. For example, if in the course of your practice as a solicitor you want to make a payment on behalf of a client, you will requisition a cheque; the bookkeeper, having received your requisition, will issue the cheque (which will be signed by an authorised person) and will then record the payment in the accounts. The bookkeeper will record two separate consequences of the payment:

(a) the firm has less cash in its bank account;

(b) the firm is now owed money by the client.

## 1.3 What do accountants do?

Accountants can be involved in one or more of a number of different aspects of managing the finances of a business.

### 1.3.1 Recording information

We have already seen that it is very important to have records so that the proprietor can make informed decisions. The accountant will follow rules that govern the way in which information is recorded. It is important that there are rules since it means that anyone who has learnt the rules can understand accounts kept by another person on the basis of those rules.

### 1.3.2 Reporting

The accountant can analyse the information contained in the day-to-day accounts, summarise it and present it to management. Management can then use that information as the basis for decisions on strategy. However, it is not just management who need financial reports. There is also a demand for information from outside the business. The Inland Revenue demands tax returns and, in the case of companies, the government, potential investors and shareholders demand published accounts. Employees may also demand information about the financial health of the business, usually as a prelude to wage negotiations.

### 1.3.3 Auditing

Not all accountants are qualified to audit accounts. Only those who are registered auditors are authorised to sign a statutory audit report.

Companies (other than 'small' companies – see below) are *required* to have their accounts examined by a qualified auditor who must provide an opinion as to whether the accounts give a 'true and fair' view of the affairs of the company and its profit (or loss) for the relevant period. The auditors will have access to all the books and documents of the company. They are under an obligation to the members of the company and are also subject to disciplinary action by their professional body for misconduct. There have been cases recently where shareholders have alleged negligence or misconduct on the part of auditors and so the process must be carried out with great care.

In addition to the statutory audit required by the Companies Acts, auditors may be invited by management to carry out an audit as a means of obtaining an independent appraisal on the efficiency of the organisation.

A 'small' company, as defined in s 249A of the Companies Act 1985 as amended, is entirely exempt from the audit requirement if its turnover is not in excess of £5.6 million and its Balance Sheet total is not more than £2.8 million. Public companies must satisfy other criteria set out in s 249B.

Small and medium-sized companies are entitled to submit abbreviated accounts.

There is an overriding provision that holders of 10% or more of a company's issued share capital may require an audit.

As from 1 September 1998, firms of solicitors are required to employ a registered auditor to give an accountant's report on the quality of the solicitor's bookkeeping insofar as it relates to money held for clients. The requirements are now set out in Part F of the Solicitors' Accounts Rules 1998. Prior to that date, solicitors were required to employ an independent accountant. The change stems from The Law Society's attempts to reduce the costs of default. It became apparent from the reports of the Monitoring Unit and from inspections carried out by the Solicitors' Complaints Bureau's Investigation Accountants that some reporting accountants were not carrying out their duties effectively and that serious breaches of the Solicitors' Accounts Rules 1998, and, in some cases, frauds, had not been identified.

### 1.3.4 Preparing Profit and Loss Accounts and Balance Sheets

All businesses need an annual statement of profits (or losses) and of assets and liabilities. These are required for the proprietor's own purposes and for the purpose of the Inland Revenue. Accountants are frequently asked to prepare these 'Final Accounts' from the day-to-day accounts kept by the bookkeeper for the business.

### 1.3.5 Dealing with HM Revenue & Customs

Accountants frequently prepare tax returns for submission to HM Revenue & Customs on behalf of individuals and businesses. They can advise on the availability of deductions, exemptions and reliefs and on the correct treatment of income and capital gains.

## 1.4 Who needs financial reports?

### 1.4.1 The proprietor

As we have already suggested, the proprietor of a business will need to know how much profit the business has made in the most recent accounting period, how much cash is in the bank and what liabilities and other assets the business has at the end of the accounting period.

The proprietor will use this information to decide what action to take in the following period. If the business is basically profitable but currently short of cash because of over-enthusiastic expansion, the proprietor may try to borrow more money to improve cash flow. If machinery is outdated, it may be desirable to scrap the existing machinery and buy something more modern. If business is thriving, the proprietor may want to consider taking on more staff and premises and expanding the scale of operations.

### 1.4.2 Taxation records

These are extremely important. The government imposes a variety of different taxes, all of which require detailed records. If the business is unincorporated, the proprietor (or proprietors, if it is a partnership) will include the profit or profit share of the business in his income tax return. If the business is incorporated, the company itself will be liable for corporation tax.

If the business employs staff, it will have to operate the PAYE (Pay As You Earn) scheme. This requires the employer to deduct income tax from the employee and to account for it to HM Revenue & Customs. Records will have to be kept of salaries so that HM Revenue & Customs can check that the correct amount of tax has been deducted and certificates of deduction of income tax can be issued to employees.

The business will also have to deduct national insurance contributions from the employees. Again, detailed records will have to be kept for the Inland Revenue.

Finally, if the business is registered for VAT (value added tax), it will need to keep records of VAT charged to customers and of VAT charged to the business by suppliers. It will have to account to the government for the correct amount of VAT every quarter.

## 1.5 Regulation of accounts

### 1.5.1 Introduction

There is a great deal of regulation of accounts. Some of it is self-imposed by the accountancy profession and some of it is imposed externally, for example, the government insists that companies produce final accounts at the end of the accounting year in a particular form.

### 1.5.2 Self-imposed regulation

Why do accountants want uniformity?

A person could prepare a set of accounts for his own use on any idiosyncratic basis he wished, but such accounts would be useless to an outsider trying to understand the affairs of the business. Clearly, if accounts are prepared on a uniform basis (ie, if the same conventions have been followed and the same practices adopted), they will be usable by anyone.

Frequently, people want to compare the accounts of one business with the accounts of another (eg, when investing or considering the purchase of a business). It is impossible to make a valid comparison unless the accounts have been prepared on a uniform basis.

The accounting profession has, therefore, tried to achieve a measure of uniformity.

### 1.5.3 Accounting standards

There are six major accountancy bodies in the UK and Ireland. They established the Accounting Standards Committee which lays down definitive standards of financial accounting and reporting. These standards describe methods of accounting for application to all financial accounts. The aim is to give a true and fair view of the financial position of an enterprise and its profit or loss. Although these standards have no statutory force, non-compliance by an accountant could lead to disciplinary action by the appropriate governing body in a similar way to disciplinary proceedings against a solicitor. The accountancy bodies could enquire into apparent failure by their members to observe the standards or to disclose departures therefrom.

In 1990, as a result of the recommendations of the Dearing Committee, the Accounting Standards Board (ASB) was established. The ASB's function is to issue (or withdraw) accounting standards on its own authority.

Accounting standards issued by the ASB are known as Financial Reporting Standards (FRSs). Before an FRS is approved, the ASB issues an 'exposure draft' for general comment. These drafts are known as Financial Reporting Exposure Drafts (FREDs). The purpose of these standards is to set out the appropriate procedures for preparing accounts to give a 'true and fair view'.

The Dearing Committee considered recommending full statutory support for accounting standards but decided against it on the basis that it would make standards too legalistic and inhibit quick change where new developments required it. The Companies Act 1989 incorporated into the Companies Act 1985 a lesser form of statutory support. However, this relates only to the accounts of companies.

Companies which are not 'medium-sized' or 'small' companies are required by Sch 4, para 36A of the Companies Act 1985 to state within their accounts whether the accounts have been prepared in accordance with applicable accounting standards and to give details of, and the reasons for, any material departures. To that extent, FRSs issued by it have an element of statutory force.

Companies which qualify as small companies may elect to adopt a single reporting standard known as the Financial Reporting Standard for Smaller Entities, rather than follow all the individual SSAPs and FRSs.

For this purpose, a 'small' company is one which satisfies two of the following criteria:

(a) turnover not more than £5.6 million;
(b) Balance Sheet total not more than £2.8 million;
(c) not more than 50 employees.

## 1.6 What does a business want from its accounts?

### 1.6.1 Information

A business needs to know:

(a) what income it has generated in a particular period; and
(b) what expenses it has incurred in the same period.

Deducting expenses from income will allow the business to calculate its net profit for the period. This is done on a *Profit and Loss Account*.

A business also needs to know:

(a) what assets it has at a given moment; and
(b) what liabilities it has at a given moment.

Assets and liabilities are listed on a *Balance Sheet*.

On a daily basis, therefore, a business must keep records of income, expenses, assets and liabilities so that periodically it can produce a Profit and Loss Account and a Balance Sheet.

### 1.6.2 Classification of items

We referred in **1.6.1** to income, expenses, assets and liabilities. How do we classify items into the appropriate categories? The classification is crucial since it is income less expenses that gives a business its profit. A mistake in classification will misstate profit.

*Income* is what the business is trying to produce. It is the result either of the labour of the business's employees or the investment of its capital.

Examples of income are professional charges for services supplied, the price charged for stock sold, interest received and insurance commission received.

*Expenses* are items paid (or payable), the benefit of which is obtained and exhausted in a relatively short period (often within a single accounting period) and where the expenditure is necessary to maintain the earning capacity of the business.

Examples of expenses are the price of stock bought for resale, gas, electricity, wages, interest paid, hire charges, petrol and repairs.

*Assets* must be carefully distinguished from expenses. Like expenses, assets are the result of expenditure. The difference is that an asset gives rise to a benefit which can be spread over a longer period and which will increase the earning capacity of the business. Examples of assets are premises, machinery, fixtures and fittings, vehicles, cash and debtors. These are often referred to as 'fixed assets'. Fixed assets are the setting in which the business operates. There is another category of assets called 'current' or 'circulating' assets which we will look at later.

*Liabilities* are amounts owing from the business. They may be short term (eg, unpaid expenses) or long term (eg, a loan from a bank). Current assets are cash, debtors and stock left over at the end of the year.

### 1.6.3 Specimen Profit and Loss Account and Balance Sheet

We have set out below a specimen set of year end (or 'Final') Accounts. In later chapters, you will see how the various items are built up.

Remember the Profit and Loss Account shows income less expenses over the year in question. The difference between the two is the net profit of the business.

The Balance Sheet lists assets and liabilities at the end of the year. It shows how solvent the business is at that point.

Example

**The AB Partnership**

**Solicitors**

**Profit and Loss account for year ended 31 December 200–**

| | | £ | £ | £ |
|---|---|---|---|---|
| **Income** | | 000 | 000 | 000 |
| Profit Costs Billed | | 478 | | |
| Less Opening Work in Progress | | (30) | | |
| Plus Closing Work in Progress | | 40 | | |
| | | | 488 | |
| Gain on Sale of Car | | | 2 | |
| Insurance Commission Received | | | 10 | |
| Interest Received | | | 20 | |
| | | | | 520 |
| **Expenses** | | | | |
| Salaries | | | 98 | |
| General: | Paid | 55 | | |
| | Prepaid | (4) | | |
| | | | 51 | |
| Administrative: | Paid | 35 | | |
| | Accrued | 3 | | |
| | | | 38 | |
| Bad Debts | | | 17 | |
| Provision for Doubtful Debts | | | 8 | |
| Depreciation on Computers @ 20% | | | 10 | |
| Depreciation on Fixtures @ 5% | | | 1 | |
| Depreciation on Cars @ 20% | | | 8 | |
| Rent Paid | | | 21 | |
| Loan Interest Paid | | | 5 | |
| | | | | (257) |
| **Net profit** | | | | 263 |
| **Appropriated** | | £ | £ | £ |
| | | **A** | **B** | |
| Interest on Capital | | 5 | 3 | 8 |
| Salary | | | 10 | 10 |
| Share of Remaining Profits (3:2) | | 147 | 98 | 245 |
| | | 152 | 111 | 263 |

**The AB Partnership**

**Solicitors**

**Balance Sheet as at 31 December 200–**

| EMPLOYMENT OF CAPITAL | | | |
|---|---|---|---|
| **Fixed Assets** | £ | £ | £ |
| | 000 | 000 | 000 |
| Leasehold premises | | 218 | |
| Fixtures | 20 | | |
| *Less*: Depreciation | (13) | | |
| | | 7 | |
| Computers | 50 | | |
| *Less*: Depreciation | (40) | | |
| | | 10 | |
| Cars | 40 | | |
| *Less*: Depreciation | (8) | | |
| | | 32 | |
| | | | 267 |
| **Current Assets** | | | |
| Work in Progress | 40 | | |
| Debtors | 80 | | |
| *Less*: Provision | (8) | | |
| Cash – Office Bank Account | 10 | | |
| Petty Cash | 1 | | |
| Prepayments | 4 | | |
| | | 127 | |
| **Current Liabilities** | | | |
| Creditors | (39) | | |
| Accrued Expenses | (3) | | |
| | | (42) | |
| **Net Current Assets** | | | 85 |
| | | | 352 |
| *Less*: Bank Loan | | | (60) |
| Client Bank Account | 150 | | |
| *Less*: Amount due to Clients | (150) | | |
| | | | 292 |
| **Net Assets** | | | |
| **Capital employed** | | | |
| Capital: A | 50 | | |
| B | 30 | | |
| | | 80 | |
| Current: A | 124 | | |
| B | 88 | | |
| | | 212 | |
| | | | 292 |

**Movement on current accounts**

| | A | B |
|---|---|---|
| | £ | £ |
| Balance from Trial Balance at 31 Dec | 2CR | 3CR |
| Profits | 152 | 111 |
| Drawings | (30) | (26) |
| | 124CR | 88CR |

### 1.6.4 Day-to-day records

Although we will be working towards preparing a set of Final Accounts, we need to look first of all at the day-to-day records a business keeps. The Final Accounts are prepared from the information contained in the day-to-day records. The system which all well-organised businesses use for their day-to-day record keeping is the double entry bookkeeping system.

## 1.7 Why use the double entry system?

There is nothing to stop anyone inventing their own personal accounting system. However, there is a great deal to be said for using the double entry system which has been developed over hundreds of years and is understood by people all over the world.

It is important to realise that, while the double entry bookkeeping system has its own internal logic, the whole system could have been set up differently. For example, we will see later that some things are recorded on the right and some on the left; the initial decision could just as easily have been to record them the other way round.

However, once you have accepted that initial decision, everything which follows builds logically.

## 1.8 Principles of double entry

Lawyers should be particularly well placed to understand the fundamental principle of double entry bookkeeping as it is rather similar to the doctrine of consideration. The principle is that any business transaction has two aspects to it.

For example, if you buy premises for £100,000 cash, you gain an asset but you lose cash. If a customer pays you £100 cash for services provided, you have earned income and gained cash. If the services are provided on a credit basis, you earn income and gain the customer's debt. When the customer pays, you lose the debt but gain cash.

The double entry system requires you to make two entries in the accounts, one for each of the two aspects. You must never record only one aspect of the transaction.

In the example of the buying of premises, you would record the gain of the premises and the loss of the cash. In the case of charging the customer, you would record the earning of income and the gain of cash or the benefit of a debt owed.

In order to record the two aspects, accounts are divided into two sides. The two aspects of any transaction are recorded on different sides of the two accounts involved. There are rules as to which side of the accounts are used to record particular aspects. There is no magic about these rules. The system would work just as well if the aspects were recorded on the opposite sides.

### 1.8.1 Rules for recording transactions

You need to learn these rules:

(1) A source of *income* is always recorded on the right of an income account.

(2) The incurring of an *expense* is always recorded on the left of an expense account.

(3) The *gain of an asset* is recorded on the left of an asset account. The *loss of an asset* is recorded on the right of an asset account.

(4) The *incurring of a liability* is recorded on the right of a liability account. The *reduction of a liability* is recorded on the left of a liability account.

(5) Cash is an asset which regularly goes up and down. The rule for assets applies to cash, but it is helpful to state it expressly:

   (a) *Increasing cash* is equivalent to gaining an asset, so it is recorded on the left of a cash account.

   (b) *Reducing cash* is equivalent to losing an asset, so it is recorded on the right of a cash account.

The following grid summarises the above and shows which items are recorded on the left of accounts and which are recorded on the right:

*Remember, every transaction has one aspect which is recorded on the left of one account and one aspect which is recorded on the right of another. You must identify the two aspects and then record each of them.*

| Expense Incurred | Income Earned |
|---|---|
| Asset Gained | Asset Lost |
| Liability Reduced/Extinguished | Liability Incurred/Increased |
| Cash Gained | Cash Paid |

Example

Your business carries out the following transactions:

(a) Business buys a machine for £20,000 cash.
It gains an asset (recorded on left of the asset account) and loses cash (recorded on right of the cash account).

(b) Business buys stock for £1,000 cash.
The purchase of stock is an expense of the business (recorded on left of the expense account); there is a loss of cash (recorded on right of the cash account).

(c) Business sells stock for £3,000.
The sale of stock earns income (recorded on right of the income account); there is a gain of cash (recorded on left of the cash account).

Transactions (b) and (c) in the above example illustrate an important point about the double entry system. Initially, you do not worry about the concept of 'profit' or 'loss'. You simply record transactions as they occur and, periodically, usually at the end of the accounting period, deduct all the expenses of the period from all the income of the period to see what, if any, profit the business has made.

When recording the initial purchase or sale of stock, you do not worry about whether the goods bought were 'worth' £1,000 or whether the sale price of £3,000 was a high or low price. You simply record what happens.

Another important principle of double entry bookkeeping is that the business is regarded as completely separate from its proprietor. Thus, when a person sets up a business and puts in some cash, you must record the transaction from the point of view of the business. The business is gaining cash but is incurring a liability; it now owes money to the proprietor. This liability to repay its proprietor is normally referred to as the 'capital' of the business.

Exercise 1A

A starts a business buying and selling goods.

(a) **Identify the two aspects involved in the following transactions and say whether they would be recorded on the right or left of the accounts.**
   (1) To start the business, A puts in £20,000 cash and a car worth £8,000.
   (2) Business borrows £100,000 from a bank.
   (3) Business buys premises for £90,000 cash.
   (4) Business buys trading stock for £1,000 cash.
   (5) Business buys trading stock for £2,000 on credit from X.
   (6) Business sells some of the trading stock for £4,000 cash.
   (7) Business sells the rest of the trading stock for £1,000 on credit to Y, a customer.
   (8) Business pays X, a supplier, £2,000.
   (9) Y, a customer, pays business £1,000.

(b) **How much cash does the business have left after the above transactions have taken place?**

(c) **Identify the income, expenses, assets and liabilities involved in the above transactions.**

(d) **Calculate the firm's profit for the year by deducting expenses from income.**

## 1.9 'Debits' and 'credits'

So far, when talking about the sides of the accounts, we have referred to the left-hand side and the right-hand side.

However, accountants use the labels 'Debit' and 'Credit'.

'Debit' is used as a label for the left-hand side and 'Credit' as a label for the right-hand side. They are shortened to DR and CR respectively.

Example

(a) Joe sets up a business and pays in £120,000 to start it.
   The business gains cash (record on left of cash account with a DR entry) and incurs a liability to its proprietor (record on right of liability account with a CR entry).

(b) Business buys premises for £100,000.
   Business loses cash (record on right of cash account with a CR entry) and gains premises (record on left of asset account with a DR entry).

### 1.9.1 Do they seem to be the wrong way round?

People tend to expect 'Debits' to be payments and 'Credits' to be receipts. This is because that is the way in which your bank statement is labelled. On your bank statement, a receipt into your bank account is labelled by the bank as a credit and a payment is labelled as a debit. For an explanation of the apparent discrepancy with your bank statement, read the following paragraph. Remember that every transaction has to be recorded with two entries – a DR and a CR.

### 1.9.2 What is recorded on my bank statement?

A bank statement is a copy of the account labelled with your name, which the bank keeps to record its dealings with you.

When you pay money into the bank, the bank receives cash and makes a left-hand (DR) entry on its cash account to record the receipt of cash. However, it also incurs a liability since it owes that money to you; it makes a right-hand (CR) entry on the account it keeps in your name to record its liability to you. The bank owes you money.

Hence, on the bank statement your bank sends you, the money paid into your account is shown as a CR entry on your account. There is also a DR entry on the bank's cash record which you do not see.

When money is paid out of your bank account, the bank loses cash and therefore makes a CR entry on its cash account to record that loss. It owes you less and makes a DR entry on your account to record the reduction in its liability to you.

## 1.10 What do accounts look like?

Accounts can be presented in a variety of different forms. The most common form of presentation is the tabular form.

| Date | Details | DR | CR | BAL |
|---|---|---|---|---|
| | | | | |

The date of the transaction is entered in the 'Date' column. The 'Details' column contains a cross-reference to the name of the account where the other part of the double entry is made as well as a brief description of the nature of the transaction. The amount is entered in the debit or credit column, as appropriate. The 'Balance' column is a running balance of the entries made in the account.

Example

Business pays four electricity bills: £1,000, £3,000, £2,000 and £1,500. Each payment will be recorded on the cash account and the electricity account. The electricity account will look as follows:

| Date | Details | DR | CR | BAL |
|---|---|---|---|---|
| 1 | Cash | 1,000 | | 1,000DR |
| 2 | Cash | 3,000 | | 4,000DR |
| 3 | Cash | 2,000 | | 6,000DR |
| 4 | Cash | 1,500 | | 7,500DR |

The cash account will have four credit entries on it amounting to £7,500.

## 1.11 Solution

Exercise 1A

(a)

| | | |
|---|---|---|
| (1) | Business gains assets (cash and car) | Business incurs liability to proprietor |
| (2) | Business gains cash | Business incurs liability to bank |
| (3) | Business gains asset (premises) | Business loses cash |
| (4) | Business incurs expense (cost of stock) | Business loses cash |
| (5) | Business incurs expense (cost of stock) | Business incurs liability to X |
| (6) | Business gains cash | Business has source of income (sale of stock) |
| (7) | Business gains asset (debt from Y) | Business has source of income (sale of stock) |
| (8) | Business extinguishes liability | Business loses cash |
| (9) | Business gains cash | Business loses asset (debt) |

(b) The business will have £32,000 cash left.

(c) *Assets* cash, car
*Liabilities* amounts owed to proprietor and to bank
*Income* sale price of goods sold
*Expenses* cost of goods purchased

Note: The business did have an additional liability, the amount it owed to X, and an additional asset, the amount Y owed. However, these have been paid in full and are, therefore, extinguished.

(d) The income is £5,000 and the expenses are £3,000. The profit is, therefore, £2,000.

# Chapter 2

# Basic Bookkeeping – The Double Entry System



## 2.1 Dealing with trading stock

In this chapter, we will consider the entries required to record basic transactions and also some more complex ones.

Example

This example illustrates how a business will record day-to-day transactions. If necessary, refer back to the grid at **1.8**.

(1) On 1 May, A starts a trading business and puts in £100,000 cash.

*Note:* The business gains cash so you make a left-hand DR entry on the cash account. The business incurs a liability to the proprietor so you make a right-hand CR entry. You need an account to record this liability. It is normal to call the account recording liability to the proprietor 'capital'.

**Cash**

| Date | Details | DR | CR | BAL |
|---|---|---|---|---|
| May | | | | |
| 1 | Capital | **100,000** | | 100,000DR |

**Capital**

| Date | Details | DR | CR | BAL |
|---|---|---|---|---|
| May | | | | |
| 1 | Cash | | **100,000** | 100,000CR |

(2) On 2 May, the business borrows £200,000 from Barcloyds Bank.

*Note:* The business gains cash (DR cash). It incurs a liability to the bank. You need an account to record this liability to the bank and you will make a CR entry on it.

**Cash**

| Date | Details | DR | CR | BAL |
|---|---|---|---|---|
| May | | | | |
| 1 | Capital | 100,000 | | 100,000DR |
| 2 | Barcloyds | **200,000** | | 300,000DR |

**Barcloyds Bank**

| Date | Details | DR | CR | BAL |
|---|---|---|---|---|
| May | | | | |
| 2 | Cash | | **200,000** | 200,000CR |

(3) On 4 May, the business buys trading stock for £20,000 cash.

*Note:* The business will lose cash and so you will CR the cash account.

The business has incurred an expense of £20,000. You need an account to record this category of expense. It is normal to call such an expense account 'purchases'. You will DR this account.

**Cash**

| Date | Details | DR | CR | BAL |
|---|---|---|---|---|
| May | | | | |
| 1 | Capital | 100,000 | | 100,000DR |
| 2 | Bank Loan | 200,000 | | 300,000DR |
| 4 | Purchases | | **20,000** | 280,000DR |

**Purchases**

| Date | Details | DR | CR | BAL |
|---|---|---|---|---|
| May | | | | |
| 4 | Cash | **20,000** | | 20,000DR |

(4) On 5 May, the business buys goods on credit from X, a supplier, for £30,000.

*Note:* As in the previous example, the business incurs an expense (DR Purchases). This time it does not pay cash immediately. Instead it incurs a liability to the supplier. You need an account to record this liability to the supplier, and you will make a CR entry in it.

**Purchases**

| Date | Details | DR | CR | BAL |
|---|---|---|---|---|
| May | | | | |
| 4 | Cash | 20,000 | | 20,000DR |
| 5 | X | **30,000** | | 50,000DR |

**Supplier X**

| Date | Details | DR | CR | BAL |
|---|---|---|---|---|
| May | | | | |
| 5 | Purchases | | **30.000** | 30,000CR |

(5) On 8 May, the business sells trading stock for £120,000 cash.

*Note 1:* The business gains cash and you will record this with a DR entry. It has a source of income which you will record with a CR entry. It is normal to call such an income account 'sales'.

*Note 2:* You could show purchased stock on the DR side of a stock account and sales of stock on the CR side of the same account, but this is not usual. It is more convenient for calculating profit at the end of the year to have separate accounts for expenses and income.

**Cash**

| Date | Details | DR | CR | BAL |
|---|---|---|---|---|
| May | | | | |
| 1 | Capital | 100,000 | | 100,000DR |
| 2 | Barcloyds | 200,000 | | 300,000DR |
| 4 | Purchases | | 20,000 | 280,000DR |
| 8 | Sales | **120,000** | | 400,000DR |

**Sales**

| Date | Details | DR | CR | BAL |
|---|---|---|---|---|
| May | | | | |
| 8 | Cash | | **120,000** | 120,000CR |

(6) On 12 May, the business sells goods for £70,000 on credit to Y.

*Note:* As in the previous example, the business has a source of income (CR Sales). This time it gains a debt rather than cash so make a DR entry on an account showing the amount owed by Y.

**Sales**

| Date | Details | DR | CR | BAL |
|---|---|---|---|---|
| May | | | | |
| 8 | Cash | | **120,000** | 120,000CR |
| 12 | Y | | **70,000** | 190,000CR |

**Y**

| Date | Details | DR | CR | BAL |
|---|---|---|---|---|
| May | | | | |
| 12 | Sales | **70,000** | | 70,000DR |

(7) On 15 May, the business pays X £30,000.
*Note:* The business loses cash (CR cash) and extinguishes a liability (DR X).

**Cash**

| Date | Details | DR | CR | BAL |
|---|---|---|---|---|
| May | | | | |
| 1 | Capital | 100,000 | | 100,000DR |
| 2 | Barcloyds | 200,000 | | 300,000DR |
| 4 | Purchases | | 20,000 | 280,000DR |
| 8 | Sales | 120,000 | | 400,000DR |
| 15 | X | | **30,000** | 370,000DR |

**X**

| Date | Details | DR | CR | BAL |
|---|---|---|---|---|
| May | | | | |
| 5 | Purchases | | 30,000 | 30,000CR |
| 15 | Cash | **30,000** | | — |

(8) On 20 May, Y pays the business £70,000.
*Note:* The business gains cash (DR cash) and loses an asset, Y's debt (CR Y).

**Cash**

| Date | Details | DR | CR | BAL |
|---|---|---|---|---|
| May | | | | |
| 1 | Capital | 100,000 | | 100,000DR |
| 2 | Barcloyds | 200,000 | | 300,000DR |
| 4 | Purchases | | 20,000 | 280,000DR |
| 8 | Sales | 120,000 | | 400,000DR |
| 15 | X | | 30,000 | 370,000DR |
| 20 | Y | **70,000** | | 440,000DR |

**Y**

| Date | Details | DR | CR | BAL |
|---|---|---|---|---|
| May | | | | |
| 12 | Sales | 70,000 | | 70,000DR |
| 15 | Cash | | 70,000 | – |

Exercise 2A

Prepare accounts to record the following transactions:

| | | |
|---|---|---|
| (1) | 1 April | Amanda decides to open an antiques shop. |
| | 3 April | She puts in her savings of £700 cash. |
| | 4 April | Business buys stock at an auction for £300 cash. |
| | 5 April | Business buys stock from Alice for £100 on credit. |
| | 6 April | Business sells some of the stock in the shop for £500 cash. |
| | 7 April | Business pays Alice £100 cash. |
| (2) | 1 June | Beryl decides to open a bookshop. |
| | 3 June | She puts in her savings of £1,000 cash. |
| | 4 June | Business buys stock on credit from Booksellers & Co for £2,000. |
| | 5 June | Business sells some stock for £2,500 cash. |
| | 6 June | Business sells some stock on credit to Brian for £300. |
| | 7 June | Business pays Booksellers & Co £2,000. |
| | 8 June | Brian pays business £250. |

## 2.2 Other types of transaction

So far we have looked at the entries required to purchase and sell goods, and to record receipts and payments of cash and amounts owing to and by the business.

We will now look at the entries you would make to record other types of transaction.

### 2.2.1 Assets

Long-lasting items purchased to improve the efficiency of the business rather than for resale, for example premises, machinery, cars, are referred to as 'fixed assets'. Each category of fixed asset will have its own account. If it is purchased for cash, the entries will be:

CR Cash account
DR Asset account

If it is purchased on credit, the entries will be:

CR Supplier's account
DR Asset account

Example

On 1 May, the business purchases a machine for £30,000 on credit from A.

*Entries:*
CR A
DR Machinery

A

| Date | Details | DR | CR | BAL |
|---|---|---|---|---|
| May 2 | Machinery | | 30,000 | 30,000CR |

Machinery

| Date | Details | DR | CR | BAL |
|---|---|---|---|---|
| May 2 | A | 30,000 | | 30,000DR |

On 1 September there is a DR balance on the cash account of £100,000. (This means the business has received £100,000 more than it has paid out.) The business pays A for the machine.

*Entries:*
DR A
CR Cash account

**A**

| Date | Details | DR | CR | BAL |
|---|---|---|---|---|
| May 2 | Machinery | | 30,000 | 30,000CR |
| Sept 1 | Cash | **30,000** | | – |

**Cash**

| Date | Details | DR | CR | BAL |
|---|---|---|---|---|
| Sept 1 | Balance | | | 100,000DR |
| 1 | A | | **30,000** | 70,000DR |

Notice that no entry is made on the machinery account so the balance of £30,000 on the machinery account remains unchanged by the payment. The balance will remain on the machinery account so long as the business retains the machine. (The machine may be depreciated – see **Chapter 5**.)

At the end of every accounting period, the business will draw up a list of its assets and liabilities on the final day of the accounting period. The list is referred to as a Balance Sheet. Asset accounts are sometimes referred to as 'real' accounts because they record tangible assets.

The purchase and sale of assets has no effect on the *profit* of a business. This is because profit is the difference between income and expenses. Assets do not affect profit. Buying an asset for cash simply means that one asset (cash) has been changed into another. Buying on credit means that the business has acquired an asset and incurred a liability which cancel each other out.

### 2.2.2 Expenses

Any business will have a variety of expenses. We have looked at purchases, but there are many others such as electricity, wages, rent and rates. A business will have an account for each category of expense. The business will receive bills periodically for these expenses. No entries are made until the expense is paid. Then you will CR the cash account and make a DR entry on the expense account.

*Entries:*

CR Cash account } when bill is paid
DR Expense account }

Example

1 May Business has a DR balance on the cash account of £10,000. (This means that the business has received £10,000 more than it has paid out.)

2 May Business receives an electricity bill of £1,000.

10 May Business pays it.

**Cash**

| Date | Details | DR | CR | BAL |
|---|---|---|---|---|
| May 1 | Balance | | | 10,000DR |
| 10 | Electricity | | **1,000** | 9,000DR |

**Electricity**

| Date | Details | DR | CR | BAL |
|---|---|---|---|---|
| May 10 | Cash | **1,000** | | 1,000DR |

As and when bills are paid during an accounting period, the DR balance on the expense account will increase. At the end of the accounting period, the total expenses will be taken into account when calculating the net profit of the business.

Expense accounts are sometimes referred to as 'nominal' accounts. This is because they do not reflect tangible assets; they reflect expenses the benefit of which will normally have been exhausted by the end of the accounting period.

You must be very careful to distinguish assets from expenses accurately because, at the end of the accounting period when you are calculating the net profit for the period, expenses reduce that profit but the cost of fixed assets does not.

### 2.2.3 Profit costs

Solicitors and other professionals do not sell trading stock to produce income. They sell their services.

When a bill is issued, the solicitor wants to record the sale (ie, the loss) of services and the gain of the debt now owed by the client to the firm. Charges for professional services are recorded as a CR entry on an income account, often called 'profit costs'. The client's debt is recorded as a DR entry on an account in the name of the client.

*Entries:*

CR Profit costs account
DR Client's account
} when bill is issued

**Example**

On 1 June, a solicitor issues a bill to A for profit costs of £1,000. (In this illustration we have not worried about what figure was in the balance column of the costs account on 1 June.)

**Profit Costs**

| Date | Details | DR | CR | BAL |
|---|---|---|---|---|
| June 1 | A | | 1,000 | XXX |

**A**

| Date | Details | DR | CR | BAL |
|---|---|---|---|---|
| June 1 | Profit Costs | 1,000 | | 1,000DR |

When the client eventually pays, the solicitor will record a receipt of cash and the loss of the debt owed by A to the business.

*Entries:*
DR Cash account
CR A's account

On 10 June, A pays solicitor amount due. (We have not worried about what figure was in the balance column of the cash account before the receipt.)

**Cash**

| Date | Details | DR | CR | BAL |
|---|---|---|---|---|
| June 10 | A | 1,000 | | XXX |

**A**

| Date | Details | DR | CR | BAL |
|---|---|---|---|---|
| June 1 | Profit Costs | 1,000 | | 1,000DR |
| 10 | Cash | | 1,000 | - |

*Note:* No entry is made on the profit costs account when the client pays the cash due. The profit costs account merely records the bill issued. It does not show whether or not clients have paid their bills.

The balance on the profit costs account will increase every time a bill is issued. The total of profit costs at the end of an accounting period will form the basis of the calculation of net profit for the period.

### 2.2.4 Other income

A business may earn income from subsidiary sources. For example, a firm of solicitors may receive most of its income from profit costs but may, in addition, earn income from interest, insurance commission and rent on premises let to tenants. A business will have an account for each category of income.

It would be possible to make entries to show that income is owed to the firm and then make entries to show the receipt of cash. However, it is more usual to make no entries until the cash is received. Then you will need a DR entry to record the receipt of cash and a CR entry on an income account to record the income. The CR entry is made on an income received account.

*Entries:*
DR Cash account
CR Income Received account

Example

On 1 March, a business, which has a debit balance of £10,000 on its cash account, receives a cheque for £100 interest.

Cash

| Date | Details | DR | CR | BAL |
|---|---|---|---|---|
| March 1 | Balance | | | 10,000DR |
| | Interest Received | 100 | | 10,100DR |

Interest Received

| Date | Details | DR | CR | BAL |
|---|---|---|---|---|
| March 1 | Cash | | 100 | 100CR |

Exercise 2B

Prepare accounts to record the following transactions:

1 July Sally starts to practise as a solicitor. She puts in £5,000 cash.
2 July Business pays £1,000 rent for office premises.
3 July Business pays £500 hire charges for office machinery.
18 July Business pays £1,000 cash in wages.
20 July Business pays £100 cash for electricity bill.
22 July Business pays £80 cash for stationery bill.
25 July Business sends out a bill for £300 profit costs to Sidney, a client.
28 July Business pays £1,000 cash in wages.
29 July Business pays £500 hire charges for office machinery.

You will see that already we have encountered a large number of accounts. Traditionally, the accounts were kept together in a bound book referred to as the 'ledger'. The accounts are often referred to as 'ledger accounts'. The cash account was usually kept in a separate book. This was convenient as the cash account was the busiest account. Because it is separate from the main ledger, the cash account is not referred to as a 'ledger account'.

## 2.3 Trial balance

Periodically, a bookkeeper checks the accuracy of the bookkeeping. This will normally be done every month and always at the end of the accounting period before the bookkeeper starts to calculate the net profit for the period.

The double entry system requires that, for every DR entry made on an account, a CR entry for an identical amount must be made on another account. If every transaction has been properly recorded, the total of DR entries will equal the total of CR entries. If an entry has been made on only one side of the accounts, or if an entry has been written incorrectly on one side of the accounts, there will be a discrepancy between the two totals.

It would, therefore, be possible to check the accuracy of bookkeeping by comparing the two totals. However, over an entire accounting period (usually one year), a bookkeeper will make a daunting number of entries. Adding them all up would be a tedious task. As a short-cut, it is possible to add together all the DR balances and then all the CR balances and, if no errors have been made, the two totals will agree. You will see why this works if you think about what a balance is. It is the difference between the DR and CR entries on each account. If the correct DR and CR entries have been made on each account, the differences between the DR and CR sides of each and every account should agree.

The process of adding together all DR and CR balances and comparing the total is referred to as preparing a Trial Balance.

Example

Look at the solution to Exercise 2B. We will use the figures to prepare a Trial Balance.

**Trial Balance**

| | DR | CR |
|---|---|---|
| | £ | £ |
| Capital | | 5,000 |
| Cash | 820 | |
| Hire Charges | 1,000 | |
| Wages | 2,000 | |
| Electricity | 100 | |
| Stationery | 80 | |
| Rent | 1,000 | |
| Profit Costs | | 300 |
| Debtors | 300 | |
| | 5,300 | 5,300 |

You will see that income and liability accounts have credit balances, while expense and asset accounts have debit balances.

Note that a cash account may have either a DR or a CR balance depending on whether the business has cash in the bank or has an overdraft.

A DR balance on the cash account indicates that the business has money, a CR balance that it has an overdraft. If a question does not tell you that a business is overdrawn, you may assume that it has money in the bank.

> **Exercise 2C**
> Prepare a Trial Balance from the following list of balances:
>
> Profit Costs £10,000. Rent £750. Rates £800. Electricity £150. Sundry Expenses £25. Postages and Telephones £175. Wages £2,500. Miscellaneous Income £325. Stationery £50. Cash £2,000. Creditors £300. Debtors £250. Fixtures and Fittings £1,405. Capital £1,750. Motor Car £4,770. Bank Loan £500.

A Trial Balance will not reveal all bookkeeping errors. For example, if one half of an entry has been omitted or written as a wrong amount, the error is revealed but no other types of error will be. There are other types of error which will not be revealed by a Trial Balance.

> **Exercise 2D**
> What types of error will not be revealed by a Trial Balance? List five possibilities.

## 2.4 Capital and drawings

As we have seen already in **Chapter 1**, whenever people start businesses, they will normally contribute some cash. The entries required to deal with this are:

*Entries:*
DR Cash account
CR Capital account

The proprietor of a business hopes that at the end of the accounting period the business will have made a net profit. Any profit made will be 'owed' to the proprietor. Hence, once the net profit has been calculated, it will be credited to the capital account to increase the amount shown as owing to the proprietor.

If you were running a business, you would almost certainly need to withdraw some cash from time to time to live on. Such withdrawals would reduce the cash in the business and would also reduce the amount the business owed you. You would make a CR entry on cash and could record the withdrawals on the DR side of the capital account. However, a large number of withdrawals would clutter the capital account, so it is usual to keep a separate account called a 'Drawings' account on which to record withdrawals.

Thus, whenever a proprietor withdraws cash:

*Entries:*
CR Cash account
DR Drawings account

At the end of the year, the balance on the drawings account may be transferred from the drawings account to the capital account so that the picture on the capital account is brought up to date.

Example

On 1 May at the start of the accounting year, A has a balance on her capital account of £30,000. During the accounting year, she withdraws £3,000 on 31 July, 31 October and 31 January.

At the end of the accounting year on 30 April, the balance on the drawings account is transferred to the capital account.

Each time cash is withdrawn:

*Entries:*

CR Cash account
DR Drawings account

**Cash**

| Date | Details | DR | CR | BAL |
|---|---|---|---|---|
| July 31 | Drawings | | **3,000** | xxx |
| October 31 | Drawings | | **3,000** | xxx |
| January 31 | Drawings | | **3,000** | xxx |

**Drawings**

| Date | Details | DR | CR | BAL |
|---|---|---|---|---|
| July 31 | Cash | **3,000** | | 3,000DR |
| October 31 | Cash | **3,000** | | 6,000DR |
| January 31 | Cash | **3,000** | | 9,000DR |

To transfer the £9,000 balance on the drawings account to the capital account:

*Entries:*

CR Drawings account
DR Capital account

**Capital**

| Date | Details | DR | CR | BAL |
|---|---|---|---|---|
| April 30 | Balance | | | 30,000CR |
| 30 | Drawings | **9,000** | | 21,000CR |

**Drawings**

| Date | Details | DR | CR | BAL |
|---|---|---|---|---|
| July 31 | Cash | 3,000 | | 3,000DR |
| October 31 | Cash | 3,000 | | 6,000DR |
| January 31 | Cash | 3,000 | | 9,000DR |
| April 30 | Capital | | **9,000** | – |

Currently, therefore, the business is shown as owing the proprietor £21,000. However, as soon as the net profit is calculated, it will be credited to the capital account (DR entry will be on Profit and Loss Account – see **Chapter 4**), thus increasing the amount shown as owing to the proprietor.

## 2.5 Cash, bank and petty cash

Most businesses operate by banking all receipts and making virtually all payments by cheque. The so-called 'cash' account is in reality a record of receipts into and payments out of the bank account. However, a business will need a small amount of cash in the office to cover small day-to-day expenses. This is referred to as 'petty cash'. A petty cash account is required to record the periodic receipts of cash from the bank and the various payments made from petty cash.

Example

A business has a DR balance on the cash account of £20,100. On 1 May, the bookkeeper withdraws £20 cash from the bank for petty cash, and, on 2 May, the firm purchases a roll of sticky tape for £2 from petty cash.

*Entries:*

To record the withdrawal of cash from the bank:
CR Cash account
DR Petty Cash account

To record the purchase of sticky tape:
CR Petty Cash account
DR Office Sundries account

**Cash**

| Date | Details | DR | CR | BAL |
|---|---|---|---|---|
| May | | | | |
| 1 | Balance | | | 20,100DR |
| 1 | Petty Cash | | 20 | 20,080DR |

**Petty Cash**

| Date | Details | DR | CR | BAL |
|---|---|---|---|---|
| May | | | | |
| 1 | Cash | 20 | | 20DR |
| 2 | Office Sundries | | 2 | 18DR |

**Office Sundries**

| Date | Details | DR | CR | BAL |
|---|---|---|---|---|
| May | | | | |
| 2 | Petty Cash | 2 | | 2DR |

Any petty cash left over at the end of the accounting period will be an asset of the firm and will be shown as such on the Balance Sheet of the firm.

## 2.6 Dishonoured cheques

A bookkeeper will record a receipt of cash on the day on which the firm receives a cheque. Occasionally, a few days after the cheque has been paid into the bank, the bank may inform the firm that the cheque has been dishonoured ('bounced'). The bookkeeper will have already recorded a receipt of cash, but it now appears that this was wrong.

The error must be rectified, and the entries made when the receipt was recorded must be reversed.

Example

On 1 June, Customer A is shown as owing the firm £100. The firm has £1,000 in the bank. On 2 June, Customer A gives the firm a cheque for £100, which the firm banks. On 9 June, the bank informs the firm that the cheque has bounced.

*Entries:*

To record receipt of cash:
DR Cash account
CR Customer A's account

**Cash**

| Date | Details | DR | CR | BAL |
|---|---|---|---|---|
| June | | | | |
| 1 | Balance | | | 1,000DR |
| 2 | A | 100 | | 1,100DR |

**Customer A**

| Date | Details | DR | CR | BAL |
|---|---|---|---|---|
| June | | | | |
| 1 | Balance | | | 100DR |
| 2 | Cash | | 100 | – |

To record the fact that the cheque has been dishonoured, you must reverse the entries you made when the cheque was received:

CR Cash account

DR Customer A's ledger account

**Cash**

| Date | Details | DR | CR | BAL |
|---|---|---|---|---|
| June | | | | |
| 1 | Balance | | | 1,000DR |
| 2 | A | 100 | | 1,100DR |
| 9 | A– Dishonoured cheque | | **100** | 1,000DR |

**Customer A**

| Date | Details | DR | CR | BAL |
|---|---|---|---|---|
| June | | | | |
| 1 | Balance | | | 100DR |
| 2 | Cash | | 100 | – |
| 9 | Cash– Dishonoured cheque | **100** | | 100DR |

Notice that the effect of recording the dishonouring of the cheque is to reduce the balance on the cash account and to restore the customer to the list of debtors of the firm. The customer will continue to be shown as a debtor until either the debt is paid or it is written off as bad (see 2.7).

The customer may tell the firm to present the cheque again a few days later when there may be sufficient funds to meet the cheque. In such a case, the firm will record a receipt of cash on the later date.

## 2.7 Bad debts

Debts are regarded as an asset of a business. Periodically, any business will review its debtors to ascertain whether any should be declared bad and written off. The effect of writing off a debt as bad is that the debtor is no longer shown as owing the firm money, and, therefore, the total of assets will be reduced. Bad debts are regarded as an expense of the business and, therefore, reduce the amount of net profit at the end of the accounting period.

A business will need a bad debts account to which all bad debts are debited.

Example

Customer B is shown as owing the firm £200. This means that there is a DR balance of £200 on the account kept to show B's indebtedness to the firm. The debt has been outstanding for some time and B cannot be traced. On 1 May, the firm decides to write off the debt as bad.

*Entries:*

To record writing off the debt:

DR Bad Debts

CR B's account

**Bad Debts**

| Date | Details | DR | CR | BAL |
|---|---|---|---|---|
| May | | | | |
| 1 | B | **200** | | 200DR |

**Customer B**

| Date | Details | DR | CR | BAL |
|---|---|---|---|---|
| May | | | | |
| 1 | Balance | | | 200DR |
| | Bad Debts | | **200** | – |

If the client paid the debt at a later stage, the firm would DR cash and CR either the Bad Debts account or a separate account called Bad Debts Recovered.

## 2.8 Errors

All sorts of errors may be made in the bookkeeping entries. Once discovered, an error must be rectified as quickly as possible. The precise entries you will need to make will depend on the sort of error made, but basically you will want to reverse any entries made wrongly (as with a dishonoured cheque) and then make the correct entry.

Example

The balance on the sales account is £200,000, and the balance on furniture is £15,000. On 10 April, the bookkeeper wants to record a purchase of furniture for £3,000. The correct CR entry is made on cash, but, instead of making the DR entry on furniture, the bookkeeper makes the DR entry on the sales account. After the error is made, the accounts look like this:

**Sales**

| Date | Details | DR | CR | BAL |
|---|---|---|---|---|
| April | | | | |
| 10 | Balance | | | 200,000CR |
| | Cash | 3,000 | | 197,000CR |

**Furniture**

| Date | Details | DR | CR | BAL |
|---|---|---|---|---|
| April | Balance | | | 15,000DR |

*Entries:*

To correct the error:

CR Sales account

DR Furniture account

**Sales**

| Date | Details | DR | CR | BAL |
|---|---|---|---|---|
| April | | | | |
| 10 | Balance | | | 200,000CR |
| | Cash | 3,000 | | 197,000CR |
| | Furniture – to correct error | | 3,000 | 200,000CR |

**Furniture**

| Date | Details | DR | CR | BAL |
|---|---|---|---|---|
| April | | | | |
| 10 | Balance | | | 15,000DR |
| | Sales – to correct error | 3,000 | | 18,000DR |

## 2.9 Suspense account

A Trial Balance which does not balance indicates that an error has been made in the double entry bookkeeping. Sometimes the bookkeeper cannot immediately locate the error made. In such a case, a suspense account is opened and an appropriate DR or CR entry is made. It is merely a temporary measure and, as soon as the error is (or errors are) located, the account is closed and the entries necessary to correct the accounts are made.

Example

The DR balances on the Trial Balance are £100 less than the CR balances. On 30 November, the bookkeeper opens a suspense account as a temporary measure. On 1 December, the bookkeeper discovers that a DR entry of £100 was omitted from the stationery account and corrects the error.

*Entries:*

When the suspense account is opened:

DR Suspense account

**Suspense**

| Date | Details | DR | CR | BAL |
|---|---|---|---|---|
| Nov 30 | Error | **100DR** | | 100DR |

When the error is discovered:

CR Suspense account

DR Stationery account

**Suspense**

| Date | Details | DR | CR | BAL |
|---|---|---|---|---|
| Nov 30 | Error | 100 | | 100DR |
| Dec 1 | Stationery | | **100** | – |

**Stationery**

| Date | Details | DR | CR | BAL |
|---|---|---|---|---|
| Dec 1 | Suspense | **100** | | xxx |

A suspense account may also be used as a temporary measure when a bookkeeper is not certain how to treat a particular item.

Example

The balance on a firm's repairs account is £1,000 and on premises £100,000.

On 1 March, the firm pays £31,500 to builders. The bookkeeper is not sure whether the payment represents repairs or an extension to existing premises. Repairs, being an expense item, would be recorded as a DR on the repairs account, but an extension, being a capital item, would be recorded as a DR entry on the premises account. As a temporary measure, until additional information can be obtained, the bookkeeper records the payment on the suspense account. On 12 March, the bookkeeper discovers that £1,500 is to be regarded as repairs and £30,000 as the cost of the extension.

The accounts will look as follows:

**Cash**

| Date | Details | DR | CR | BAL |
|---|---|---|---|---|
| March 1 | Suspense | | 31,500 | xxx |

**Suspense**

| Date | Details | DR | CR | BAL |
|---|---|---|---|---|
| March 1 | Cash | 31,500 | | 31,500DR |
| 12 | Repairs | | 1,500 | 30,000DR |
| | Premises | | 30,000 | – |

Repairs

| Date | Details | DR | CR | BAL |
|---|---|---|---|---|
| March<br>12 | <br>Balance<br>Suspense | <br><br>1,500 | | <br>1,000DR<br>2,500DR |

Premises

| Date | Details | DR | CR | BAL |
|---|---|---|---|---|
| March<br>12 | <br>Balance<br>Suspense | <br><br>30,000 | | <br>100,000DR<br>130,000DR |

Exercise 2E

An extract from the Trial Balance of X Co is set out below.

**X Co**
**Trial Balance**

| | DR | CR |
|---|---|---|
| | £ | £ |
| Credit Sales | | 30,000 |
| Debtors | 3,000 | |
| (including B £500) | | |
| Cash | 10,000 | |

Show the entries necessary to record the following transactions:

1 May X delivers a bill to A for credit sales of £200.

2 May A pays, but X mistakenly records the receipt as coming from B.

3 May X discovers the mistake and corrects it.

4 May B sends X a cheque for £500 in payment of the amount due.

5 May Bank tells X that B's cheque has been dishonoured.

6 May X writes off B's debt as bad.

## 2.10 Solutions

Exercise 2A

(1)

Capital

| Date | Details | DR | CR | BAL |
|---|---|---|---|---|
| April<br>3 | <br>Cash | | <br>700 | <br>700CR |

Cash

| Date | Details | DR | CR | BAL |
|---|---|---|---|---|
| April<br>3<br>4<br>6<br>7 | <br>Capital<br>Purchases<br>Sales<br>Alice | <br>700<br><br>500<br> | <br><br>300<br><br>100 | <br>700DR<br>400DR<br>900DR<br>800DR |

Purchases

| Date | Details | DR | CR | BAL |
|---|---|---|---|---|
| April<br>4<br>5 | <br>Cash<br>Alice | <br>300<br>100 | | <br>300DR<br>400DR |

Alice

| Date | Details | DR | CR | BAL |
|---|---|---|---|---|
| April<br>5<br>7 | <br>Purchases<br>Cash | <br><br>100 | <br>100<br> | <br>100CR<br>– |

**Sales**

| Date | Details | DR | CR | BAL |
|---|---|---|---|---|
| April<br>6 | Cash | | 500 | 500CR |

(2)

**Capital**

| Date | Details | DR | CR | BAL |
|---|---|---|---|---|
| June<br>3 | Cash | | 1,000 | 1,000CR |

**Cash**

| Date | Details | DR | CR | BAL |
|---|---|---|---|---|
| June | | | | |
| 3 | Capital | 1,000 | | 1,000DR |
| 5 | Sales | 2,500 | | 3,500DR |
| 7 | Booksellers & Co | | 2,000 | 1,500DR |
| 8 | Brian | 250 | | 1,750DR |

**Purchases**

| Date | Details | DR | CR | BAL |
|---|---|---|---|---|
| June<br>4 | Booksellers & Co | 2,000 | | 2,000DR |

**Booksellers & Co**

| Date | Details | DR | CR | BAL |
|---|---|---|---|---|
| June | | | | |
| 4 | Purchases | | 2,000 | 2,000CR |
| 7 | Cash | 2,000 | | – |

**Sales**

| Date | Details | DR | CR | BAL |
|---|---|---|---|---|
| June | | | | |
| 5 | Cash | | 2,500 | 2,500CR |
| 6 | Brian | | 300 | 2,800CR |

**Brian**

| Date | Details | DR | CR | BAL |
|---|---|---|---|---|
| June | | | | |
| 6 | Sales | 300 | | 300DR |
| 8 | Cash | | 250 | 50DR |

Exercise 2B

**Cash**

| Date | Details | DR | CR | BAL |
|---|---|---|---|---|
| July | | | | |
| 1 | Capital | 5,000 | | 5,000DR |
| 2 | Rent | | 1,000 | 4,000DR |
| 3 | Hire | | 500 | 3,500DR |
| 18 | Wages | | 1,000 | 2,500DR |
| 20 | Electricity | | 100 | 2,400DR |
| 22 | Stationery | | 80 | 2,320DR |
| 28 | Wages | | 1,000 | 1,320DR |
| 29 | Hire | | 500 | 820DR |

**Capital**

| Date | Details | DR | CR | BAL |
|---|---|---|---|---|
| July<br>1 | Cash | | 5,000 | 5,000CR |

**Rent**

| Date | Details | DR | CR | BAL |
|---|---|---|---|---|
| July<br>2 | Cash | 1,000 | | 1,000DR |

**Wages**

| Date | Details | DR | CR | BAL |
|---|---|---|---|---|
| July | | | | |
| 18 | Cash | 1,000 | | 1,000DR |
| 28 | Cash | 1,000 | | 2,000DR |

**Hire Charges**

| Date | Details | DR | CR | BAL |
|---|---|---|---|---|
| July | | | | |
| 3 | Cash | **500** | | 500DR |
| 29 | Cash | 500 | | 1,000DR |

**Stationery**

| Date | Details | DR | CR | BAL |
|---|---|---|---|---|
| July 22 | Cash | 80 | | 80DR |

**Electricity**

| Date | Details | DR | CR | BAL |
|---|---|---|---|---|
| July 20 | Cash | 100 | | 100DR |

**Profit Costs**

| Date | Details | DR | CR | BAL |
|---|---|---|---|---|
| July 25 | Sidney | | 300 | 300CR |

**Sidney**

| Date | Details | DR | CR | BAL |
|---|---|---|---|---|
| July 25 | Profit Costs | 300 | | 300DR |

*Note*: It would be misleading to label the 'Hire of Machinery' account as 'Machinery'. The title 'Machinery' would suggest that the business owned a fixed asset, whereas in fact it has simply paid hire charges. A fixed asset will continue to be a benefit to the business so long as the asset remains usable, whereas the benefit of hire charges ceases as soon as the period of hire expires. In accounting terms, hire charges are 'expenses' which reduce net profit, whereas assets are something tangible owned by the business which are a continuing benefit.

Exercise 2C

**Trial Balance**

| | DR | CR |
|---|---|---|
| | £ | £ |
| Profit Costs | | 10,000 |
| Rent | 750 | |
| Rates | 800 | |
| Electricity | 150 | |
| Sundry Expenses | 25 | |
| Postage and Telephones | 175 | |
| Wages | 2,500 | |
| Miscellaneous Income | | 325 |
| Stationery | 50 | |
| Cash | 2,000 | |
| Creditors | | 300 |
| Debtors | 250 | |
| Fixtures and Fittings | 1,405 | |
| Capital | | 1,750 |
| Motor Car | 4,770 | |
| Bank Loan | | 500 |
| | 12,875 | 12,875 |

Exercise 2D

A Trial Balance will not reveal the following types of error.

(1) *Both parts of an entry omitted* The Trial Balance still balances but the accounts are clearly inaccurate.

(2) *Compensating errors* If two errors are made which cancel each other out, the Trial Balance will balance, but the accounts are clearly inaccurate.

(3) *Errors of classification* An entry may be made on the right side but on the wrong *type* of account. For example, an asset may be purchased and, instead of debiting the asset account, the bookkeeper debits an expense account. The Trial Balance will balance but the accounts are not accurate. When the net profit is calculated at the end of the accounting period, expenses will be overstated and assets understated.

(4) *Wrong account used* The bookkeeper may make an entry on the correct side and on the correct type of account, but on the wrong example of the type. For example, a bill is delivered to client X but the DR entry is made on client Y's account. The Trial Balance will balance but the accounts are inaccurate.

(5) *Reversed entries* The bookkeeper may record the correct amounts on the correct accounts, but may DR the account which should be credited and vice versa. The Trial Balance will balance, but the accounts are not accurate.

Exercise 2E

**Sales**

| Date | Details | DR | CR | BAL |
|---|---|---|---|---|
| May | | | | |
| 1 | Balance | | | 30,000CR |
| 1 | A | | 200 | 30,200CR |

**A**

| Date | Details | DR | CR | BAL |
|---|---|---|---|---|
| May | | | | |
| 1 | Credit Sales | 200 | | 200DR |
| 3 | Cash | | 200 | – |

**Cash**

| Date | Details | DR | CR | BAL |
|---|---|---|---|---|
| May | | | | |
| 1 | Balance | | | 10,000DR |
| 2 | B | 200 | | 10,200DR |
| 3 | B – correction of error | | 200[1] | 10,000DR |
| 3 | A | 200[1] | | 10,200DR |
| 4 | B | 500 | | 10,700DR |
| 5 | B – dishonoured cheque | | 500 | 10,200DR |

[1] These entries cancel each other out. You could omit them completely and correct the error more simply by making a DR entry on B's account and a CR entry on A's account.

**B**

| Date | Details | DR | CR | BAL |
|---|---|---|---|---|
| May | | | | |
| 1 | Balance | | | 500DR |
| 2 | Cash | | 200 | 300DR |
| 3 | Cash – correction of error | 200 | | 500DR |
| 4 | Cash | | 500 | – |
| 5 | Cash – dishonoured cheque | 500 | | 500DR |
| 6 | Bad Debts | | 500 | – |

**Bad Debts**

| Date | Details | DR | CR | BAL |
|---|---|---|---|---|
| May | | | | |
| 6 | B | 500 | | 500DR |

# Chapter 3

# Final Accounts – Preparation of Profit and Loss Account



## 3.1 Purpose of Final Accounts

So far we have looked at the bookkeeping entries made by a firm to record its day-to-day business. These entries give the firm information on every single transaction carried out, for example, payment of a gas bill, purchase of a fixed asset, delivery of a bill to a client, receipt of cash from a client in payment of costs.

This information is required so that periodically (usually once a year) the business can calculate its net profit and list its assets and liabilities. As we saw in **Chapter 2**, net profit is calculated on a Profit and Loss Account, assets and liabilities are listed on a Balance Sheet. These end of year accounts are referred to as 'Final Accounts'.

## 3.2 Differences between Final Accounts of trading businesses and professional businesses

The Final Accounts of a trading business differ from those of a business providing professional services.

Both businesses have a Balance Sheet. A professional business has a Profit and Loss Account. This Profit and Loss Account shows income from professional charges and any other sources (eg, interest received, commission received) less its expenses. The difference between the two is its net profit.

A trading business has a Profit and Loss Account, but it also has a preliminary account called a Trading Account.

This Trading Account shows income from sales less the cost of those sales (ie, the cost of buying the trading stock). The difference between the two is the gross profit. The gross profit is then carried forward to start the Profit and Loss Account, and the expenses of the business are deducted from that gross profit. The difference between the two is the net profit.

We will consider the preparation of the Profit and Loss Account of a professional business first and then the preparation of a Trading Account for a trading business.

## 3.3 The Profit and Loss Account

### 3.3.1 The period covered

The accounting period will normally (but not necessarily) be one year. It is important that the Profit and Loss Account is headed with the period to which it relates.

> Examples
>
> Profit and Loss Account for ABC & Co for year ended 30 September [200–]
>
> Profit and Loss Account for ABC & Co for 1 October [200–] to 30 September [200–].

### 3.3.2 Classification of items

The profit or loss calculated on the Profit and Loss Account is the result of subtracting expenses from income. It is, therefore, vital that you can accurately identify these items and distinguish them from assets and liabilities of the business. If necessary, re-read **1.6.2.**

Exercise 3A

Study the following list of items. Identify those which will appear on the Profit and Loss Account as income and those which will appear there as expenses.

| | | | |
|---|---|---|---|
| Premises | Capital | Interest received | Stationery |
| Rent paid | Drawings | Interest paid | Creditors |
| Machinery | Profit costs | Insurance commission received | Debtors |
| Wages | Bank loan | Gas | |
| Repairs | Cash | Electricity | |

*Note*: Those items which are neither income nor expenses will be assets or liabilities and will appear on the Balance Sheet.

It is important to distinguish income receipts from capital receipts. A firm may sell its premises; the receipt of cash is a capital receipt and does not in itself affect the profitability of the firm. The firm has simply transformed one asset, premises, into a different sort of asset, cash. There will be changes on the firm's Balance Sheet, but nothing will appear on the Profit and Loss Account. However, it may be that an asset is sold for *more* or *less* than the value recorded for that asset in the firm's accounts. The resulting gain or loss over the recorded value would represent a profit or loss and would affect the firm's profitability. That profit or loss would appear on the firm's Profit and Loss Account. See **5.3.2**. It is important to distinguish capital profits from trading profits on the Profit and Loss Account. Failure to do so will make the Profit and Loss Account misleading.

> Example
>
> A professional partnership buys premises for £150,000. Two years later, it sells them for £150,000. After the sale, the Balance Sheet will show cash instead of premises. Nothing will be shown on the Profit and Loss Account in respect of the sale.

Had the premises been sold for £200,000, the gain of £50,000 over the recorded value of the premises would have been shown on the Profit and Loss Account as additional income of the firm.

Had the premises been sold for £100,000, the resulting loss of £50,000 would have appeared on the Profit and Loss Account as an additional expense.

The disposal of assets is dealt with in more detail in **Chapter 5**.

### 3.3.3 Preparation

Once you have identified the income and expense accounts, you will transfer the balances on those accounts to the Profit and Loss Account.

Expenses are transferred to the DR side of the Profit and Loss Account; income is transferred to the CR side of the Profit and Loss Account.

The Profit and Loss Account is usually set out vertically going down the page instead of in the normal tabular fashion. Instead of having a DR column next to a CR column, it has a DR section set out below the CR section. This is easier for non-accountants to understand. Despite its unusual appearance, the Profit and Loss Account is part of the Double Entry System. Accountants talk of expenses being 'debited' to the Profit and Loss Account and income 'credited' to it.

Example

Ann, a solicitor in sole practice, has the following income and expense accounts for the year 1 March [200–] to 28 February [200–]. The balances are transferred to the Profit and Loss Account and the ledger accounts for the current year are closed. Here is an extract from the Trial Balance prepared for Ann at the end of the year.

**Ann, a firm**

**Extract from Trial Balance 28 February 200–**

| | DR | CR |
|---|---|---|
| Profit Costs | | 120,000 |
| Interest Received | | 20,000 |
| General Expenses | 10,000 | |
| Salaries | 30,000 | |

Ann's Profit and Loss Account will show income less expenses and will look like this:

**Profit and Loss Account for Ann for year ended 28 February 200–**

| | £ | £ |
|---|---|---|
| **Income** | | |
| Profit Costs | 120,000 | |
| Interest Received | 20,000 | |
| | | 140,000 |
| **Expenses** | | |
| Salaries | 30,000 | |
| General Expenses | 10,000 | |
| | | (40,000) |
| NET PROFIT | | 100,000 |

The balance on the Profit and Loss Account, ie, the difference between the income side and the expenses side (£100,000), will represent the net profit.

The balance on the Profit and Loss Account (£100,000 in the above example) is transferred to the capital account.

If you think about it, you will see why. The net profit is 'owed' to the proprietor of the business; the capital account is the account which shows how much the business 'owes' the proprietor.

Assume that Ann contributed £120,000 cash to the business when she started it, and that during the first year she withdrew £20,000 cash. At the end of the first year, her net profit was £100,000. Her capital account will appear as follows:

**Capital**

| | DR | CR | BAL |
|---|---|---|---|
| Cash – Original Contribution | | 120,000 | 120,000CR |
| Cash – Drawings | 20,000 | | 100,000CR |
| Net Profit for year | | 100,000 | 200,000CR |

Exercise 3B

Prepare a Profit and Loss Account for Smith for the year ended 31 December 200– based on the Trial Balance set out below. Use the vertical form of presentation.

**Trial Balance as at 31 December 200–**

| | £ | £ |
|---|---|---|
| Profit Costs | | 18,462 |
| Wages and Salaries | 14,629 | |
| Motor Expenses | 520 | |
| Rent and Rates | 2,820 | |
| Stationery | 111 | |
| General Expenses (including Electricity) | 105 | |
| Fixtures and Fittings | 6,500 | |
| Motor Vehicles | 6,200 | |
| Debtors | 1,950 | |
| Creditors | | 1,538 |
| Cash at Bank | 1,654 | |
| Petty Cash | 40 | |
| Drawings | 895 | |
| Capital | | 15,424 |
| | 35,424 | 35,424 |

## 3.4 Trading businesses

### 3.4.1 Need for Trading Account

A trading business must produce a Trading Account as well as a Profit and Loss Account. The Trading Account calculates the difference between income from selling goods and the cost of goods sold. The result is called 'gross profit'. The Trading Account must be headed with the period to which it relates.

### 3.4.2 Preparation of Trading Account

The balance on the sales account for the year will be transferred to the Trading Account as income. The balance on the purchases account for the year will be transferred to the Trading Account as an expense.

The balance on the Trading Account, ie, the difference between the sales income and the cost of buying trading stock, will represent the gross profit. It will be carried down to start the Profit and Loss Account.

Example

A business, ABC & Co, has the following balances on its sales and purchases accounts for the year 1 January to 31 December 200–. The balances are transferred to the Trading Account.

ABC & Co

**Extract from Trial Balance as at 31 December 200–**

| | DR | CR |
|---|---|---|
| **Sales** | | **400,000** |
| **Purchases** | **280,000** | |

Its Trading Account will show sales less the cost of the goods sold.

**Trading Account for ABC & Co for year ended 31 December 200–**

| | | £ |
|---|---|---|
| | Sales | 400,000 |
| Less | Cost of goods sold | (280,000) |
| | Gross profit | 120,000 |

The gross profit is carried forward to start the Profit and Loss Account.

### 3.4.3 The 'cost of goods sold'

In the example of ABC & Co, we took the balance on the purchases account as the cost of goods sold. Frequently, it will be necessary to make an adjustment to allow for the value of stock left over at the end of the year. We will consider this in more detail in **Chapter 5**.

## 3.5 Solutions

Exercise 3A

| **Expenses** | **Income** |
|---|---|
| Rent paid | Profit costs |
| Wages | Interest received |
| Repairs | Insurance commission received |
| Interest paid | |
| Gas | |
| Electricity | |
| Stationery[1] | |

[1] You may have wondered whether to classify stationery as an asset or as an expense item. It is correct to classify it as an expense since the purchase of stationery is recurrent and the benefit of it is normally exhausted relatively quickly. (Any stationery which is left over at the end of the accounting period will be shown on the Balance Sheet as an asset. See **Chapter 5**.)

The remaining items represent assets or liabilities which will appear on the Balance Sheet.

Exercise 3B

**Profit and Loss Account for Smith for year ended 31 December 200–**

| | £ | £ |
|---|---|---|
| **Income** | | |
| Profit Costs | | 18,462 |
| **Expenses** | | |
| Wages and Salaries | 14,629 | |
| Motor Expenses | 520 | |
| Rent and Rates | 2,820 | |
| Stationery | 111 | |
| General Expenses | 105 | |
| | | (18,185) |
| **NET PROFIT** | | 277 |

# Chapter 4
# Final Accounts – Preparation of Balance Sheet



## 4.1 The Balance Sheet

### 4.1.1 The date of preparation

The Balance Sheet is a list of the assets and liabilities of the business. It lists assets and liabilities on the last day of the accounting period and is accurate only for that one day. It must be headed with that date.

> Example
> Balance Sheet for ABC & Co as at 31 December [year].

### 4.1.2 Assets and liabilities

As we saw at **3.3.3**, the balances on income and expense accounts for the year are transferred to the Profit and Loss Account to calculate net profit. The remaining accounts represent assets and liabilities. The balances on the accounts are not transferred. If a business has an asset or a liability on the evening of the last day of an accounting period, it will still have that asset or liability on the morning of the first day of the following accounting period. The balances on these accounts are carried down to start off the ledger accounts for the next period. The values of these assets and liabilities are listed on the Balance Sheet. Notice that the Balance Sheet is not an account and is not part of the double entry system. It is simply a list which summarises information already available to the proprietor in the accounts.

## 4.2 Preparation

Originally, a Balance Sheet was prepared in 'horizontal' form. It listed liabilities on the left and assets on the right. However, it is now more common to use a vertical presentation (shown at **4.2.2**). Remember that capital is a liability of the business. It represents the amount owing to the proprietor. The modern Balance Sheet is divided into two parts. One part shows the value of assets less liabilities owed to third parties. The other part shows the amount owed to the proprietor as capital. The two amounts should be the same.

### 4.2.1 Order of items

By convention, assets are listed in decreasing order of permanence (or, to put it another way, in increasing order of liquidity).

Thus, fixed assets are shown before current assets. Fixed assets are those which are bought not for resale but to improve the efficiency of the business, for example, premises, machinery. Premises are always shown first in the list of fixed assets.

Current (or circulating) assets are short-term assets which turn from one into another.

[cash → trading stock or work in progress → debtors → cash]

Stock or work in progress is always shown as the first current asset followed by debtors and cash.

Liabilities are divided into current and long term. Current liabilities are those which are repayable in 12 months or less from the date of the Balance Sheet. Long-term liabilities are those repayable more than 12 months from the date of the Balance Sheet.

Current liabilities are deducted from current assets to give a figure called net current assets (sometimes referred to as 'working capital'). This is an important figure for a business. It represents the liquid funds available to it. A business may have substantial assets and be very profitable, but, if it has insufficient liquid assets, it will be unable to meet its debts as they fall due and will be unable to continue trading. The Balance Sheet therefore highlights the net current assets figure.

Long-term liabilities are deducted from the total of fixed and net current assets to give a figure for the net assets of the business.

Net assets will always equal the new figure for capital.

### 4.2.2 Example

In the example set out below, we show the assets section first and the liabilities section second, labelling the sections 'Employment of Capital' and 'Capital Employed' respectively. However, it is perfectly possible to show the Balance Sheet the other way round with the liabilities section first. Different titles are often used for the two sections of the vertical Balance Sheet. The assets section is often titled simply 'Assets' and the liabilities section is often labelled 'Financed By' or 'Represented By'.

The business has just borrowed £100,000 from the bank on a five-year loan. The cash is in the bank at the moment although eventually the business will spend the cash on additional fixed assets. The Balance Sheet will appear as set out below.

Note that the Employment of Capital section (assets less liabilities owed to third parties) comes to £110,000 and is the same as the amount owed to the proprietor as capital.

Example

**Balance Sheet as at 30 September 200–**

| | £ | £ |
|---|---|---|
| **EMPLOYMENT OF CAPITAL** | | |
| **Fixed Assets** | | |
| Premises | 50,000 | |
| Machinery | 50,000 | |
| | | 100,000 |
| **Current Assets** | | |
| Debtors | 10,000 | |
| Cash | 102,000 | |
| **Less Current Liabilities** | | |
| Creditors | (2,000) | |
| **Net Current Assets** | | 110,000 |
| | | 210,000 |
| **Less Long-term Liabilities** | | |
| Five-year Bank Loan | | (100,000) |
| **Net Assets** | | **110,000** |
| **CAPITAL EMPLOYED** | | |
| **Capital** | | |
| Opening balance | 80,000 | |
| Net profit | 60,000 | |
| Drawings | (30,000) | |
| | | **110,000** |

### 4.2.3 Client bank account

A firm of solicitors will have an additional asset – a bank account containing money held for clients. This asset will always be equalled by the amount the firm 'owes' its clients. The two items are normally shown as self-cancelling items after net current assets.

Example

| | £ | £ |
|---|---|---|
| **Net Current Assets** | | 110,000 |
| Client bank account | 100,000 | |
| Due to clients | (100,000) | |

Exercise 4A

Prepare a Balance Sheet for Smith as at 31 December 200– based on the Trial Balance set out in Exercise 3B. Use the vertical form of presentation.

## 4.3 Solution

Exercise 4A

**Balance Sheet for Smith as at 31 December 200–**

| | £ | £ |
|---|---|---|
| **Employment of Capital** | | |
| **Fixed Assets** | | |
| Fixtures and Fittings | 6,500 | |
| Motor Vehicles | 6,200 | |
| | | 12,700 |
| **Current Assets** | | |
| Debtors | 1,950 | |
| Cash at Bank | 1,654 | |
| Petty Cash | 40 | |
| | 3,644 | |
| **Less Current Liabilities** | | |
| Creditors | (1,538) | |
| **Net Current Assets** | | 2,106 |
| **Net Assets** | | 14,806 |
| **Capital Employed** | | |
| **Capital** | | |
| Opening Balance | 15,424 | |
| Net profit | 277 | |
| Drawings | (895) | |
| | | 14,806 |

# Chapter 5
# Adjustments



## 5.1 What figures for income and expenses?

### 5.1.1 The concept of accruals

During the accounting period, entries are made on the ledger accounts as and when expenses are actually paid. Thus, if an electricity bill of £100 has been received but not yet paid, there will be no entries in the accounts.

The Final Accounts of most businesses are prepared rather differently on what is called the 'accruals basis'. The accruals basis requires that income and expenditure are recorded in the period *to which they relate* rather than that in which payment or receipt happens to occur. The Final Accounts must include all expenses which relate to the period, irrespective of whether the expense has yet been paid or whether bills have yet been received. So far as income is concerned, the accruals basis requires the Final Accounts to include all income 'earned' during the period, irrespective of whether cash has yet been received or whether bills have yet been delivered.

Conversely, if an expense has been paid in the current accounting period which actually relates to an earlier or later period, it will not be included in the current Final Accounts; neither will income received in the current accounting period which actually relates to an earlier or later period be included. Instead, such items will be included in the Final Accounts for the appropriate period.

Think of the process of determining which items relate to which period as 'matching'. You are trying to 'match' the expense to the period in which the benefit of the expense was obtained and to 'match' the income to the period in which the work producing the income was done.

The detail of the entries that need to be made in the accounts will vary depending on the type of income or expense involved, but the principle of 'matching' remains the same.

Exercise 5A

You are preparing Final Accounts for Smith & Co for the accounting year ending 31 December 2005. Decide which of the following items relate to the accounting year ending 31 December 2005.

(a) Electricity bill paid 10 January 2005 for period July–December 2004

(b) Electricity bill paid 10 July 2005 for period January–June 2005

(c) Electricity bill unpaid for period July–December 2005

(d) Stationery bill paid 30 November 2005. Three-quarters of the stationery purchased remains in the stationery cupboard on 1 January 2006.

(e) Rent for new premises paid in advance on 28 December 2005 for period January–March 2006

(f) Work done for clients during 2005 but not yet billed by 31 December 2005 is estimated at £15,000

### 5.1.2 Outstanding expenses

As and when expenses are paid during an accounting period, entries are made on the cash account and on the relevant expense account.

By the end of an accounting period, a DR balance will have built up on each expense ledger account. An unpaid bill increases the amount of the expense correctly attributable to the accounting period and must be added to the DR balance on the expense account to increase it. The increased expense is then shown on Profit and Loss as the true expense for the current accounting period. The amount of the unpaid liability is shown on the Balance Sheet as a current liability.

*Note:* The expense has been added to this year's profits but will not actually be paid until the following year. When it is paid, the bookkeeper must make sure that the expense is not included a second time. He does this by carrying forward a CR entry to start the expense account for the following period. Having a CR entry already made on the expense account at the start of the period means that, when the expense is finally paid, the balance on the expense account will return to zero.

Adjustments will be made *after* the preparation of the Trial Balance at the end of the accounting period.

You will never be required to make the entries to adjust the ledger accounts, but a full example of the entries is given below for completeness.

### Example

On 31 December, AB & Co are preparing their Final Accounts for Year 1. There was a balance on the administrative expenses account of £35,000 on 31 December Year 1, but there was an unpaid bill of £3,000. This bill was finally paid on 30 January Year 2.

On 31 December Year 1, before any adjustments, the administrative expenses account looked like this:

**Administrative Expenses Year 1**

| | DR | CR | BAL |
|---|---|---|---|
| Dec<br>31 Balance | | | 35,000DR |

To make the adjustment for the outstanding expense, the entries are as follows:

*Entries:*

DR Administrative Expenses ledger account for Year 1 } with the out-
CR Administrative Expenses ledger account for Year 2 } standing expenses

**Administrative Expenses Year 1**

| | DR | CR | BAL |
|---|---|---|---|
| Dec<br>31 Balance<br>31 Adjustment | <br><br>**3,000** | | <br>35,000DR<br>38,000DR |

**Administrative Expenses Year 2**

| Date | DR | CR | BAL |
|---|---|---|---|
| Jan<br>1 Adjustment | | **3,000** | 3,000CR |

The Profit and Loss Account for Year 1 will show the new balance on the administrative expenses account of £38,000.

The Balance Sheet will have an additional current liability of £3,000.

On 30 January Year 2 when the bill is paid, the entries will be as follows:

*Entries:*

CR Cash

DR Administrative Expenses ledger account Year 2

**Cash**

| | DR | CR | BAL |
|---|---|---|---|
| Jan<br>30 Electricity | | <br>**3,000** | xx<br>xx |

**Administrative Expenses Year 2**

| Date | DR | CR | BAL |
|---|---|---|---|
| Jan<br>1 Adjustment<br>30 Cash | <br><br>**3,000** | <br>3,000 | <br>3,000CR<br>– |

You can see that, once the old bill is paid in Year 2, the balance on the administrative expenses account for Year 2 returns to zero, ready to start recording the Year 2 expenses.

*Note:* The Profit and Loss Account and Balance Sheet position is shown in the Specimen Accounts at **1.6.3**. The Profit and Loss Account shows the adjusted balance for administrative expenses. The Balance Sheet has an additional current liability: accrued expenses of £3,000.

### 5.1.3 Prepayments

As and when expenses are paid during an accounting period, entries are made on the cash account and on the relevant expense account.

By the end of an accounting period, a DR balance will have built up on each expense ledger account.

An amount paid in the current period, the benefit of which will not be received until the following period, reduces the amount of the expense correctly attributable to the current accounting period and should be deducted from the DR balance on the current period's account to reduce it. The reduced expense is then shown on Profit and Loss as the true expense for the current accounting period.

The amount of the prepayment is shown on the Balance Sheet as a current asset (usually after cash). The 'asset' is the benefit of the payment. It allows the business to use something in the future without any future payment.

*Note:* The amount of the payment in advance is carried forward as a DR entry to start the expense account for the following period.

This ensures that, although no cash payment will be made in the following period to reflect the expense, there will be a DR entry on the expense account to increase the expenses for the following period to the appropriate level.

You will never be required to adjust the ledger accounts, but a full example of the entries is given below for completeness.

Example

On 31 December, AB & Co are preparing their Final Accounts for Year 1. There was a balance on the general expenses account of £55,000 on 31 December Year 1, but £4,000 of it is a prepayment relating to Year 2. On 31 December Year 1, before any adjustment, the general expenses account looked like this:

**General Expenses Year 1**

| | DR | CR | BAL |
|---|---|---|---|
| Dec<br>31 Balance | | | <br>55,000DR |

To make the adjustment for the prepayment, the entries are as follows:

*Entries:*

CR General Expenses ledger account for Year 1 } with the prepayment
DR General Expenses ledger account for Year 2 }

**General Expenses Year 1**

| | DR | CR | BAL |
|---|---|---|---|
| Dec<br>31 Balance<br>31 Adjustment | | <br><br>4,000 | <br>55,000DR<br>51,000DR |

**General Expenses Year 2**

| Date | DR | CR | BAL |
|---|---|---|---|
| Jan<br>1 Adjustment | <br>4,000 | | <br>4,000DR |

You can see that the general expenses account starts Year 2, with an expense of £4,000 already recorded.

*Note*: The Profit and Loss Account and Balance Sheet position is shown in the specimen Accounts at **1.6.3**. The Profit and Loss Account shows the adjusted balance for general expenses. The Balance Sheet has an additional current asset, a prepayment of £4,000.

### 5.1.4 Work in progress

A firm of solicitors (or other business which provides services) will want to adjust its profit costs account at the end of the year to reflect the value of work in progress at that date.

As and when bills are issued during the accounting period, the amount of profit costs will be recorded on the costs account and the client's ledger account. By the end of an accounting period, a CR balance will have built up on the profit costs ledger account. Some work will have been done but not yet billed.

The estimated value of work done but not yet billed increases the profit costs properly attributable to the current period and must be added to the balance on the costs account. The increased balance on the costs account must be shown on Profit and Loss. It is usual, however, to show the costs actually billed and the value of work in progress at the end of the year as two separate items, which are added together on Profit and Loss.

The value of work in progress at the end of the year is shown on the Balance Sheet as a current asset. It is normally shown as the first of the current assets.

*Note:* The value of work in progress is carried forward as a DR entry to start the costs account for the following period. This is to ensure that, when the bills are issued in the following period, the value of work in progress which has already been attributed to the current accounting period is not attributed a second time to the following period.

It is normal to show the value of work in progress at the start of the year as a deduction on Profit and Loss from the value of bills issued during the year.

For accounting periods ending on or after 22 June 2005 there will be some changes to the way work in progress is calculated for professional firms. The right to payment will normally be treated as accruing gradually as the work is done. The result is that much of work in progress will be shown as part of the debtors figure on the Balance Sheet instead of as a separate item.

Example

On 1 January Year 1, Jay & Co start a practice. During Year 1, bills are issued for profit costs of £30,000.

On 31 December Year 1, estimated work in progress is £3,000.
During Year 2, bills are issued for costs of £40,000.
On 31 December Year 2, estimated work in progress is £4,000.
During Year 3, bills are issued for costs of £50,000.
On 31 December Year 3, estimated work in progress is £5,000.
The Profit and Loss Account for Years 1, 2 and 3 will look as follows:

**Profit and Loss Account for Year ended 31 December Year 1**

| | | £ | £ |
|---|---|---|---|
| | Costs Billed | 30,000 | |
| *plus* | Work in progress at end of year | 3,000 | |
| | | | 33,000 |

**Profit and Loss Account for Year ended 31 December Year 2**

| | | £ | £ |
|---|---|---|---|
| | Costs Billed | 40,000 | |
| *less* | Work in progress at start of year | (3,000) | |
| *plus* | Work in progress at end of year | 4,000 | |
| | | | 41,000 |

**Profit and Loss Account for Year ended 31 December Year 3**

| | | £ | £ |
|---|---|---|---|
| | Costs Billed | 50,000 | |
| *less* | Work in progress at start of year | (4,000) | |
| *plus* | Work in progress at end of year | 5,000 | |
| | | | 51,000 |

The Balance Sheet for 31 December Year 1 will show work in progress as a current asset of £3,000, that for Year 2 will show £4,000 and that for Year 3 will show £5,000.

The Specimen Accounts at **1.6.3** show a firm which billed £478,000 in profit costs but had £30,000 work in progress at the start of the year. It estimated the value of its work in progress at the end of the year as £40,000.

### 5.1.5 Adjustment for closing stock on Trading Account

When we calculated gross profit on the Trading Account earlier, we deducted the cost of goods sold from sales and we used the purchases figure to represent the cost of goods sold. However, the purchases figure does not by itself represent the correct value for cost of goods sold. It is necessary to make an adjustment for the value of any stock purchased during the year and left unsold at the end of the year.

To see why this is so, consider the following example.

**Example**

X starts a trading business. In Year 1, X purchases goods for £3,000. During the year, X sells goods for £7,000. At the end of the year, X has goods left over which cost £1,000 to buy and which X hopes to sell for £2,500.

To buy the goods *which X sold* cost X £3,000 less £1,000. The Trading Account set out below shows this calculation:

**Trading Account for X**
**Year 1**

| | | £ | £ |
|---|---|---|---|
| | Sales | | 7,000 |
| *Less* | Cost of Goods Sold | | |
| | Purchases | 3,000 | |
| | *less* Closing Stock | (1,000) | |
| | | | (2,000) |
| | GROSS PROFIT | | 5,000 |

The 'closing stock' is an asset of the firm. It will be valued at the lesser of cost or realisable value and will be carried forward to start the next accounting period where it will be referred to as 'opening stock'. The value of opening stock will also have to be taken into account when calculating the cost of goods sold in the next accounting period.

In Year 2, X purchases goods for £5,000, sells goods for £12,000 and has goods left over at the end of the year which cost £2,000.

In Year 2, X has available for sale not just the goods purchased in Year 2 but also the stock purchased in Year 1 and left over. The value of opening stock will, thus, increase the cost of goods sold.

The Trading Account set out below shows this calculation:

**Trading Account for X**
**Year 2**

| | | £ | £ |
|---|---|---|---|
| | Sales | | 12,000 |
| *Less* | Cost of Goods Sold | | |
| | Purchases | 5,000 | |
| | *plus* Opening Stock | 1,000 | |
| | *less* Closing Stock | (2,000) | |
| | | | (4,000) |
| | GROSS PROFIT | | 8,000 |

You will see from the above example that the cost of goods sold is calculated as follows:

Purchases + Opening stock – Closing stock = Cost of goods sold

By convention, stock is valued at the *lesser* of acquisition or realisable value. It is, therefore, necessary to inspect the goods at the end of the accounting period to check for deterioration and pilferage. When you are analysing accounts, always look critically at the figure given for closing stock. The value given may not be a realistic assessment of the value of the stock. Overvaluing stock is an easy way to make a profit figure look better. Look at the following example.

**Example**

In its first year of trading, X & Co has sales of £20,000 and purchases of £10,000.

We have set out below the Trading Account on the basis that:

(a) closing stock is valued at £1,000;

(b) closing stock is valued at £7,000.

**(a) Trading Account for X & Co**
**Year 1**

| | | £ | £ |
|---|---|---|---|
| | Sales | | 20,000 |
| *Less* | Cost of Goods Sold | | |
| | Purchases | 10,000 | |
| | *less* Closing Stock | (1,000) | |
| | | | (9,000) |
| | GROSS PROFIT | | 11,000 |

(b) **Trading Account for X & Co**
**Year 1**

| | | £ | £ |
|---|---|---|---|
| | Sales | | 20,000 |
| *Less* | Cost of Goods Sold | | |
| | Purchases | 10,000 | |
| | *less* Closing Stock | (7,000) | |
| | | | (3,000) |
| | GROSS PROFIT | | 17,000 |

You will see that increasing the value for closing stock has the effect of increasing gross profit. Obviously, therefore, it is very important that the closing stock figure should be accurate. If it is not, the gross profit figure will also be inaccurate.

The value of closing stock is an asset of a trading business and as such must be shown on the Balance Sheet. It is a current asset.

Exercise 5B

Study the Trial Balance of Daniel Deronda & Co, set out below.

**Trial Balance as at 31 December 200–**

| | DR | CR |
|---|---|---|
| | £ | £ |
| Sales | | 109,083 |
| Purchases | 89,621 | |
| Opening Stock | 1,000 | |
| Wages and Salaries | 14,629 | |
| Motor Expenses | 520 | |
| Rates | 2,820 | |
| Stationery | 261 | |
| General Expenses (including Electricity) | 205 | |
| Fixtures and Fittings | 2,500 | |
| Motor Vehicles | 2,200 | |
| Debtors | 1,950 | |
| Creditors | | 1,788 |
| Cash at Bank | 1,654 | |
| Petty Cash | 40 | |
| Drawings | 895 | |
| Capital | | 5,424 |
| Rent Received | | 2,000 |
| | 118,295 | 118,295 |

(a) Prepare the Final Accounts for Daniel Deronda & Co for the 12 months ending 31 December 200–.

(b) Prepare Final Accounts for Daniel Deronda & Co for the 12 months ending 31 December 200–, taking into account the following adjustments:

(i) Closing stock at 31 December was £2,548.

(ii) The firm has received an electricity bill for £80 which it has not yet paid. There is unused stationery amounting to £20.

### 5.1.6 Income received in advance

The principle of 'matching' income and expenditure to the appropriate accounting period extends to all types of income and expenditure.

For example, a firm may receive some rent from a tenant in one accounting period which relates wholly or partly to a later period. Only the portion of rent which is correctly attributable to the current period will appear on the Profit and Loss Account.

### 5.1.7 Bad and doubtful debts

#### 5.1.7.1 Bad debts

It was mentioned in **Chapter 3** that a business will have to write off debts as bad from time to time.

*Entries:*
DR Bad Debts account
CR Customer's ledger account

The bad debts account is an expense account. Some debts will be written off as bad during the accounting period. In addition, at the end of an accounting period, a business may review debtors to consider whether any further debts need to be written off as bad. The balance on the bad debts account will be shown on Profit and Loss as an expense reducing the net profit.

After writing off any further debts considered to be bad, the remaining debtors will be shown on the Balance Sheet as a current asset.

Exercise 5C
At the end of an accounting period, you have already written off £1,500 debts as bad. Your remaining debtors amount to £20,000. You decide to write off a further £1,000 of debts as bad.

(a) What figure will you show on the bad debts account?
(b) What figure will you show on Profit and Loss for bad debts?
(c) What figure will you show on the Balance Sheet for debtors?

#### 5.1.7.2 Doubtful debts

At the end of an accounting period, a business will be shown as owed on paper a certain amount by debtors. However, the business will know from past experience that it never manages to collect all its debts.

It would therefore be inaccurate to calculate net profit on the basis that all debtors will pay and inaccurate to include the full debtors figure on the Balance Sheet. An adjustment must be made for doubtful debts.

A business will calculate the value of debtors it thinks may never pay and reduce the current year's net profit by this amount. This is referred to as a 'provision for doubtful debts'. It will DR the amount of this provision to the bad debts account, and this will increase the figure for bad debts shown on Profit and Loss.

*Note:* The amount of provision will be carried down as a CR balance to start the bad debts account for the following period. The effect of starting the year with a CR balance on bad debts is that, when debts are written off as bad during the accounting period, there will be no expense to be taken to Profit and Loss until sufficient bad debts are written off to exhaust the credit balance on the bad debts account.

The ledger account is frequently referred to as a 'bad *and doubtful* debts account'.

The amount of the 'provision for doubtful debts' will be shown on the Balance Sheet as a deduction from debtors.

The Specimen Accounts at **1.6.3** show a business which, at the date of the Trial Balance, had written off £15,000 of debts as bad and had £82,000 of debtors. It then decided to write off an additional debt of £2,000. Having reviewed its debtors, it concluded that £8,000 of them were doubtful, and it therefore made a provision for doubtful debts of £8,000.

**Exercise 5D**

The Trial Balance for Elliot & Co prepared on 31 December shows that debtors are £31,000 and that bad debts already written off are £4,000. The firm wants to write off as bad the debt of Jones, who owes £1,000. It reviews its remaining debtors and concludes that 5% of them are doubtful; it therefore makes a provision of 5% of debtors.

(a) What figure will appear on the Profit and Loss account for *bad* debts? Do not include provision for doubtful debts in your answer to this part of the question.

(b) What figure will appear on the Profit and Loss account for doubtful debts?

(c) What figure will appear on the Balance Sheet for debtors?

(d) Will Jones be shown as owing the firm money?

**Exercise 5E**

Freda is a solicitor in practice on her own. Her accounting period is 1 July to 30 June. As at 30 June 200–, her bookkeeper prepares the following Trial Balance:

**Trial Balance as at 30 June 200–**

| | | | **DR** | **CR** |
|---|---|---|---|---|
| | | | £ | £ |
| Capital | | | | 30,000 |
| Drawings | | | 20,000 | |
| **Costs** | Bills delivered during year | 80,000 | | |
| | Work in progress at start of year | (4,000) | | 76,000 |
| Premises | | | 60,000 | |
| Wages | | | 20,000 | |
| Electricity | | | 5,000 | |
| Stationery | | | 2,000 | |
| Travel | | | 500 | |
| Expenses | | | | |
| Rates | | | 2,200 | |
| Cash – Office Bank Account | | | 250 | |
| Petty Cash | | | 50 | |
| Debtors | | | 4,100 | |
| Creditors | | | | 3,100 |
| Bank Loan | | | | 5,500 |
| Loan Interest | | | 1,500 | |
| Bad Debts | | | 1,000 | |
| Interest Received | | | | 2,000 |
| Client Bank Account | | | 100,000 | |
| Due to Clients | | | | 100,000 |
| | | | 216,600 | 216,600 |

There are outstanding electricity expenses of £200 to take into account, and stationery stock left over at the end of the year amounts to £300. Closing work in progress is estimated at £7,000. A provision is to be made for doubtful debts of £175.

After the Trial Balance has been prepared, the bookkeeper finds a cheque for £350 from a debtor in settlement of the debtor's account. This cheque was received the week before but was not recorded in the accounts as the bookkeeper had temporarily overlooked it. The bookkeeper wishes to adjust the accounts to allow for the receipt of the money before preparing the accounts.

An employee of Freda's explains to the bookkeeper that she paid travel expenses of £25 from her own pocket the previous week and requires reimbursement. The bookkeeper gives the employee £25 from petty cash and adjusts the travel expenses account before preparing the Final Accounts.

For questions (1)–(5) below, tick which *one* of the alternative statements you think is correct.

(1) **In relation to the £200 outstanding electricity bill:**

(a) The £200 will increase the amount shown on Profit and Loss for electricity. It will not appear on the Balance Sheet.

(b) The £200 will reduce the amount shown on Profit and Loss for electricity and will appear on the Balance Sheet as a current asset.

(c) The £200 will increase the amount shown on Profit and Loss for electricity and will appear on the Balance Sheet as a current asset.

(d) The £200 will increase the amount shown on Profit and Loss for electricity and will appear on the Balance Sheet as a current liability.

(2) **In relation to the prepaid stationery stock of £300:**

(a) The £300 will increase the amount shown on Profit and Loss for stationery. It will not appear on the Balance Sheet.

(b) The £300 will reduce the amount shown on Profit and Loss for stationery and will appear on the Balance Sheet as a current asset.

(c) The £300 will increase the amount shown on Profit and Loss for stationery and will appear on the Balance Sheet as a current asset.

(d) The £300 will increase the amount shown on Profit and Loss for stationery and will appear on the Balance Sheet as a current liability.

(3) **The receipt of £350 in settlement of a debtor's bill will:**

(a) Increase debtors.

(b) Reduce debtors.

(c) Reduce bad debts.

(d) Have no effect on debtors.

(4) **The receipt of £350 as in (3) above will:**

(a) Reduce cash.

(b) Increase profit costs.

(c) Increase cash.

(d) Reduce profit costs.

(5) **The payment of £25 from petty cash to reimburse the employee for travel expenses will:**

(a) Reduce the balance on the cash account.

(b) Increase current liabilities.

(c) Increase travel expenses.

(d) Reduce current liabilities.

## 5.2 Depreciation

Many fixed assets lose some of their value each year, for example cars, fixtures and fittings.

### 5.2.1 Profit and Loss Account

This annual loss of value is a hidden expense of the business and must be shown on Profit and Loss as an item reducing net profit.

Example

X & Co buys a car in Year 1 for £15,000. By the end of Year 5 it is worn out and has a scrap value of only £100. Over the five years, it has depreciated by £14,900. To look at it another way, it has cost X & Co £2,980 a year to keep the car for the five years. The Profit and Loss Accounts for those years must show the annual expense of keeping the car.

### 5.2.2 Balance Sheet

The Balance Sheet will not show just the original purchase price of the asset. Instead, it will show the value at which the asset is 'carried' in the firm's accounts. This is the original purchase price with a deduction for the amount of depreciation incurred to date. This depreciation is referred to as 'accumulated depreciation'.

Example

X & Co's accounting year ends on 31 December. X & Co bought a car at the beginning of Year 1 for £15,000. Each year, X & Co depreciates the car by £2,000. At the end of Year 3, X & Co will have depreciated the car three times (once at the end of Years 1, 2 and 3). Accumulated depreciation will therefore amount to £6,000. The Balance Sheet as at 31 December Year 3 would include the following item for cars:

| **Fixed Assets** | | |
|---|---|---|
| | £ | £ |
| Car | 15,000 | |
| less Depreciation | (6,000) | |
| | | 9,000 |

*Note 1:* The £9,000 in the above example is referred to as the 'book value' of the car – its value in X & Co's books or accounts.

*Note 2:* The Profit and Loss Account *each year* will record the loss in value over the one-year period. Thus, each year, the depreciation expense shown on Profit and Loss will be £2,000.

*Note 3:* Each year, the amount of accumulated depreciation shown on the Balance Sheet will increase by £2,000.

### 5.2.3 Calculation

There are different methods of calculating the amount of depreciation, for example, the 'straight line' method and the 'reducing balance' method.

In this book, we will look only at the 'straight line' method.

A firm using the straight line method will decide on the likely life of an asset, for example, 10 years or four years.

The loss in value is spread evenly over the projected life of the asset. Thus, if the projected life is 10 years, each year the business will use up 10% of the asset's original value. If the projected life is four years, each year the asset will be reduced by 25% of its original value.

The reason that this method is called 'straight line' is that, each year, the same amount of depreciation is written off. If the asset is kept for the whole of its projected life, the value of the asset will eventually be reduced to zero.

There are different ways of making the entries for depreciation. The simplest way is to DR the depreciation directly to the Profit and Loss Account as an expense and to CR a 'provision for depreciation' account. For brevity, we will refer to it as a 'depreciation' account. This is done *after* the preparation of the final Trial Balance. The CR balance on the depreciation ledger account will be carried down to start the account for the following period.

The longer the asset is kept, the more depreciation will be written off and the bigger the carried forward CR balance on the depreciation account will be. Remember that the carried forward balance on the depreciation account represents accumulated depreciation *from earlier years*.

*Entries:*

DR Profit and Loss Account }
CR Depreciation account } Current year

The increased CR balance on the depreciation account will then be carried down to the depreciation account for the following year.

**Example**

X & Co buys a machine in Year 1 for £10,000. X & Co decides to depreciate it by 10% pa. Each year, after the preparation of the Trial Balance, £1,000 will be charged to Profit and Loss as an expense, and £1,000 will be added to the balance on the depreciation account. The increased balance on the depreciation account will be shown on the Balance Sheet as a deduction from the value of the asset.

Thus, the Profit and Loss Account for each of the 10 years will appear as follows:

**X & Co**
**Profit and Loss Account Years 1–10**

| | £ |
|---|---|
| Expenses | |
| Depreciation | **1,000** |

However, the Balance Sheet for each of the 10 years will appear as follows:

X & Co

**Balance Sheet end of Year 1**

| | £ | £ |
|---|---|---|
| Machinery | 10,000 | |
| Depreciation | (1,000) | |
| | | 9,000 |

**Balance Sheet end of Year 2**

| | £ | £ |
|---|---|---|
| Machinery | 10,000 | |
| Depreciation | (2,000) | |
| | | 8,000 |

**Balance Sheet end of Year 3**

| | £ | £ |
|---|---|---|
| Machinery | 10,000 | |
| Depreciation | (3,000) | |
| | | 7,000 |

**Balance Sheet end of Year 4**

| | £ | £ |
|---|---|---|
| Machinery | 10,000 | |
| Depreciation | (4,000) | |
| | | 6,000 |

This depreciation continues until, at the end of Year 10, the value of the machine is reduced to zero.

*Note:* The other method of recording depreciation (the 'reducing balance' method) requires the firm to write off a percentage of the value of the asset as reduced by depreciation to date. This has the merit of recording the greatest drop in the value of the asset in the first year of the asset's life. Each year, less depreciation will be written off.

### 5.2.4 Date of purchase and sale

It is common practice:

(a) to depreciate all assets held at the end of an accounting period for an entire accounting period irrespective of the point in the period at which the purchase was made;

(b) not to depreciate assets sold part way through an accounting period.

This has the merit of simplifying calculations.

**Example**

The accounting period of X & Co is 1 January–31 December. In February, X & Co sells a car which it has owned for several years and purchases a replacement. It purchases a second car in November.

At the end of the accounting period on 31 December, the new car will be depreciated for a full year.

No depreciation for the current year will be recorded for the car sold.

**Exercise 5F**

A buys a car for her business for £20,000 on 1 July Year 1. Cars are depreciated by 10% pa using the straight line basis. A's accounting year ends on 31 December.

For questions (1) and (2) below, indicate which *one* of the alternative statements you think is correct.

(1) (a) The Profit and Loss Account for year ended 31 December Year 1 shows depreciation of £1,000.
(b) The Profit and Loss Account for year ended 31 December Year 2 shows depreciation of £2,000.
(c) The Profit and Loss Account for year ended 31 December Year 3 shows depreciation of £4,000.
(d) The Profit and Loss Account for year ended 31 December Year 4 shows depreciation of £6,000.

(2) (a) On 31 December Year 1, the book value of the car shown on the Balance Sheet is £20,000.
(b) On 31 December Year 1, the book value of the car shown on the Balance Sheet is £18,000.
(c) On 31 December Year 4, the book value of the car shown on the Balance Sheet is £14,000.
(d) On 31 December Year 4, the book value of the car shown on the Balance Sheet is £10,000.

The Specimen Accounts at **1.6.3** show a firm which depreciates assets as follows:

(a) fixtures 5%;
(b) computers 20%;
(c) cars 20%.

Fixtures have been depreciated for 13 years, computers for four years and cars for one year.

You can see that the Profit and Loss Account shows one year's depreciation, but that the Balance Sheet shows the original value of the asset less the total accumulated depreciation to date.

**Exercise 5G**

The following information is extracted from the accounts of Brown, a sole trader, for the year ended 31 May 200–.

| | £ |
|---|---|
| Sales | 422,168 |
| Purchases | 292,350 |
| Capital Account | 58,125 |
| Bank Loan | 15,000 |
| Drawings | 33,600 |
| Fixtures, Furniture and Office Equipment at cost | 22,500 |
| Accumulated depreciation on Fixtures, Furniture and Office Equipment at start of year | 11,000 |
| Motor Cars at cost | 20,000 |
| Accumulated depreciation on Motor Cars at start of year | 8,000 |
| Lease at cost | 7,893 |
| Creditors | 90,970 |
| Debtors | 26,781 |
| Cash at Bank (Office Account) | 2,519 |

| | |
|---|---:|
| Petty Cash Balance | 50 |
| Interest Received | 7,896 |
| Opening Stock | 14,322 |
| Bad Debts | 320 |
| Miscellaneous Income | 2,330 |
| General Expenses | 54,047 |

The following additional information is relevant:

(a) Closing Stock is valued at £16,217.

(b) During the year, Brown purchased some reproduction antique furniture for use in the office. Due to an error made by the supplier, the amount paid by the firm in respect thereof included the sum of £500 in payment for furniture for Brown's private use. No adjustment has yet been made in respect of this error.

(c) Miscellaneous Income includes the sum of £100 representing rent received in respect of the following year.

(d) Depreciation is to be charged (straight line basis) at the following rates:

| | |
|---|---|
| Fixtures, Furniture and Office Equipment | 5% per annum |
| Motor Cars | 10% per annum |

(e) In addition to the above adjustments, there are bills outstanding at the end of the year in respect of General Expenses which have not yet been accounted for, and these amount to £496.

(f) Additional bad debts amounting to £450 are to be written off.

For questions (1)–(9) tick which *one* of the alternative statements you think is correct.

(1) **With regard to the £450 written off as additional bad debts, the Profit and Loss Account will show:**

- (a) Bad debts of £320.
- (b) Bad debts of £450.
- (c) Bad debts of £770.
- (d) Debtors of £26,781 – £770 = £26,011.

(2) **With regard to the £450 written off as additional bad debts, the Balance Sheet will show:**

- (a) Bad debts of £450.
- (b) Bad debts of £770.
- (c) Debtors of £26,781 – £770 = £26,011.
- (d) Debtors of £26,781 – £450 = £26,331.

(3) **Closing Stock will be:**

- (a) Added to Purchases on the Trading Account.
- (b) Deducted from Purchases on the Trading Account.
- (c) Shown on the Balance Sheet as an addition to capital.
- (d) Shown on the Balance Sheet as a deduction from capital.

(4) **Opening Stock will be:**

- (a) Added to Purchases on the Trading Account.
- (b) Deducted from Purchases on the Trading Account.
- (c) Shown on the Balance Sheet as an addition to capital.
- (d) Shown on the Balance Sheet as a current liability.

(5) **The £500 for Brown's private furniture will:**

- (a) Be shown on Profit and Loss as an expense.

(b) Reduce the value of the furniture shown on the Balance Sheet.
(c) Increase Brown's capital balance.
(d) Not affect Brown's capital balance.

(6) **The £100 of rent received relating to the following year will:**
(a) Only increase miscellaneous income on Profit and Loss. It will not affect the Balance Sheet.
(b) Only reduce miscellaneous income on Profit and Loss. It will not affect the Balance Sheet.
(c) Increase miscellaneous income on Profit and Loss and be shown as a current asset on the Balance Sheet.
(d) Reduce the miscellaneous income on Profit and Loss and be shown as a current liability on the Balance Sheet.

(7) **Depreciation on cars on Profit and Loss will be:**
(a) £800.
(b) £8,880.
(c) £2,000.
(d) £10,000.

(8) **Depreciation on cars shown on the Balance Sheet will be:**
(a) £8,000.
(b) £2,000.
(c) £10,000.
(d) £8,800.

(9) **Outstanding expenses of £496 will:**
(a) Increase expenses on Profit and Loss.
(b) Reduce expenses on Profit and Loss.
(c) Have no effect on Profit and Loss.
(d) Have no effect on the Balance Sheet.

## 5.3 Revaluation

Assets which are not depreciated, such as premises, will continue to be recorded at their acquisition value. Over time, the real value may increase. As it does so, the value recorded in the accounts will become increasingly inaccurate.

The proprietor of a business may decide to revalue the asset. The increase in value 'belongs' to the proprietor. The entries are, therefore, as follows:

DR increase in value to asset account
CR increase in value to capital account

A proprietor may decide to revalue just before admitting a partner. The result is to reserve the benefit of the increase in value to date to the original proprietor.

Exercise 5H

Ruddle has been in practice as a solicitor for some years, and he decides to admit Trant into the firm as a partner with effect from 1 January Year 10.

The firm's accountant produces the following list of balances for the year ended 31 December Year 9.

| | £ |
|---|---|
| Capital account (at 1 January Year 9) | 100,000 |
| Cash at Bank – Client account: | |

| | | |
|---|---|---|
| Deposit account | 660,000 | |
| Current account | 47,896 | |
| Office account | 6,427 | (credit) |
| Petty Cash | 50 | |
| Clients' Ledger balances: | | |
| Office account | 35,946 | |
| Client account | 707,896 | |
| Drawings | 55,500 | |
| Profit Costs | 392,568 | |
| Opening Work in Progress | 29,644 | |
| Interest Received | 22,567 | |
| Sundry Creditors | 20,463 | |
| Administrative and General Expenses | 323,465 | |
| Freehold Premises | 90,000 | |
| Furniture and Library at cost | 15,000 | |
| Motor Cars at cost | 39,420 | |
| Provision for Depreciation at start of Year 9: | | |
| Furniture and Library | 4,500 | |
| Motor Cars | 15,768 | |
| Bank Loan | 26,732 | |

(a) Ruddle decides that premises will be revalued by £160,000 on 31 December Year 9 before admitting Trant.

(b) Depreciation is to be charged at the following rates (straight line basis):

Furniture and Library 15% pa

Motor Cars 20% pa

(c) Interest Received includes the sum of £800 which had been paid into the office bank account by the bank in error. The money belonged to another customer of the bank, and it has not yet rectified the error. You have made no entries as yet to correct the error.

For questions (1)–(6) below tick which *one* of the alternative statements you think is correct.

(1) **On the Balance Sheet prepared on 31 December Year 9:**
- (a) Premises will be shown at their acquisition value of £90,000.
- (b) Premises and capital will both be increased by £160,000.
- (c) Premises will be increased by £90,000.
- (d) The capital account of Ruddle will be increased by £90,000.

(2) **On the Profit and Loss Account for year ended 31 December Year 9, the increase in value of premises will:**
- (a) Be shown as additional income.
- (b) Be shown as additional expenses.
- (c) Be shown as a deduction from expenses.
- (d) Not be shown.

(3) **Depreciation on furniture and library will be:**
- (a) £2,250 on Profit and Loss.
- (b) £1,500 on Profit and Loss.
- (c) £4,500 on Profit and Loss.
- (d) £450 on Profit and Loss.

(4)
- (a) £4,500 on the Balance Sheet.
- (b) £6,750 on the Balance Sheet.

(c) £2,250 on the Balance Sheet.

(d) £1,500 on the Balance Sheet.

(5) **Depreciation on motor cars will be:**

(a) £15,768 on Profit and Loss.

(b) £7,884 on Profit and Loss.

(c) £7,884 on the Balance Sheet.

(d) £15,768 on the Balance Sheet.

(6) **The £800 received in error as interest received will:**

(a) Reduce interest received.

(b) Increase income on Profit and Loss.

(c) Reduce cash on the Balance Sheet.

(d) Increase capital on the Balance Sheet.

## 5.4 Disposal of a fixed asset

### 5.4.1 Disposal at 'book' value

When an asset is sold, the business will lose the asset and gain cash.

Exercise 5I

(1) What changes would you need to make to the ledger accounts set out below to record the sale of premises for £180,000?

**Premises**

| | DR | CR | BAL |
|---|---|---|---|
| Balance | | | 180,000DR |

**Cash**

| | DR | CR | BAL |
|---|---|---|---|
| Balance | | | 20,000DR |

(2) Would the transaction have any effect on:

(a) the Profit and Loss Account; and/or

(b) the Balance Sheet?

The loss of the asset and the receipt of cash must be recorded on the ledger accounts as in question (1) of **Exercise 5I.** Provided the asset is sold for exactly the value at which it is recorded in the accounts of the business, no gain or loss over book value arises as a result of the transaction. The only effect of the sale will be on the Balance Sheet where there will be fewer fixed assets and more cash. Total assets on the Balance Sheet remain the same.

No entries are made on the Profit and Loss. This is because the Profit and Loss Account records *income* receipts and expenditure. The sale of an asset gives rise to a *capital* receipt and, thus, has no effect on Profit and Loss.

### 5.4.2 Disposal not at 'book' value

It is fairly unusual for an asset to be sold for exactly the amount recorded in the accounts. If the asset is sold for *more* than its book value, the excess will be a *profit* on the sale. The profit will be recorded on the Profit and Loss Account and will increase net profit. If the asset is sold for *less* than its book value, there will be a loss on the sale. The loss will be recorded on the Profit and Loss Account and will reduce the net profit.

Note that only the *excess or shortfall* over book value is recorded on Profit and Loss.

It is important to differentiate profits and losses of this type from *trading* profits and losses. Failure to do so will make the Final Accounts misleading.

In May 2000, British Airways reported a small net profit. Inspection of the accounts revealed that there was a substantial trading loss. The profit had been made on the sale of assets.

Accounts should show profit resulting from trading activities and other items such as gains and losses on sale of assets separately.

Exercise 5J

Premises recorded in the accounts at £170,000 are sold for £200,000.

(a) What is the gain over book value?

(b) What will be recorded on Profit and Loss?

(c) What effect will the sale have on the Balance Sheet, assuming the Balance Sheet is prepared immediately after the sale?

## 5.5 Solutions

Exercise 5A

(a) This expense relates to an earlier accounting period, and will not be included in the Profit and Loss Account for the current year even though it is paid in the current period.

*Note:* The amount of the expense will have been included in the previous year's Profit and Loss Account.

(b) This expense relates to the current accounting year and will be included in the Profit and Loss Account for the current year.

(c) This expense relates to the current accounting year, and will be included in the current Profit and Loss Account even though not yet paid.

The firm has an outstanding liability which must be shown on the Balance Sheet at the end of the year.

(d) The stationery bill should be apportioned. One-quarter of the stationery purchased has been used in the current accounting period; three-quarters will not be used until the following period.

Therefore, one-quarter of the bill should be shown as an expense on the current Profit and Loss Account, and three-quarters should be carried forward as an expense to the Profit and Loss Account for the following period.

The value of the stock remaining is an asset of the firm and must be shown on the Balance Sheet as such.

(e) The rent has been paid in the current accounting period, but the benefit will not be obtained until the following period.

Therefore, the whole of the expense should be carried forward to the Profit and Loss Account for the following period.

The firm has an asset, the right to occupy the premises for three months without further payment. The right of occupation is an asset and should be shown as a current asset on the Balance Sheet at the end of the year.

(f) The work has been done in the current accounting period and therefore the benefit of it should be attributed to the current accounting period. It will be included on the current Profit and Loss Account as additional income. The value of the work done will be shown as a current asset on the Balance Sheet at the end of the year.

Exercise 5B

(a)

**Trading and Profit and Loss Account for Daniel Deronda & Co for year ended 31 December 200–**

| | | £ | £ |
|---|---|---|---|
| **Sales** | | | 109,083 |
| *Less* | **Cost of Goods Sold** | | |
| | Purchases | 89,621 | |
| | *Plus* Opening Stock | 1,000 | |
| | | | (90,621) |
| **Gross Profit** | | | 18,462 |
| *Plus* | Rent Received | | 2,000 |
| *Less Expenses* | | | |
| | Wages | 14,629 | |
| | Motor Expenses | 520 | |

| | £ | £ |
|---|---|---|
| Rates | 2,820 | |
| Stationery | 261 | |
| General Expenses (including Electricity) | 205 | |
| | | (18,435) |
| **Net Profit** | | 2,027 |

**Balance Sheet for Daniel Deronda & Co as at 31 December 200–**

| | £ | £ |
|---|---|---|
| **Employment of Capital** | | |
| **Fixed Assets** | | |
| Fixtures and Fittings | 2,500 | |
| Motor Vehicles | 2,200 | |
| | | 4,700 |
| **Current Assets** | | |
| Debtors | 1,950 | |
| Cash at Bank | 1,654 | |
| Petty Cash | 40 | |
| **Current Liabilities** | | |
| Creditors | (1,788) | |
| **Net Current Assets** | | **1,856** |
| | | 6,556 |
| **Capital Employed** | | |
| Balance as at 1 January | 5,424 | |
| Drawings | (895) | |
| Net profit | 2,027 | |
| | | 6,556 |

(b) (i) The cost of goods sold must be found by adding £1,000 (opening stock) and deducting £2,548 (closing stock). Closing stock must be shown as a current asset.

(ii) General expenses must be increased by the outstanding electricity bill of £80.

The £80 must be shown on the Balance Sheet as a current liability.

Stationery must be reduced by £20, which must be shown on the Balance Sheet as a current asset prepayment.

**Trading and Profit and Loss Account for Daniel Deronda & Co for year ended 31 December 200–**

| | £ | £ |
|---|---|---|
| **Sales** | | 109,083 |
| *Less* **Cost of Goods Sold** | | |
| Purchases | 89,621 | |
| *plus* Opening Stock | 1,000 | |
| *less* Closing Stock | (2,548) | |
| | | (88,073) |
| **Gross profit** | | 21,010 |
| *plus* Rent Received | | 2,000 |
| | | 23,010 |
| *less* Expenses | | |
| Wages and Salaries | 14,629 | |
| Motor Expenses | 520 | |
| Rates | 2,820 | |
| Stationery | 241 | |
| General Expenses | 285 | (18,495) |
| **Net Profit** | | 4,515 |

**Balance Sheet for Daniel Deronda & Co**
**as at 31 December 200–**

| | £ | £ |
|---|---|---|
| **Employment of Capital** | | |
| **Fixed Assets** | | |
| Fixtures and Fittings | 2,500 | |
| Motor Vehicles | 2,200 | 4,700 |
| **Current Assets** | | |
| Stock | 2,548 | |
| Debtors | 1,950 | |
| Cash at Bank | 1,654 | |
| Petty Cash | 40 | |
| Prepayment | 20 | |
| | 6,212 | |
| **Current Liabilities** | | |
| Creditors | (1,788) | |
| Accruals | (80) | |
| **Net Current Assets** | | 4,344 |
| **Net Assets** | | 9,044 |
| **Capital employed** | | |
| Capital | | |
| Balance as at 1 January | 5,424 | |
| Net Profit | 4,515 | |
| | 9,439 | |
| Drawings | (895) | |
| | | 9,044 |

Exercise 5C

(a) £2,500. Bad debts *were* £1,500; you have now written off a further £1,000.

(b) £2,500.

(c) £19,000. The debtors on the last day of the accounting period, having already written off bad debts of £1,500, *were* £20,000. You then wrote off a further £1,000, which will reduce debtors to £19,000.

Exercise 5D

(a) £5,000. Bad debts were £4,000, but the firm writes off an additional £1,000.

(b) £1,500. Debtors were £31,000, but an additional £1,000 of debts was written off as bad. Once a debt is written off, it ceases to be shown as an asset as part of the debtors figure. Thus, the debtors figure is reduced by £1,000 to £30,000. Five per cent of £30,000 is £1,500.

(c) The debtors figure has been reduced to £30,000, and this will be shown on the Balance Sheet. However, a provision of £1,500 has been made, and this must be shown on the Balance Sheet as a deduction from £30,000:

| | £ |
|---|---|
| Debtors | 30,000 |
| Provision | (1,500) |
| | 28,500 |

Thus, the final value of debtors shown on the Balance Sheet will be £28,500.

(d) No. Jones will not be shown as a debtor of the firm. His account has been closed and no longer has a DR balance. Only people who are still expected to pay are shown as debtors of a firm. Once a debt is written off as bad, it ceases to be an asset of the firm.

Exercise 5E

(1) (d) Outstanding expenses increase expenses shown on Profit and Loss and are shown on the Balance Sheet as a current liability.

(2) (b) Prepaid amounts reduce expenses shown on Profit and Loss and are shown on the Balance Sheet as current assets.

(3) (b)
(4) (c) } The cash received from a debtor will increase cash and reduce debtors. It will have no other effect.

(5) (c) The payment of petty cash to reimburse an employee for travel expenses will reduce petty cash and increase travel expenses (thereby reducing net profit). It will have no other effect.

Exercise 5F

(1) (b) Each year, the Profit and Loss Account shows a charge for depreciation of 10% of the acquisition value. Thus, each year the charge is £2,000.

(2) (b) The book value shown on the Balance Sheet is acquisition value less accumulated depreciation to date. At the end of Year 1, there has been one charge to depreciation, hence the book value is £18,000. At the end of Year 4, there have been four charges to depreciation, hence the book value is £12,000.

Exercise 5G

(1) (c) The full amount of bad debts written off during the year is shown on Profit and Loss (£320 + £450). Debtors do not appear on Profit and Loss. They are an asset.

(2) (d) The debtors figure shown on the Trial Balance already reflects the fact that £320 has been written off. When an additional £450 is written off, the debtors figure must be reduced further (£26,781 – £450). Bad debts do not appear on the Balance Sheet. They are an expense.

(3) (b) Closing stock is subtracted from purchases on the Trading Account and is shown on the Balance Sheet as a current asset.

(4) (a) Opening stock is added to purchases on the Trading Account. It is not shown as a separate item on the Balance Sheet.

(5) (b) The adjustment has no effect on the Profit and Loss Account. The value of furniture held by the firm must be reduced on the Balance Sheet. Brown owes the firm £500, and this will be shown on the Balance Sheet by *reducing* the balance on his capital account by £500.

(6) (d) This receipt is partly attributable to the following period. Thus, income shown on Profit and Loss for the current period must be reduced and the Balance Sheet must show that £100 is 'owed' to the next accounting period as a current liability.

(7) (c) The charge to depreciation shown on Profit and Loss is 10% of the acquisition value:

$$\frac{10}{100} \times £20{,}000 = £2{,}000$$

(8) (c) Accumulated depreciation must be shown on the Balance Sheet. This is depreciation already accumulated from previous years, shown on the Trial Balance as £8,000 plus the current year's depreciation of £2,000.

£8,000 + £2,000 = £10,000

(9) (a) Outstanding expenses increase expenses on Profit and Loss and are shown as a *current liability* on the Balance Sheet.

Exercise 5H

(1) (b) Premises and capital accounts are both increased by £160,000.

(2) (d) An increase in value resulting from a revaluation does not appear on Profit and Loss.

(3) (a) Depreciation on furniture charged to Profit and Loss is 15% of the acquisition value shown on the Trial Balance:

$$\frac{15}{100} \times £15{,}000 = £2{,}250$$

(4) (b) Accumulated depreciation shown on the Balance Sheet is the total of accumulated depreciation from previous years plus current depreciation:

£4,500 + £2,250 = £6,750

(5) (b) Depreciation on cars charged to Profit and Loss is 20% of the acquisition value shown on the Trial Balance:

$$\frac{20}{100} \times £39{,}420 = £7{,}884$$

Accumulated depreciation shown on the Balance Sheet is:

£7,884 + £15,768 = £23,652

(6) (a) The £800 must be deducted from interest received since it is *not* income of the firm. It has not yet been removed from the bank account, and, therefore, cash cannot be reduced. However, £800 is owed to the bank. Hence, there is an additional current liability.

Exercise 5I

(1) You will have no premises but more cash. Therefore, you must reduce the balance on the premises account to zero and increase the balance on cash by £180,000 to £200,000.

*Entries:*

| | |
|---|---|
| CR Premises | £180,000 |
| DR Cash | £180,000 |

(2) (a) It will have no effect on Profit and Loss. The Profit and Loss account records income receipts and expenditure. This is a capital receipt.

(b) There will be no premises on the Balance Sheet. Hence, fixed assets will be reduced. There will be more cash on the Balance Sheet. Hence, current assets will be increased. Overall, total assets will remain the same.

Exercise 5J

(a) Book value was £170,000. The sale was for £200,000. Therefore, the gain over book value is £30,000.

(b) Only the gain over book value, £30,000, is recorded on Profit and Loss. Thus, the net profit of the business will be increased by £30,000.

(c) Premises will no longer be shown in the fixed assets section of the Balance Sheet. Fixed assets will, therefore, be reduced by £170,000.

Cash will be increased by £200,000. Overall, therefore, the assets of the business will have been increased by £30,000.

The Capital Employed section will also be increased by £30,000, since the net profit of the business goes up by £30,000 and net profit is shown in the Capital Employed section of the Balance Sheet representing an amount owed to the proprietor by the business.

An extract from the Profit and Loss Account is shown below:

**Profit and Loss Account year ended [date]**

| | £ | £ |
|---|---|---|
| **Income** | | |
| Profit Costs | | xxx |
| Profit on Sale of Premises | | 30,000 |

# Chapter 6
# Partnerships



## 6.1 Introduction

In a partnership, capital is contributed by a number of different people (the partners) and the firm's profit is 'owed' to those partners. Separate records will have to be kept for each partner showing:

(a) the amount of capital contributed;

(b) the amount of profit 'owed' at the end of each year by the business to the partner;

(c) the amount of cash withdrawn from the business during the year by the partner.

The accounts of a partnership will have to show this information. There will, therefore, be some differences between the accounts of a sole practitioner and the accounts of a partnership.

Both trading and professional businesses can be run through the medium of a partnership. In this chapter, for convenience, we shall use a solicitor's firm for our illustrations.

## 6.2 How do partnership accounts differ from a sole trader's accounts?

### 6.2.1 Capital accounts

(a) Each partner will have a capital account in his or her own name. This account will show the amount contributed by the partner.

Example

A and B set up a partnership and contribute £30,000 and £20,000 respectively as capital.

**A – Capital**

| Date | Details | DR | CR | BAL |
|---|---|---|---|---|
| | Cash | | 30,000 | 30,000CR |

**B – Capital**

| Date | Details | DR | CR | BAL |
|---|---|---|---|---|
| | Cash | | 20,000 | 20,000CR |

The Balance Sheet will show separately the balance on each capital account.

**Balance Sheet as at [date]**

| | £ | £ |
|---|---|---|
| Capital | | |
| A | 30,000 | |
| B | 20,000 | |
| | | 50,000 |

(b) The capital account will also show the partner's share of an increase (or decrease) in value of an asset recorded in the accounts by way of revaluation.

The ratio in which partners are to share increases and decreases in the value of capital assets may be set out in the partnership agreement. If the partnership agreement is silent on this point, the partners will share capital increases and decreases in the ratio in which they agreed to share profits and losses.

Example

A and B in the previous example agreed that they would share increases and decreases in the capital value of assets in the ratio 2:1.

After a few years, they agree to increase the value of premises by £90,000.

A – Capital

| Date | Details | DR | CR | BAL |
|---|---|---|---|---|
| | Balance | | | 30,000CR |
| | Revaluation of premises | | 60,000 | 90,000CR |

B – Capital

| Date | Details | DR | CR | BAL |
|---|---|---|---|---|
| | Balance | | | 20,000CR |
| | Revaluation of premises | | 30,000 | 50,000CR |

*Note:* The DR balance on the premises account will be increased by £90,000.

### 6.2.2 Profit sharing

A well-drawn partnership agreement should set out the profit sharing ratio. If it is silent, the partners will share profits and losses equally.

A partnership agreement may provide that partners are to receive 'interest' on capital (common where capital contributions are unequal) and/or 'salaries' (common where some partners are required to work longer hours than others).

In the case of a sole practitioner, interest paid to lenders and salaries paid to employees are expenses which reduce net profit for tax purposes. However, so-called 'interest' and 'salaries' allowed to partners are not regarded by the Inland Revenue as expenses for tax purposes. The Inland Revenue regards such items as 'preferential appropriations' of profit. In other words, the partners must calculate net profit without regard to 'interest on capital' and 'salaries due to partners'. The partners must then take that net profit figure and appropriate it to the various partners in accordance with the terms of the partnership agreement, appropriating 'interest' and 'salaries' first, and then any balance to the partners in the agreed profit sharing ratio.

Unless the partnership agreement provides otherwise, 'salaries' and 'interest' must be appropriated to partners by the partnership irrespective of whether the net profit is sufficient to cover the amount due. The result may be to produce a loss for the year which must then be appropriated among all partners in the agreed profit sharing ratio. A well-drafted partnership agreement should, therefore, provide that salaries and interest are due only if profits are sufficient to cover them.

### 6.2.3 The appropriation account

The Profit and Loss Account of a partnership is prepared in exactly the same way as the Profit and Loss Account of a sole practitioner. However, as stated above, 'salaries' and 'interest' due to partners are not shown on the Profit and Loss Account.

The Profit and Loss Account is extended to an appropriation account on which the allocation of net profit among partners is shown.

Example

X and Y set up in partnership. X contributes capital of £5,000 and Y contributes £2,000.

The net profit for the year has been calculated at £21,700. The partnership agreement provides for interest on capital of 10% pa, a salary for Y of £1,000 pa and remaining profits to be divided 3:1.

**Profit and Loss Account for X Y & Co year ended [date]**

| | £ | £ | £ |
|---|---|---|---|
| Net Profit | | | 21,700 |
| **Appropriations** | X | Y | |
| Interest on Capital | 500 | 200 | 700 |
| Salary | – | 1,000 | 1,000 |
| Profits | 15,000 | 5,000 | 20,000 |
| | 15,500 | 6,200 | 21,700 |

### 6.2.4 Current account

The appropriation of net profit is 'owed' to each partner. A sole practitioner credits net profit direct to the capital account. In the case of a partnership, it is usual to have a separate current account for each partner to which the appropriation of net profit (including salary and interest) is credited and to which drawings are debited. The reason for separating capital and current accounts is that many partners are entitled to interest on capital contributed. It is therefore desirable to keep the capital contribution of each partner readily accessible and unaffected by subsequent appropriations of profits and drawings.

Example

Continuing the previous example, if X had withdrawn £10,000 and Y £8,000 during the first year, their current accounts would appear as follows:

**X – Current**

| | DR | CR | BAL |
|---|---|---|---|
| Drawings | 10,000 | | 10,000DR |
| Appropriations | | 15,500 | 5,500CR |

**Y – Current**

| | DR | CR | BAL |
|---|---|---|---|
| Drawings | 8,000 | | 8,000DR |
| Appropriations | | 6,200 | 1,800DR |

The CR balance on X's current account shows that X has withdrawn less than his full entitlement to profit, so the business 'owes' him £5,500. The DR balance on Y's current account shows that Y has withdrawn more than his full entitlement to profit, and so Y owes the business £1,800.

A well-drafted partnership agreement should limit the drawings partners are free to make without the agreement of other partners.

Exercise 6A

Parsley, Thyme and Sage are in partnership as solicitors. The partnership agreement provides for interest on capital of 10% pa. Thyme is to receive a salary of £9,000 pa and Sage a salary of £10,000 pa. Remaining profits are to be shared in the ratio 2:2:1.

The Trial Balance of Parsley, Thyme and Sage extracted at 31 December 200– is as follows:

**Trial Balance 200–**

| | | DR | CR |
|---|---|---|---|
| | | £ | £ |
| **Capital:** | Parsley | | 120,000 |
| | Thyme | | 80,000 |
| | Sage | | 10,000 |
| **Current:** | Parsley | | 2,000 |
| | Thyme | | 1,000 |
| | Sage | 2,800 | |
| Bank Loan | | | 34,750 |
| Premises | | 150,000 | |
| Office Equipment | | 29,300 | |
| Library | | 22,700 | |
| Vehicles | | 9,700 | |
| Profit costs | | | 260,000 |
| Interest Received | | | 20,250 |
| General Expenses | | 152,300 | |
| Interest Paid on Bank Loan | | 3,750 | |
| Travel Expenses | | 4,200 | |
| Debtors | | 171,000 | |
| Creditors | | | 20,000 |
| Office Bank Account | | 2,250 | |
| Client Bank Account | | 400,000 | |
| Due to Clients | | | 400,000 |
| | | 948,000 | 948,000 |

Prepare a Profit and Loss and Appropriation Account from the above figures.

### 6.2.5 The Balance Sheet

The capital and current account balances of each partner are shown separately on the Balance Sheet under the general heading of capital employed. A DR balance on a current account is subtracted from the other balances in the capital employed section.

Example

Continuing the previous example, the Balance Sheet will appear as follows:

**Balance Sheet for X Y & Co as at [date]**

| | | £ | £ |
|---|---|---|---|
| **Capital Employed** | | | |
| Capital | X | 5,000 | |
| | Y | 2,000 | |
| Current | X | 5,500 | |
| | Y | (1,800) | |
| | | | 10,700 |

### 6.2.6 Details of movements on partners' current accounts

You will notice that, in the previous example, we showed only the final balances for the current accounts on the Balance Sheet. This is because the Balance Sheet would be very cluttered if full details of salaries, interest, profit shares and drawings were included, especially where there are several partners. It would be difficult to pick out the important figures. However, it is clearly desirable to provide information as to how the balances were arrived at. It is, therefore, usual to provide an appendix to the Balance Sheet which sets out the detailed picture of movements on partners' current accounts.

A common form of presentation is set out in the example below.

**Example**

Details of movements on current accounts

| | A | B |
|---|---|---|
| | £ | £ |
| Balance at start of accounting period | 2,000CR | 2,000CR |
| Appropriations | 40,000 | 34,000 |
| Drawings | (22,000) | (18,000) |
| Closing balance | 20,000CR | 18,000CR |

**Exercise 6B**

Prepare a Balance Sheet and details of movements on partners' current accounts from the figures given in Exercise 6A and your calculation of net profit from that exercise.

## 6.3 Partnership changes

The number of partners may change part of the way through an accounting period either because a new partner is admitted or because an old partner leaves. This will affect the accounts as follows.

(a) Any contribution or removal of capital will be recorded immediately and any drawings will be recorded as and when they occur.

(b) The Profit and Loss Account will be prepared for the whole accounting period in the normal way and a net profit figure produced for the whole accounting period in the normal way.

(c) The net profit will then be apportioned on a time basis to the period before and the period after the change.

(d) Two appropriation accounts will be prepared, one allocating the pre-change profit in accordance with the pre-change partnership agreement and one allocating the post-change profit in accordance with the post-change partnership agreement.

**Revision Exercise 6C**

Do not attempt this exercise unless you have studied **Chapter 5**.

A and B are the partners in a firm of solicitors, AB & Co.

Their partnership agreement provides that partners are to receive interest on capital of 10% pa and that B is to receive a salary of £10,000 pa (profits permitting). Remaining profits are to be divided in the ratio 3:2.

The following Trial Balance is extracted from the accounts at the end of the current accounting year.

**Prepare Final Accounts including Movements on Partners' Current Accounts for the current year.**

*Note:* The Specimen Accounts at **1.6.3** form the solution to this exercise.

**AB & Co Solicitors**

**Trial Balance as at 31 December 200–**

| | £ 000 | £ 000 |
|---|---|---|
| Current Accounts | | |
| A | | 2 |
| B | | 3 |
| Drawings | | |
| A | 30 | |
| B | 26 | |
| Capital | | |
| A | | 50 |
| B | | 30 |
| Leasehold Premises | 218 | |
| Fixtures | 20 | |
| Depreciation on Fixtures | | 12 |
| Computers | 50 | |
| Depreciation on Computers | | 30 |
| Cars | 40 | |
| Debtors | 82 | |
| Office Bank Account | 10 | |
| Petty Cash | 1 | |
| Profit Costs Billed | | 478 |
| Opening Work in Progress | 30 | |
| Interest Received | | 20 |
| Insurance Commission Received | | 10 |
| Salaries | 98 | |
| General Expenses | 55 | |
| Administrative Expenses | 35 | |
| Bad Debts | 15 | |
| Rent Paid | 21 | |
| Loan Interest Paid | 5 | |
| Bank Loan | | 60 |
| Creditors | | 39 |
| Gain on Sale of Car | | 2 |
| Client Bank Account | 150 | |
| Due to Clients | | 150 |
| | 886 | 886 |

The following matters need to be taken into account:

(1) Work in Progress at the end of the year is estimated at £40,000.

(2) The partnership wishes to write off as bad an additional debt of £2,000. After reviewing its remaining debtors, it concludes that 10% of its remaining debtors are doubtful and that it needs to make a Provision for Doubtful Debts of 10% of remaining debtors.

(3) There are prepaid General Expenses of £4,000 which relate to the following year.

(4) There are accrued Administrative Expenses of £3,000.

(5) Depreciation is allowed on the straight line basis as follows:

Fixtures at 5%;
Computers at 20%;
Cars at 20%.

*Note:* During the current year, the partnership sold its previous car, making a gain of £2,000 over its book value, and acquired the present car for £40,000.

## 6.4 Taxation of partnerships

Each individual partner makes a tax return claiming personal allowances. The senior partner of the firm makes a return of partnership income. The Inland Revenue then makes a joint assessment to tax in the partnership name. This assessment is based on each partner's share of profit less reliefs and charges and supplies the senior partner with information on the method of calculation so that the tax burden can be apportioned among its partners.

The tax liability does not appear on the Profit and Loss or Appropriation Account of the partnership. You will see when you come to look at company accounts that the taxation of companies is different. A company has its own tax liability which is shown on its Appropriation Account.

## 6.5 Solutions

Exercise 6A

**Parsley, Thyme and Sage**

**Profit and Loss Account for year ended 31 December 200–**

| | | £ | £ |
|---|---|---|---|
| Income | | | |
| | Costs Billed | 260,000 | |
| | Interest Received | 20,250 | |
| | | | 280,250 |
| Expenses | | | |
| | General Expenses | 152,300 | |
| | Interest on Bank Loan | 3,750 | |
| | Travel Expenses | 4,200 | |
| | | | (160,250) |
| NET PROFIT | | | 120,000 |

**Appropriations**

| | **Parsley** | **Thyme** | **Sage** | |
|---|---|---|---|---|
| | £ | £ | £ | £ |
| **Interest** | 12,000 | 8,000 | 1,000 | 21,000 |
| **Salary** | – | 9,000 | 10,000 | 19,000 |
| **Profits** | 32,000 | 32,000 | 16,000 | 80,000 |
| | 44,000 | 49,000 | 27,000 | 120,000 |

Exercise 6B

**Movements in Partners' Current Accounts**

| | Parsley | Thyme | Sage |
|---|---|---|---|
| | £ | £ | £ |
| Opening Balance | 2,000 | 1,000 | (2,800) |
| Appropriations | 44,000 | 49,000 | 27,000 |
| | 46,000 | 50,000 | 24,200 |

**Parsley, Thyme and Sage**

**Balance Sheet as at 31 December 200–**

| | | £ | £ |
|---|---|---|---|
| **Employment of Capital** | | | |
| | Premises | 150,000 | |
| | Office Equipment | 29,300 | |
| | Library | 22,700 | |
| | Cars | 9,700 | |
| | | | 211,700 |
| **Current Assets** | | | |
| | Debtors | 171,000 | |
| | Office Bank Account | 2,250 | |
| | | 173,250 | |
| **Current Liabilities** | | | |
| | Creditors | (20,000) | |
| **Net Current Assets** | | | 153,250 |
| | Client Bank Account | 400,000 | |
| | Due to Clients | (400,000) | |
| | | | 364,950 |
| **Less Long-Term Liabilities** | | | |
| | Bank Loan | | (34,750) |
| **Net Assets** | | | **330,200** |
| **Capital Employed** | | | |
| Capital: | Parsley | 120,000 | |
| | Thyme | 80,000 | |
| | Sage | 10,000 | |
| Current: | Parsley | 46,000 | |
| | Thyme | 50,000 | |
| | Sage | 24,200 | |
| | | | 120,200 |
| | | | **330,200** |

# Chapter 7
# Company Accounts (1)



## 7.1 Introduction

The accounts of a company are prepared on exactly the same accounting basis as those of a sole trader or a partnership. There are, however, some differences in the form of the accounts because of the different legal nature of a company. We will look first at the way in which a company records the raising of capital.

A company is a separate legal individual from its owners. It can enter into contracts in its own name and has its own tax liabilities.

A company is owned by its members (called 'shareholders') who buy a 'share' in the company.

Companies are run by the directors who, in the case of small companies, will often be the shareholders; in the case of large companies the directors and shareholders will be different.

Why do people buy shares? There are two main reasons:

(a) People who wants to run a business will often choose to do it through the medium of a limited company because there is less financial risk to the owners. The only liability that shareholders have is to pay the cost of the share to the company. If the company runs into financial difficulties, it may be wound up as insolvent but the shareholders will not be asked to cover the debts (unless they have entered into personal guarantees with creditors or lenders).

To provide some protection for creditors of companies, it is not normally permissible to return amounts representing the initial capital contributions to the shareholders during the lifetime of the capital.

The owners of the business can withdraw profits from the company either by paying themselves a salary for acting as a director (if appropriate) or by withdrawing profits in the form of dividends (see (b) below).

If the business is successful the owners will often be able to sell the shares to third parties. They will receive a price based on the value of the company's assets at the date of the sale plus something for the 'goodwill' of the business generated by their successful past trading.

(b) A person who wants to invest money will often buy shares in a company as a way of profiting from a successfully managed business without having to fund the whole of the cost of the business. Each year the directors of the company will review the profits of the company and will decide how much of the profit, if any, can be returned to the shareholders as a cash dividend.

For example, a company with 40,0000 £1 shares may make a £100,000 profit in a particular year. The directors may decide that they need to retain £80,000 within the company to cover expected liabilities and future expansion but that they can pay £20,000 to the shareholders. Each shareholder will receive 50p per £1 share held. Dividends are normally paid at the end of the company's trading period although some companies will make smaller payments during the year. Dividends paid at the end of the year are referred to as 'final' dividends; those paid during the year are referred to as 'interim' dividends.

There is an element of uncertainty for investors as they depend on the decision of the directors as to the amount they will receive by way of dividend. Directors may decide, if profits are low or if substantial expansion is required, to pay no dividends in a particular year.

The level of dividends paid by many companies is often quite low and many people who invest in shares do so to obtain capital growth.

For example, Fred sets up a company. He contributes £10,000 and his father contributes £40,000. In return Fred is issued with one-fifth of the shares in the company and his father is issued with four-fifths. The company's assets are currently £50,000, the cash contributed, so if Fred's father tried to sell his shares he would probably get £40,000. Suppose that the company trades successfully for the next ten years and the assets increase to £1m. If a third party offers to buy the shares, Fred's father would receive four-fifths of £1m (£800,000). The third party would then own the shares and would receive any future dividends and the benefit of any further increases in asset values.

## 7.2 Raising capital by issuing shares

### 7.2.1 Issuing shares

When a company issues shares, the entries are the same as those made when a sole practitioner or partner introduces capital, except that a share capital account is used. Thus, if a company issues 100,000 £1 shares for £100,000 in cash, the entries will be:

**Cash**

| | DR | CR | BAL |
|---|---|---|---|
| Share Capital | 100,000 | | 100,000DR |

**Share Capital**

| | DR | CR | BAL |
|---|---|---|---|
| Cash | | 100,000 | 100,000CR |

**Question** Why do you think a company does not have a separate capital account for each shareholder?

**Answer** (1) There could be an enormous number of different shareholders, so that having a separate capital account for each one would be unmanageable.

(2) Since shareholders can sell their shares, the company would have to keep updating the names of the different capital accounts.

### 7.2.2 Issuing shares at par

A company may issue shares either at par or at premium. (It is not possible for shares to be issued at a discount; see Companies Act 1985, s 100.) Each share has a nominal or par (ie, face) value, eg £1. The issue of shares at par means that the shares are 'sold' to the shareholder for their nominal value; the accounting entries would be the same as in the above illustration. If a Balance Sheet were drawn up at this stage, it would appear as follows:

**Balance Sheet as at [date]**

| | £ |
|---|---|
| ASSETS | |
| Cash | 100,000 |
| FINANCED BY | £ |
| Share Capital | 100,000 |

### 7.2.3 Issuing shares at a premium

The issue of shares at a premium means that the shares are 'sold' to the shareholders for more than their nominal value. Thus, a share with a nominal value of £1 may be issued to a shareholder for £1.50; the premium is 50p. In such a case, the entries are as follows:

*Entries:*

DR the cash account with the *total amount* received from the shareholder, ie, the nominal value of the share *plus* the amount of the premium;

CR the share capital account with the *nominal value* only of the share; and

CR the share premium account with the amount of *the premium.*

Example

A company issues £10,000 worth of shares, each with a nominal value of £1, at a premium of 10%. This means that the company will receive £11,000 from the shareholders (ie, the premium is £1,000).

The following entries would appear in the accounts.

**Cash**

| | DR | CR | BAL |
|---|---|---|---|
| Share Capaital<br>Share Premium | 10,000<br>1,000 | | 10,000DR<br>11,000DR |

**Share Capital**

| | DR | CR | BAL |
|---|---|---|---|
| Cash | | 10,000 | 10,000CR |

**Share premium**

| | DR | CR | BAL |
|---|---|---|---|
| Cash | | 1,000 | 1,000CR |

(b) If a Balance Sheet were drawn up at this point, what would it look like?

**Balance Sheet as at 200–**

| | £ | £ |
|---|---|---|
| ASSETS | | 11,000 |
| Cash | | |
| | £ | £ |
| FINANCED BY | | |
| Share Capital | 10,000 | |
| Share Premium | 1,000 | |
| | | 11,000 |

You will see that the premium forms part of the capital employed by the company but is shown separately from the share capital account, which is limited to the nominal value of the shares (or, if less, their paid-up value). The premium represents a surplus on the issue of the shares. However, the surplus it represents cannot as a matter of law be returned to the shareholders during the lifetime of the company (except in exceptional cases). This is because of the company law rules on maintenance of capital. Therefore, the balance on the share premium account generally remains unaltered unless it is used for one of a limited number of permitted purposes (eg, writing off the expenses of forming the company).

### 7.2.4 Different types of shares

A company may issue shares of different types (ordinary, preference or deferred shares) and also shares of the same type carrying different rights (eg, voting and non-voting ordinary shares). Preference shareholders are entitled, assuming that a dividend is in fact declared, to a share in any profit made by the company in priority to any other shareholders. If there is only a small profit, the preference shareholders may receive a dividend and the ordinary shareholders nothing.

Different classes of preference share may be issued.

(a) The shares may be 'cumulative'. This means that preference shareholders have the right to receive arrears of dividend for years when no dividend was paid as well as the dividend for the current year before any amount is paid to the ordinary shareholders.

(b) 'Participating preference shares' give the right to participate in the distribution of any surplus profits after a stated percentage dividend has been paid to the ordinary shareholders and may also carry the right to share in any surplus assets on a winding-up.

(c) 'Redeemable preference shares' are those issued on terms that they will be repaid by the company at some time in the future. A company may also issue redeemable ordinary shares (Companies Act 1985, s 159).

The important point to appreciate is that, whatever type of share is issued, the basic *entries* are precisely the same, even though the shares will be recorded in different ledger accounts and will be shown separately in the Balance Sheet.

Exercise 7A

A company issues 50,000 8% preference shares of £1 each and 200,000 £1 ordinary shares at par for cash.

(a) What entries would appear in the accounts?

**Cash Account**

| Date | Details | DR | CR | BAL |
|---|---|---|---|---|
| | | | | |

**Ordinary Share Capital Account**

| Date | Details | DR | CR | BAL |
|---|---|---|---|---|
| | | | | |

**8% Preference Share Capital**

| Date | Details | DR | CR | BAL |
|---|---|---|---|---|
| | | | | |

(b) If a Balance Sheet were drawn up at this point, what would it look like?

**Balance Sheet as at [date]**

| | £ | £ |
|---|---|---|
| ASSETS | | |
| Cash | | |
| | £ | £ |
| FINANCED BY | | |
| 8% £1 Preference Shares | | |
| £1 Ordinary Shares | | |

### 7.2.5 The requirements of FRS4

The aim of Financial Reporting Standard 4 (FRS4) is to introduce greater consistency into the accounting treatment of 'capital instruments' (ie, long-term debts and share capital). It has been obligatory for companies to observe FRS4 in respect of periods ending on or after 22 June 1994.

It requires that the total of 'Shareholders' funds', by which it means share capital and reserves (but excluding minority interests – see below), be shown on the face of the Balance Sheet. Further, shares must be divided into 'equity' and 'non-equity'. Non-equity shares are shares which have a meaningful restriction on the rights which attach to them. The restriction may be as to the right to participate in profits or in assets on a winding-up. Equity shares are those which have no such restriction. The accounts must distinguish the types of share and must include a summary of rights attaching (eg, rights to dividends, when redeemable and for how much, what priority and what entitlement on winding-up, what voting rights).

### 7.2.6 Company buying its own shares

Sections 162–181 of the Companies Act 1985 permit a company, provided various conditions are complied with, to purchase its own shares (in the case of a private company, out of capital). Once purchased, the shares are cancelled and the issued share capital reduced by the nominal amount of the shares. However, except in the case of a private company purchasing out of capital, the overall share capital of the company is not reduced. This is because the shares must be purchased either from the proceeds of a new issue or from distributable profits. If new shares are issued, there is obviously no reduction in capital. If the shares are purchased from distributable profits, the company is required to make a transfer to a capital redemption reserve. This reserve (dealt with in more detail later in this chapter) is subject to the ordinary rules as to reduction of share capital.

## 7.3 Raising capital by borrowing

### 7.3.1 Issuing debentures at par

If a company borrows money, it will commonly do so by issuing debentures. A debenture is a document evidencing a loan made to the company. Thus, if a company issues debentures of £50,000, this basically means that the company is borrowing £50,000.

To record borrowing £50,000 by issuing a 12% debenture, the accounts would appear as follows:

**Cash Account**

| Date | Details | DR | CR | BAL |
|---|---|---|---|---|
| | 12% Debenture | 50,000 | | xxx<br>xxx |

**12% Debenture Account**

| Date | Details | DR | CR | BAL |
|---|---|---|---|---|
| | Cash | | 50,000 | 50,000CR |

A debenture differs from a share in that a debenture holder has no proprietary interest in the company (ie, he is not a 'member' of the company), and the payment of interest on a debenture is not dependent on the making of profits by the company.

From the point of view of the company, this has advantages and disadvantages.

> Exercise 7B
>
> You are the major shareholder of Company X. You wish to raise additional capital of £50,000 and are trying to decide whether to issue more shares or to borrow.
>
> What are the advantages and disadvantages of each course of action?

### 7.3.2 Issuing debentures at a discount

A company may issue debentures at par or at a discount. If debentures are issued at a discount, this means that the debenture holder pays less than the nominal value.

It is necessary to make entries regarding the discount both to record the expense incurred by the company in issuing the debenture and to ensure that the true liability of the company is shown in the debenture account, since the company will have to pay the full nominal value of the debenture on redemption.

### 7.3.3 The requirements of FRS4

The Companies Act 1985 requires companies to show on the face of the Balance Sheet the division between amounts falling due within and after 12 months from the date of the Balance Sheet (ie, to distinguish current and long-term liabilities). However, the accountancy profession has its own requirements. FRS4 requires a more detailed breakdown to be disclosed. Debts should be analysed between amounts falling due:

(a) in one year or less, or on demand;
(b) between one and two years;
(c) between two and five years;
(d) in five years or more.

## 7.4 A company's Profit and Loss Account

A company, like a partnership, has an appropriation section at the end of its Profit and Loss Account. The whole account is often referred to as the 'Profit and Loss and Appropriation Account'. In essence, the Profit and Loss Account of a company is the same as that of a partnership. However, minor differences occur in the types of expense which may appear on a company's Profit and Loss Account. These differences flow from the fact that a company is a separate legal person with its own legal identity separate from its shareholders and directors. A salary paid to a director is, from the company's point of view, an expense incurred in earning profit and will therefore appear on the Profit and Loss Account as an expense; a 'salary' paid to a partner under the terms of the partnership agreement is merely a method of allocating the profit and will appear on the appropriation section of the account.

Exercise 7C

(a) Partner A in the partnership AB & Co is entitled under the terms of the partnership agreement to a salary of £10,000 pa. Where does this appear on the Profit and Loss and Appropriation Account?

(b) Director A of the company AB & Co Ltd is entitled to a salary of £10,000 pa. Where does this appear on the Profit and Loss and Appropriation Account?

## 7.5 The use of the appropriation section of a company's Profit and Loss Account

This shows the purposes for which profit will be used. There are three main purposes: taxation, dividends and retention of profits.

Usually, taxation and dividends items are not *paid* until after the end of the accounting period. However, the allocation of profit to cover these items will appear on the appropriation section of the account.

It is essential to appreciate that entries in the appropriation section of the Profit and Loss Account (whether of a partnership or company) do not involve the actual payment of money. All that is happening is that the profit as shown in the Profit and Loss section is being earmarked for various purposes. The question of paying out money for those purposes is a totally separate matter and will be recorded on the ledger accounts and cash account of the company as and when payment is made.

### 7.5.1 Taxation

The first item to be considered after the net profit has been ascertained is the company's liability to corporation tax on that profit. Until this has been provided for, the directors are in no position to make a decision on the declaration of a dividend. Corporation tax is not normally payable until nine months after the end of the accounting period. Thus, the company will show on its appropriation account that a certain amount of profit is needed to pay the company's tax bill. The amount due to the Inland Revenue will appear on the Balance Sheet as a current liability.

Example

A company has share capital of £20,000. In its first year of trading, it has income of £60,000 and expenses of £50,000. It estimates that corporation tax of £2,500 will be payable.

(a) After providing for tax, only £7,500 of profit will be left.

**Profit and Loss Account for year ending [date]**

| | £ | £ |
|---|---|---|
| Net Profit before tax | | 10,000 |
| **Appropriated** | | |
| Tax | | (2,500) |
| Post-tax profit | | 7,500 |

(b) The Provision for Tax will appear in the Current Liabilities section of the Balance Sheet as follows:

**Balance Sheet as at [date]**

| | | £ | £ |
|---|---|---|---|
| | **ASSETS** | £ | £ |
| | **Fixed Assets** | | xxxx |
| | Current Assets | xxxx | |
| *less* | Current Liabilities | | |
| | Creditors | (xxx) | |
| | Provision for Tax | (2,500) | |
| | **Net Current Assets** | | xxx |
| | | | xxxx |
| | | £ | £ |
| | FINANCED BY | | |
| | Share Capital | | xxxx |

When the company *pays* its tax, the provision will disappear from the current liabilities section and cash will be reduced in the current assets section.

Large companies are treated rather differently for tax purposes. A 'large' company for this purpose is one whose profits in the accounting period in question do not exceed the upper limit for the small companies' rate of tax (currently £1.5m). Such a company has to pay its corporation tax in four instalments.

In practice, the first payment will be made six months and 14 days after the start of the company's accounting period and subsequent payments will be made quarterly. So, a large company with a 12-month accounting period and a 31 December year-end will pay its first instalment on 14 July and the next three instalments at quarterly intervals (ie, 14 October and the following 14 January and 14 April). (It will have to estimate its taxable profit to do this.) Hence, at the date of its Balance Sheet, two instalments of tax will have been paid and the rest will still be outstanding.

### 7.5.2 Dividends

A dividend represents a distribution of part of the net profit to the owners of the company (ie, the shareholders). A company is most unlikely to distribute the whole of its profit after tax, either because it needs to retain some (eg, for expansion) or because the profit is not actually available in the form of cash. Profit may be represented by any assets (eg, stock, debtors or fixed assets).

The directors will decide how much dividend can in their opinion safely be distributed to the shareholders. The amount of this proposed dividend will be shown on the appropriation section of the Profit and Loss Account. The company cannot actually *pay* the dividend until the shareholders approve its size in the annual general meeting, which will take place after the end of the accounting period. Hence, the dividend will appear in the Balance Sheet prepared at the end of the accounting period as a current liability.

This is the timetable:

(a) accounting period ends;

(b) accountant draws up the final accounts;

(c) directors consider the final accounts and decide how much dividend to recommend;

(d) annual general meeting takes place at which the shareholders agree (or disagree) the size of the dividend;

(e) company actually pays the dividend.

Example

The previous example showed a company which had a net profit of £10,000 and which had made provision for taxation of £2,500. Imagine now that the directors of the company recommend a dividend of £3,500. The directors therefore propose retaining £4,000 within the company. This retention is referred to as a 'Reserve'. The appropriation section of the Profit and Loss Account will appear as follows:

**Profit and Loss Account for year ending [date]**

| | £ | £ |
|---|---|---|
| Profit before tax | | 10,000 |
| **Appropriated** | | |
| Taxation | 2,500 | |
| Post-tax profit | | 7,500 |
| Dividend | 3,500 | |
| Reserve | 4,000 | |
| | | 7,500 |

The Balance Sheet set out below shows the proposed dividend.

**Balance Sheet as at [date]**

| | | £ | £ |
|---|---|---|---|
| | **ASSETS** | | |
| | **Fixed Assets** | | xxxx |
| | Current Assets | xxxx | |
| *less* | Current Liabilities | | |
| | Creditors | (xxx) | |
| | Proposed dividend | (3,500) | |
| | Provision for taxation | (2,500) | |
| | **Net Current Assets** | | xxx |
| | | | 24,000 |
| | FINANCED BY | | |
| | Share Capital | 20,000 | |
| | Profit and Loss Reserve | 4,000 | |
| | | | 24,000 |

The £4,000 retained within the company allows the directors to fund future expansion and cope with inflation; it is shown on the Balance Sheet as retained profit (otherwise known as a 'reserve': see **7.5.4**). In any event, since much of the profit will not be in the form of cash, it could not all have been distributed by way of dividend.

### 7.5.3 Interim dividends

A company may choose to pay a dividend (known as an 'interim dividend') during its accounting period. The amount of the interim dividend must be shown in the appropriation section of the Profit and Loss Account, since a portion of the company's profit has been allocated to this purpose. However, since an interim dividend has already been paid by the date of the Balance Sheet, it is not shown on the Balance Sheet as a liability. Only the amount of the final dividend needs to be shown as a liability.

Exercise 7D

A company pays an interim dividend of £12,000 during its financial year. When the final accounts for the year are subsequently drawn up, a post-tax profit of £65,000 is revealed and the directors decide to recommend a final dividend (ie, in addition to the interim dividend) of £15,000. What will appear on the Profit and Loss Account and on the Balance Sheet in respect of the company's dividends?

**Profit and Loss Account for year ending [date]**

| | £ | £ |
|---|---|---|
| Post-tax profit | | 65,000 |
| *less* **Dividends:** | | |
| Interim | | |
| Final | | |

**Balance Sheet as at [date]**

| | £ | £ |
|---|---|---|
| Current Liabilities | | |
| Proposed Dividend | | |

### 7.5.4 What is a reserve?

Once provision has been made for taxation and dividends, the balance of the net profit is retained in the business.

This retained profit is referred to as 'reserved profit' or 'reserves'.

The retained profit is profit which could have been distributed to the shareholders had there been sufficient liquid funds within the company and had the directors decided to distribute it. The reserve is therefore 'owed' to the shareholders and will be shown on the Balance Sheet as a liability. The amount of a reserve is normally shown on the Balance Sheet immediately after the share capital, and the two figures together are referred to as 'shareholders' funds'.

Look at this company's appropriation account and the section of the Balance Sheet dealing with shareholders' funds. Before the calculation of profit at the year end, the company had reserves of £20,000.

**Profit and Loss Account for year ending [date]**

| | £ | £ |
|---|---|---|
| Profit before tax | | 20,000 |
| **Appropriations** | | |
| Taxation | | (5,000) |
| Post-tax profit | | 15,000 |
| Dividend | | (8,000) |
| Reserved profit | | 7,000 |

**Balance Sheet as at [date]**

| | £ | £ |
|---|---|---|
| Share Capital | 25,000 | |
| Reserves | 27,000 | |

The retained profits are often referred to as a 'Profit and Loss Reserve'.

The reason why a reserve has no direct equivalent in the accounts of a sole trader or partnership is that the only method by which shareholders can become entitled to profits in the form of cash is by declaration of a dividend.

In the case of a sole practitioner or partnership, however, the business is not a separate legal entity from its owner(s), so that any profit belongs immediately to the owner(s). Whether this profit can actually be drawn out of the business is a totally different matter and will depend (among other things) on the availability of cash in the business. If profits of an unincorporated business remain undrawn, they will not be shown as 'reserves' in the Balance Sheet but will increase the capital account of a sole trader or, in the case of a partnership, the capital or current accounts of the partners.

In the case of a company, the balance of profit remaining after provision for tax has been made (ie, net profit after tax) is, in theory, wholly available to the shareholders. The decision as to how much of the profit to recommend for withdrawal in this way is made not by the shareholders, however, but by the directors. In fact, only a part of this balance will be allocated to the shareholders by way of dividend. There are several reasons for this, including lack of available cash and the need to retain profits to provide for expansion or merely to maintain adequate working capital to cope with inflation. Whatever the reason for the non-distribution of the whole of the net profit, the profit retained will be added to reserves.

We will look in more detail at types of reserves in **7.5.6**.

### 7.5.5 Other appropriation account items

Although taxation, dividends and reserves represent the main allocations of profit, other items may occasionally appear in the appropriation section of a company's Profit and Loss Account, for example, 'write-offs'.

When the expression 'written off against profits' is used, what this in fact means is that a debit entry is made in the appropriation section, with a corresponding credit entry in the account of the item which is being written off.

Examples of items which may be dealt with in this way are goodwill purchased on the takeover of a business and company formation expenses.

Each of these items will initially appear as a debit balance in its respective account. When, for example, goodwill is purchased, the entries will be DR goodwill account, CR cash. It is common practice, however, for the balance to be written off against profits in the appropriation section. This is because the 'asset' of goodwill is not a tangible asset and its value is, therefore, speculative. When the goodwill is written off, the entries made will be CR goodwill account, DR appropriation account. Similar entries would be made for other such 'assets' written off in this way.

### 7.5.6 Types of reserves

#### 7.5.6.1 General and specific reserves

It is often difficult for people not directly involved in the management of the company (eg, shareholders, employees) to understand why large amounts of profit are being retained within the company instead of being returned to the shareholders as dividends or being used to pay salaries for employees. It is quite common, therefore, for directors to indicate why profits are being retained by attaching labels to portions of retained profit, such as 'preference share redemption reserve' or 'debenture redemption reserve'. However, it is important to realise the labels are for convenience only; the reserves remain undistributed profits *owed* to shareholders.

Exercise 7E

Study the following Balance Sheet. What changes will result when the debenture is redeemed?

**Balance Sheet as at [date]**

| | | £ | £ |
|---|---|---|---|
| | ASSETS | | |
| | **Fixed Assets** | | 40,000 |
| | Current Assets | | |
| | Cash | 25,000 | |
| *less* | Current Liabilities | | |
| | Creditors | (5,000) | |
| | **Net Current Assets** | | 20,000 |
| | | | 60,000 |
| *less* | **Liabilities payable in more than 12 months** | | |
| | Debenture | | (10,000) |
| | | | 50,000 |
| | FINANCED BY | £ | £ |
| | Share Capital | 20,000 | |
| | Debenture Redemption Reserve | 10,000 | |
| | Profit and Loss Reserve | 20,000 | |
| | | | 50,000 |

### 7.5.6.2 Capital and revenue reserves

Capital reserves are reserves which, for legal or practical reasons, are not available for distribution by way of dividend. Although the Companies Act 1967 abolished the legal necessity for distinguishing between capital and revenue reserves in the Balance Sheet, it is still necessary to show a few capital reserves separately (eg, a capital redemption reserve and a share premium account).

A capital reserve may be created by retaining profits for a specific purpose (eg, the purchase of fixed assets), or it may arise through some activity unconnected with the earning of profits. Thus, when a company issues shares at a premium, it is required to show the surplus over the nominal value of the shares on a share premium account (see **7.2.3**).

When redeemable shares are redeemed, the company must make entries in its books to credit an amount equal to the nominal value of the shares to a capital redemption reserve, so that the capital of the company is not reduced.

A capital redemption reserve is required where a company buys back shares out of profits. To avoid reducing its capital, the company is required to transfer to a capital redemption reserve an amount equivalent to the nominal share capital bought back and cancelled.

Transfers to this reserve are also required where shares are purchased partly out of the proceeds of a fresh issue and partly from distributable profits and where a private company purchases shares out of capital. The precise rules as to the amount which needs to be transferred differ.

A revaluation reserve arises when a company decides to revalue its assets. As in the case of a partnership, if the value of assets shown in the Balance Sheet is increased, there must be a corresponding increase in the capital employed section of the Balance Sheet. Unlike a partnership, however, it is not the capital accounts which will record this increase; instead, a reserve account will be opened which will be credited with the revaluation increase. A revaluation reserve is a capital reserve. Having a capital reserve does not justify payment of dividends since no profit has actually been realised as a result of the revaluation.

Example

A company decides to revalue its fixed assets. The revaluation produces a net increase of £100,000 over the assets' previous book value of £140,000. The Balance Sheet will therefore appear as follows:

**Balance Sheet as at [date]**

| | After Revaluation | (Before Revaluation) |
|---|---|---|
| | £ | £ |
| ASSETS | | |
| **Fixed Assets** | 240,000 | 140,000 |
| **Net Current Assets** | 180,000 | 180,000 |
| | 420,000 | 320,000 |
| | £ | £ |
| FINANCED BY | | |
| Share Capital | 100,000 | 100,000 |
| Capital Reserve (Revaluation) | 100,000 | – |
| Profit and Loss Reserve (Retained profits) | 220,000 | 220,000 |
| | 420,000 | 320,000 |

Which items have changed?

A new reserve has been created, fixed assets have increased and net current assets remain unchanged.

Most reserves are revenue reserves. A revenue reserve may be created by retaining profits for a specific purpose (eg, to even out dividend declarations over a number of years) or merely by retaining profit generally. In either case, the assets represented by the reserve profit can be used for the payment of dividends in future years, always assuming that the necessary cash is available. This last caveat is extremely important. A company may have made a large profit over the year's trading, but at the end of the year it may have no cash. The profit may be represented by increased stocks, debtors or fixed assets.

#### 7.5.6.3 Reserve funds

As stated above, retaining profit for a particular purpose does not mean that the cash will be available for that purpose when it is required in the future. Although the value of the assets as a whole will have increased as a result of making a profit, the increase is likely to be in the form of extra fixed assets or trading stock, rather than extra cash. Therefore, in order to ensure that the required amount of cash is available, it will be necessary at the same time as profit is retained within the business to set aside an equivalent amount of cash in a reserve fund (sometimes called a 'sinking fund'). This will be a fund of easily realisable investments which can be used when needed.

Exercise 7F

A company has issued debentures with a nominal value of £40,000 redeemable after eight years. To cover the redemption of the debenture, the company decides to retain £5,000 of its net profit after tax each year for eight years. To ensure that it has cash available at the relevant time, the company decides to create a sinking fund by purchasing £5,000 worth of government stocks each year.

The Balance Sheet of the company at the end of the first year would include the following:

**Balance Sheet as at [End Yr 1]**

| ASSETS | £ |
|---|---|
| **Fixed Assets** | xxxxx |
| Debenture Redemption Sinking Fund | 5,000 |
| **Net Current Assets** | xxxxx |
| *less* Debenture | (40,000) |
| FINANCED BY | |
| Share Capital | xxxxx |
| Debenture Redemption Reserve | 5,000 |
| Profit and Loss Reserve | xxxxx |

At the end of each succeeding year, the balances on both the reserve and sinking fund accounts would be increased by £5,000 so that, by the time the debentures became redeemable, the Balance Sheet would include the following:

**Balance Sheet as at [End Yr 8]**

| ASSETS | £ |
|---|---|
| **Fixed Assets** | xxxxx |
| Debenture Redemption Sinking Fund | 40,000 |
| **Net Current Assets** | xxxxx |
| *less* Debenture | (40,000) |
| FINANCED BY | |
| Share Capital | xxxxx |
| Debenture Redemption Reserve | 40,000 |
| Profit and Loss Reserve | xxxxx |

How will the Balance Sheet change when the sinking fund investments are used to redeem the debenture?

### 7.5.6.4 Capitalisation of reserves

The result of retaining part of the net profit in the business is that, after a number of years, a company will have built up substantial reserves of undistributed profit. Although these reserves are in theory 'owed' to the shareholders, in reality they will be represented by fixed assets and net current assets, and there will not be sufficient cash to pay the shareholders everything 'owed'. To recognise this state of affairs, the company may decide to capitalise some of these reserves by making a bonus issue of shares to its members. The company will receive no cash in return for the shares, so, instead of making a debit entry on the cash account, the debit entry will be made on the profit and loss reserve account.

Exercise 7G

A company with an issued share capital of 20,000 £1 ordinary shares and a profit and loss reserve of £25,000 decides to make a 'one for two' bonus issue (ie, one bonus share for every two shares currently held).

(a) What entries will be made to record this in the ledger account below?

**Share Capital – £1 Ordinary**

| Date | Details | DR | CR | BAL |
|---|---|---|---|---|
| | Balance | | | 20,000CR |

**Profit and Loss Reserve**

| Date | Details | DR | CR | BAL |
|---|---|---|---|---|
| | Balance | | | 25,000CR |

(b) What changes will be made to the Balance Sheet of the company after the bonus issue?

**Balance Sheet**

| | (before) | (after) |
|---|---|---|
| | £ | £ |
| Share Capital | 20,000 | |
| Profit and Loss Reserve | 25,000 | |

(c) Will there be any changes to the assets section of the Balance Sheet?

The effect of a bonus issue is, therefore, that each shareholder will own a greater number of shares, but the value of each share will be less since the shares as a whole will still be represented by the same total value of assets. In addition, future dividends are likely to be declared at a lower rate because a similar amount of net profit will have to be apportioned among a larger number of shares.

Exercise 7H

For questions (1)–(3), study the following extract from the appropriation account and Balance Sheet.

**Profit and Loss Account for year ending [date]**

| | £ |
|---|---|
| Profit before tax | **100,000** |
| **Appropriated** | |
| Tax @ 20% | (20,000) |
| Profit after tax | **80,000** |
| Dividend | (37,000) |
| Reserved profit | 43,000 |

**Balance Sheet as at [date]**

| | |
|---|---|
| Share Capital | 100,000 |
| Reserves | 100,000 |

For questions (1) and (2), tick which one of the alternatives you think is correct.

(1) **Assume nothing has been written off against reserves. On last year's Balance Sheet, reserves would have been:**

(a) £100,000.

(b) £143,000.

(c) £57,000.

(d) £43,000.

(2) **Assume in addition to its final dividend of £37,000, the company had paid an interim dividend of £8,000 half-way through the accounting year:**

(a) The Balance Sheet will show a liability for dividends of £45,000.

(b) The Balance Sheet will show a liability for dividends of £8,000.

(c) The Balance Sheet will show a liability for dividends of £37,000.

(d) The Balance Sheet will show none of the above.

For questions (3) and (4), study the following Balance Sheet.

**Balance Sheet as at [date]**

| | £ | £ |
|---|---|---|
| **Fixed Assets** | | 300,000 |
| Current Assets | | |
| Cash | 300,000 | |
| Others | 100,000 | |
| Current Liabilities | (200,000) | |
| **Net Current Assets** | | 200,000 |
| *less* Debenture | | (100,000) |
| | | 400,000 |
| Share Capital | | |
| Ordinary | | 50,000 |
| Redeemable Preference Shares | | 100,000 |
| Debenture Redemption Reserve | | 100,000 |
| Redeemable Preference Share Reserve | | 100,000 |
| Profit and Loss Reserve | | 50,000 |
| | | 400,000 |

Tick which one of the following alternatives you think is correct.

(3) **Assume you pay off the debenture:**

(a) The debenture redemption reserve will disappear.

(b) Reserves will be reduced by £100,000.

(c) A capital reserve of £100,000 will be created.

(d) Cash will be reduced by £100,000.

(4) **Assume you redeem the preference shares:**

(a) The redeemable preference share reserve will disappear.

(b) The capital of the company will be reduced by £100,000.

(c) The company must create a capital redemption reserve of £100,000.

(d) Assets will not be reduced.

For question (5), study the following extract from a Balance Sheet.

**Balance Sheet as at [date]**

| | £ |
|---|---|
| Share Capital £1 ordinary | 50,000 |
| Reserves | 550,000 |
| | 600,000 |
| Assets | 600,000 |

(5) **Assume the company decides to make a 'two for one' bonus issue against reserves. Which one of the following alternatives is correct?**

(a) Assets will be reduced by £100,000.

(b) Reserves will increase by £100,000.

(c) Reserves will be reduced by £100,000.

(d) Share capital will be increased by £50,000.

## 7.6 Solutions

Exercise 7A

(a)

**Cash**

| | DR | CR | BAL |
|---|---|---|---|
| 8% Preference Share Capital | 50,000 | | 50,000DR |
| Ordinary Share Capital | 200,000 | | 250,000DR |

**Ordinary Share Capital**

| | DR | CR | BAL |
|---|---|---|---|
| Cash | | 200,000 | 200,000CR |

**8% Preference Share Capital**

| | DR | CR | BAL |
|---|---|---|---|
| Cash | | 50,000 | 50,000CR |

(b)

**Balance Sheet as at [date]**

| | £ | £ |
|---|---|---|
| ASSETS | | |
| Cash | | 250,000 |
| FINANCED BY | £ | £ |
| 8% £1 Preference Shares | 50,000 | |
| Ordinary Shares | 200,000 | |
| | | 250,000 |

Exercise 7B

**Shares**

**Advantages**

(i) Dividends need only be paid if profits are sufficient.

(ii) Shares are not normally bought back by the company so, once issued, the company has no further capital liability to the shareholder during the lifetime of the company.

**Disadvantage**

(i) Your majority shareholding will be diluted (unless the new shares are non-voting, but such shares may not be attractive to purchasers).

**Debentures**

**Advantages**

(i) Once the fixed rate of interest has been paid, any surplus profits are available to shareholders.

(ii) Debenture holders have no vote at meetings, so your majority position is safe.

**Disadvantages**

(i) The fixed rate of interest *must* be paid even when profits are poor.

(ii) The debenture will have to be redeemed, so cash will have to be made available.

Exercise 7C

(a) On the appropriation section. A partner's 'salary' is merely a preferential appropriation of profit (ie, it represents what the parties have decided to do with their net profit, not an item of expense which reduces the net profit).

(b) On the Profit and Loss Account. The directors are quite separate from the company. Salaries paid to directors are true expenses which reduce the net profit of the company.

Exercise 7D

**Profit and Loss Account for year ending [date]**

| | | £ | £ |
|---|---|---|---|
| | Post-tax profit | | 65,000 |
| *less* | **Dividends** | | |
| | Interim | (12,000) | |
| | Final | (15,000) | |

**Balance Sheet as at [date]**

| | £ | £ |
|---|---|---|
| **Current Liabilities** | | |
| Proposed Dividend | | 15,000 |

Exercise 7E

**Balance Sheet as at [date]**

| | | £ | £ |
|---|---|---|---|
| | ASSETS | | |
| | **Fixed Assets** | | 40,000 |
| | Current Assets | | |
| | Cash | 15,000 | |
| *less* | Current Liabilities | | |
| | Creditors | (5,000) | |
| | **Net Current Assets** | | 10,000 |
| | | | 50,000 |
| | | £ | £ |
| | FINANCED BY | | |
| | Share Capital | 20,000 | |
| | Debenture Redemption Reserve | 10,000 | |
| | Profit and Loss Reserve | 20,000 | |
| | | | 50,000 |

Cash has been reduced by £10,000. The debenture of £10,000 has disappeared. Notice that the debenture redemption reserve has remained on the Balance Sheet. This is because it is merely undistributed profit 'owed' to the shareholders. Nothing has been distributed to the shareholders, so this 'liability' remains. The company may decide to relabel the reserve.

Exercise 7F

| | £ |
|---|---|
| ASSETS | |
| Fixed Assets | xxxxx |
| Net Current Assets | xxxxx |
| | xxxxx |
| | £ |
| FINANCED BY | |
| Share Capital | xxxxx |
| Debenture Redemption Reserve | 40,000 |
| Profit and Loss Reserve | xxxxx |
| | xxxxx |

Note that the debenture liability has disappeared, as has the sinking fund. However, the reserved profits remain as they have not been returned to shareholders.

Exercise 7G

(a)

**Share Capital**

| | DR | CR | BAL |
|---|---|---|---|
| Balance | | | 20,000CR |
| Bonus Shares | | 10,000 | 30,000CR |

**Profit and Loss Reserve**

| | DR | CR | BAL |
|---|---|---|---|
| Balance | | | 25,000CR |
| Bonus Shares | 10,000 | | 15,000CR |

(b)

**Balance Sheet as at [date]**

| | (before) | (after) |
|---|---|---|
| | £ | £ |
| Share Capital | 20,000 | 30,000 |
| Profit and Loss Reserve | 25,000 | 15,000 |
| | 45,000 | 45,000 |

(c) No. Assets have neither been received nor disposed of.

Exercise 7H

(1) (c) This year's reserved profits will be added to accumulated reserves. As the result is £100,000, last year's reserves must have been £100,000 less £43,000, ie, £57,000.

(2) (c) Since the interim dividend has already been paid, it will have no effect on the Balance Sheet, which shows liability *to pay* dividends in the future.

(3) (d) Reserves are retained profits and cannot be reduced unless distributed to shareholders, used to write off allowable items or capitalised. The effect of repaying the debenture will be to remove a liability (the debenture) and to remove cash.

(4) (c) Because a company is not normally allowed to reduce its capital, it must create a capital reserve when shares are redeemed. The preference share redemption reserve does not disappear (see answer to question (4)). Assets will be reduced since cash will leave the company.

(5) (c) Each shareholder will receive two shares for every one share held. Therefore, the company will issue 100,000 £1 shares. Share capital will increase by £100,000. Reserves will be reduced by £100,000. Assets will not be affected.

# Chapter 8
# Company Accounts (2)



This chapter deals with additional items which you might encounter on a company balance sheet.

## 8.1 Consolidated accounts

### 8.1.1 Parents and subsidiaries

It is very common for a company which is expanding its business activities either to acquire control of other companies or to compartmentalise parts of its own organisation so that each part can be run as a separate company (this is sometimes described as 'ring fencing' hazardous parts of the company's business undertaking).

The resulting business combinations are referred to as 'groups'. The controlling company is referred to as the 'parent' and the controlled company as the 'subsidiary'.

As early as 1948, it was realised that shareholders in the parent company needed additional financial statements to show the combined results of all the companies in the group if they were to be able to assess performance of their company.

Whenever a company becomes a 'parent', the Companies Act 1985 requires that, in addition to preparing the normal final accounts of each of the companies in the group, it must produce:

(a) a consolidated Balance Sheet showing the financial state of the parent company and its subsidiary undertakings; and

(b) a consolidated Profit and Loss Account showing the profit or loss of the group.

Thus, although each company retains its own legal identity and must prepare its own final accounts, the requirements as to group accounts reflect the commercial reality that the group as a whole is a single unit. (There are certain exceptions to the requirement that consolidated accounts be produced, see **8.1.2**.)

### 8.1.2 Statutory definition of a 'parent'

Sections 229 and 230 of the Companies Act 1985 (as amended by the Companies Act 1989) require group accounts to be prepared by a 'parent undertaking'. Section 258 defines the term as follows:

> An undertaking is a parent to its subsidiary if:
>
> (1) it holds a majority of voting rights in its 'subsidiary'; or
>
> (2) it is a member of the 'subsidiary' and can appoint or remove directors who are able to exercise a majority of the voting rights at board meetings; or
>
> (3) it is a member of the subsidiary with sole control, pursuant to an agreement with other shareholders or members of a majority of voting rights in it; or
>
> (4) it has the right to exercise a dominant influence over the subsidiary by reason of provisions in its memorandum, articles, or a control contract; or

(5) it has a minimum stake in the subsidiary (generally, at least 20%) and, either, actually exercises a dominant influence over the subsidiary, or is managed on a unified basis with the subsidiary.

There is no obligation to produce group accounts where *the group* comes within the definition of 'small' or 'medium-sized'. Also, an intermediate parent company which is itself included in consolidated accounts does not generally have to produce group accounts; it must, however, file a copy of these consolidated accounts with the Registrar of Companies together with its own accounts.

### 8.1.3 'Share' or 'asset' takeovers

Sometimes, instead of buying shares in the other company, the acquiring company buys the *assets* of the other, which may well then be wound up (having sold all its assets, it now has only cash left). The difference between the two methods is that, in the case of a 'share takeover', the acquiring company becomes a 'parent', whereas, with an 'asset takeover', the companies remain quite separate.

Thus, only a 'share' takeover gives rise to a group of companies, and in the rest of this section we shall not consider an 'assets' takeover further.

### 8.1.4 FRS6 mergers

According to FRS6, a 'merger' is a business combination which results in the creation of a new reporting entity, formed from the combining parties in which the shareholders of those parties come together in partnership. No party obtains control or is seen to be dominant. The accounts of the new entity are prepared on a different basis to that on which the consolidated accounts of a parent and subsidiary are prepared.

Merger accounting is not dealt with further in this book.

### 8.1.5 The consolidated Balance Sheet

#### 8.1.5.1 Elimination of inter-company items

The consolidated Balance Sheet must show the assets and liabilities of the group as a whole.

It will not show an item owed by one company to the other as this is merely an internal matter.

> Example
>
> Company A buys all the shares in Company B for £10,000, thereby getting the use of all Company B's assets which are valued at £10,000. Company A has an asset – its investment in Company B – which will be recorded on its Balance Sheet at the price paid. Company B has a liability – it owes the value of its share capital and its retained profits to its only shareholder, Company A.
>
> Company A's asset and Company B's liability cancel each other out. Therefore, when preparing the consolidated Balance Sheet for the group, these inter-company items are excluded from the consolidated Balance Sheet.

The consolidated Balance Sheet for a group will show:

(a) the share capital of the parent;

(b) the reserves of the parent and any reserves of the subsidiary retained since the original investment by the parent;

(c) the current year's reserved profits for both companies as calculated on the current consolidated Profit and Loss Account;

(d) the assets of both companies excluding the parent's original investment in the subsidiary;

(e) any liabilities owed by the companies to outsiders excluding the share capital and reserves owed by the subsidiary to the parent.

#### 8.1.5.2 Goodwill and capital reserves

In the previous example, the parent company acquired the shares of the subsidiary for exactly the value of its assets. Sometimes, a parent company may pay more for the shares in the subsidiary than the apparent value of the subsidiary's assets. Sometimes, the parent may pay less.

A parent company which pays more for its subsidiary's shares than the book value of the assets is paying an additional amount for 'goodwill'. Goodwill is classified as an intangible fixed asset.

> Example
>
> Parent acquires all the shares of Child for £12,000. The book value of Child's assets is only £10,000.
>
> Parent has paid £2,000 for goodwill.

The 'extra' paid by the parent for the goodwill represents an asset which is not cancelled out by the subsidiary's liability, and so it must be shown on the consolidated Balance Sheet.

Goodwill is classified as an intangible fixed asset, and, because of its intangible nature, companies often write off its value. They can either do this against profits over a period of time or against reserves as soon as the goodwill is acquired.

A parent company which pays less for its subsidiary's share than the book value of the assets is making a profit (albeit unrealised). Because the parent has made a profit on the transaction, the subsidiary's liability does not cancel out the parent's asset. The profit must be shown on the consolidated Balance Sheet. A profit owing to the shareholders but not distributed to them is a reserve. In this case, the reserve is described as a 'capital' reserve and will appear as such on the consolidated Balance Sheet.

### 8.1.6 The consolidated Profit and Loss Account

This must show the income and expenses of the group as a whole. It will not show the dividend paid by the subsidiary to the parent as this is merely an internal matter.

The consolidated Profit and Loss Account for the group will show:

(a) the income of the parent and subsidiary excluding any dividend paid by the subsidiary to the parent;

(b) the expenses of the parent and subsidiary;

(c) the appropriation of profit excluding any dividend paid by the subsidiary to the parent.

### 8.1.7 Minority interests

One of the situations where a company becomes a 'parent' is where one company holds more than half the nominal value of the equity share capital of another company, with corresponding voting rights. It is therefore quite common for a 'group' to exist where part of the share capital of a subsidiary company is owned by shareholders who are not otherwise connected with the group. There is still a requirement that consolidated accounts be produced, but they will have to reflect the interest of the minority shareholders. The minority shareholders are, in effect, owners of a proportion of the group's assets.

#### 8.1.7.1 The Balance Sheet

The consolidated Balance Sheet will include the whole of the subsidiary's assets and outside liabilities. It will specify the interest of the minority shareholders, who for this purpose are shown as outside creditors.

FRS4 requires that minority interests be analysed into equity and non-equity interests. The values can be shown in the notes to the accounts, but the wording of the Balance Sheet must disclose that non-equity interests have been included. In the following example, we assume that the minority interests are equity interests.

Example

L Ltd is a company which had assets of £95,000 (fixed: £52,000; net current: £43,000). It acquires 60% of the issued share capital in M Ltd for £9,000. The remaining 40% of the issued share capital (£6,000) stayed in the ownership of outsiders. M Ltd has assets of £15,000 (fixed: £11,000; net current: £4,000). The share capital and reserves of L Ltd are £40,000 and £64,000

The consolidated Balance Sheet for the group will appear as follows:

**Consolidated Balance Sheet for L and M Group**

| | | £ | £ |
|---|---|---|---|
| ASSETS | | | |
| Fixed Assets: | **L Ltd** | 52,000 | |
| | **M Ltd** | 11,000 | |
| Net Current Assets: | **L Ltd** | 43,000 | |
| | **M Ltd** | 4,000 | |
| | | | 110,000 |
| FINANCED BY | | | |
| Share Capital | | 40,000 | |
| Reserves | | 64,000 | |
| Interest of Minority Shareholders | | 6,000 | |
| | | | 110,000 |

You will see that the consolidated Balance Sheet shows *all* the assets of the two companies. This is correct, as the group has the use of all the assets. The interest of the minority shareholders appears as a liability.

#### 8.1.7.2 The Profit and Loss Account

The existence of a minority shareholding in a subsidiary company will affect the entries appearing in a consolidated Profit and Loss Account for the group.

It is necessary to calculate the proportion of the subsidiary's net profit after tax which is attributable to the minority shareholders. This is then deducted on the appropriation section of the Profit and Loss Account before appropriations are made for dividends and reserves.

## 8.2 Deferred taxation

Provision for taxation appears in the appropriation section of the Profit and Loss Account and in the Balance Sheet as a current liability. Frequently, company accounts also include an item called 'provision for *deferred* tax' in this section of the final accounts. What is a provision for deferred taxation?

### 8.2.1 The concept

Accountants like to spread expenses evenly over the period to which they relate. Straight line depreciation is an example of this (see **Chapter 5**).

HM Revenue & Customs is not concerned with matching income and expenses to the appropriate period in the same way. Depreciation is not regarded as a deductible expense for tax purposes, so the tax liability of a company must be calculated on its net profit before deducting depreciation.

Although depreciation is non-deductible for tax purposes, companies are allowed to deduct capital allowances when calculating their taxable profit. The rules on the amount which can be deducted in the form of capital allowances vary according to the policies of the current government. Thus, net profit and taxable profit may be very different figures.

In some tax years, companies have been allowed large 'first year' capital allowances on the cost of purchasing fixed assets. In years when this is possible, the company obtains a great deal of tax relief in the year in which the allowance is claimed, resulting in a low tax bill and large post-tax profits for that year. Once the allowance has been claimed, there will be little or no tax relief for later years, which means bigger tax bills and, therefore, smaller post-tax profits for those years.

A distorting effect on a company's post-tax profit is produced by the fact that the benefit of the capital allowance on the purchase of an item of plant or machinery is usually greater *initially* than the figure treated as an annual accounting expense for depreciation. (Correspondingly, in later years it is generally smaller.) In simple terms, one might say that, from an accounting point of view, too much tax relief is being allowed initially and, as a result, too much tax will be charged in later years.

Accountants would describe such a situation by saying that a timing difference exists.

### 8.2.2 Object of deferred tax accounting

The object of deferred tax accounting is to restate the tax liability shown on the Profit and Loss Account as though timing differences did not exist and to iron out the distortions which they produce.

Accountants deal with timing differences by creating a provision for tax in a year in which they consider too little tax is being charged. They use that provision in later years to reduce the burden of the tax charged against current profits. The non-accountant may feel this to be an interesting but superfluous adjustment. However, this is not the case. Consider the following.

> **Example**
>
> You are looking at the accounts of a business. You find that the post-tax profit in 2004 is very high, while the post-tax profit in 2005 is very low. Would this decrease in profitability alarm you?
>
> Clearly, at first sight, a slump in profitability *would* alarm you, since it suggests a slump in trading profit.
>
> However, there might be an explanation not linked to declining trading profit. It is possible that, in 2004, the business received large capital allowances, which reduced its tax liability and thus increased its post-tax profit. In 2005, the business may have received lower capital allowances, which increased its tax liability, thus reducing its post-tax profit.

It is clearly unsatisfactory that the figure for post-tax profit, which is used by many as a yardstick for a company's performance, should be liable to such fluctuations.

*Note:* Even if the reduction in capital allowances is the explanation for the fall in profit, there might still be some cause for alarm. Has the business got sufficient cash to pay its tax bill? Have the people running the business foreseen the increase in tax and budgeted appropriately?

### 8.2.3 A basic illustration

First, consider how, in the absence of deferred tax accounting, the accounts of the following business (AB Ltd) would appear. For convenience, the example assumes an unchanging corporation tax rate of 40% for all of the years mentioned, and also that 100% capital allowances were available to the company. These assumptions highlight the problems caused by timing differences and make the illustration easier to follow.

> **Example**
>
> AB Ltd is a company which in recent years was making (after depreciation and other overheads) a profit of £10,000 per annum. Assume that in the first year covered by the example, it bought a machine for £10,000. The machine has an expected working life of four years, so that (calculated on the straight line basis) depreciation is for accounting purposes being treated as an annual expense of £2,500.
>
> Since depreciation does not qualify as a deductible expense for tax purposes, the £2,500 will have to be added back to determine the profit on which tax is payable.
>
> The company took a 100% capital allowance in the year of acquisition in respect of the machine.
>
> You will see from the example that the capital allowance has a distorting effect on the post-tax profit figures because the tax relief is taken in the first year and not spread over the machine's working life.

| Year | | Taxable profit £ | Tax @ 40% £ | Post-tax profit £ |
|---|---|---|---|---|
| 1 | | 12,500 | | |
| | less allowance | (10,000) | | |
| | | 2,500 | 1,000 | 9,000 |
| 2 | | 12,500 | 5,000 | 5,000 |
| 3 | | 12,500 | 5,000 | 5,000 |
| 4 | | 12,500 | 5,000 | 5,000 |

Over the four-year period, the company pays £16,000 in tax. If this were spread evenly over the four-year period, the company would pay £4,000 pa. From the point of view of accountants, who like to spread expenses evenly over the periods to which they relate, this means that in Year 1 the company paid £3,000 too little in tax. This is referred to as an 'originating difference'. In each of the next three years, the company pays £1,000 too much. This is referred to as a 'reversing difference'.

To iron out this distortion, AB Ltd should create in Year 1 a provision for deferred tax equal to the amount of tax 'saved' as a result of the excess tax relief (the originating difference). This provision would be shown on the Profit and Loss Account in Year 1, and would have the effect of reducing the post-tax profit for that year. In subsequent years, the provision would be used, and therefore shown on the Profit and Loss Account as a deduction from the taxation figure. This would have the effect of increasing the post-tax profit for subsequent years.

**Example**

The Profit and Loss Account for Year 1 should show the actual tax paid as well as a provision for the amount of tax saved as a result of the excessive relief.

(a) Using the figures from the example above, it will be necessary to create a provision of £3,000 for Year 1:

**Profit and Loss Account for Year 1**

| | £ | £ |
|---|---|---|
| Net Profit | | 10,000 |
| Tax | 1,000 | |
| *plus* Provision | 3,000 | |
| | | (4,000) |
| Post-tax Profit | | 6,000 |

In subsequent years, the account will have to show the actual tax paid of £5,000 pa. However, part of the provision created in Year 1 on the Profit and Loss Account will be used to reduce the amount finally shown as charged against profits.

(b) Each year, £1,000 of the provision will be used to reduce the amount of tax charged in the Profit and Loss Account.

**Profit and Loss Account for Years 2, 3 and 4**

| | £ | £ |
|---|---|---|
| Net Profit | | 10,000 |
| Tax | 5,000 | |
| *less* Provision | (1,000) | |
| | | (4,000) |
| Post-tax Profit | | 6,000 |

### 8.2.3.1 The deferred tax account

The provision created in Year 1 in the previous example will be credited to a deferred tax account. Roughly speaking, the balance on that account represents an expectation of paying tax in the future. The provision will be shown on the Balance Sheet as a long-term liability.

In subsequent years, the balance on the deferred tax account will be reduced as the provision is used.

### 8.2.4 Deferred tax and changes in rates of taxation

It is necessary to adjust the amount of provision made in the light of changes to the prevailing tax rates.

The arithmetical calculation of the amount of the provision can be complex and is not something a solicitor would expect to do.

### 8.2.5 Significance for solicitors

It is obvious that the calculation of the annual deferred tax charge is extremely complex. Accountants must calculate the actual amount of the originating difference for the year, then make allowance for any items of deduction. In addition, they must consider the impact of changes in the rates of corporation tax. Thus, a provision which originally was adequate may have become either inadequate or too great, and may therefore require adjustment.

As a solicitor, when looking at a set of accounts, you will probably not want (or be able) to check the calculation. However, you should certainly be concerned if no provision at all has been made, since this may mean that the business will face heavy tax bills in the future without any provision. This would mean a dramatic fall in post-tax profits. You should also ask whether correct accounting practice has been followed in calculating the amount of provision.

FRS 10 'Reporting Financial Performance' requires company accounts for accounting periods, ending on or after 23 January 2002, to be prepared showing a full provision for deferred tax. Up to then, companies had been able to make more limited provision.

# Chapter 9
# How to Read Accounts



## 9.1 The purposes of reading accounts

In broad terms, the purposes of reading the accounts of a business are:

(a) to assess its current performance; and
(b) to predict its future prospects.

Certain questions come immediately to mind, for example:

(a) Is the present level of profitability satisfactory?
(b) Is the profitability likely to improve in the future?
(c) Can the business meet its current liabilities?
(d) Will it be able to meet its current liabilities next year and the year after?
(e) Are investors in the business receiving a satisfactory return on their investment?
(f) Will they be doing better or worse in five years' time?

## 9.2 Who will want to read accounts and why?

The following people are likely to be interested in reading accounts:

(a) *Investors* To assess the level of risk and return.
(b) *Managers* To make sure that the business is performing to its potential.
(c) *Lenders* To ensure that the debt will be repaid and the business can pay interest.
(d) *Inland Revenue* To assess the profits for tax.
(e) *Potential purchasers* To consider whether the business is worth buying.
(f) *Employees* To negotiate terms and conditions of employment.

Bear in mind that not all of those interested will be able to get full information about the business they are assessing. Obviously, managers will be able to get all the necessary information, but how much an investor will be able to find out will depend largely on how much of an investment is involved – the larger the amount, the more influence a potential investor will have when demanding information.

## 9.3 The limitations of accounts

You must be able to understand what is in the accounts, but looking at accounts alone may provide a misleading picture of the state of a business. Accounts are produced only *after* events have occurred.

Furthermore, accounts can produce information of only a financial nature. Thus, a Balance Sheet will only list assets and liabilities of the business. It will not indicate the health or otherwise of labour relations, despite the fact that many people would regard good staff relations as a very important asset. A poor trade reputation would be regarded by many people as a liability, but it has no place on a financial statement.

There may also be matters entirely beyond the control of management, such as a declining market for the firm's products. In other words, the accounts provide only part of the information needed in the analysis of the position of a business.

## 9.4 What information do you need?

It is important to have a general picture of the firm that you are investigating:

(a) It is large or small?
(b) Is it growing or contracting?
(c) What is the nature of its business?
(d) Does it operate in an expanding or declining market?
(e) Does it depend heavily on a particular product or products?

The questions which you should ask depend on the circumstances and are largely a matter of common sense.

### 9.4.1 Public companies

A public company must prepare an annual report. The report has two main purposes:

(a) It complies with the requirements of the Companies Act 1985 to produce certain information and accounts.
(b) It gives the company an opportunity to promote itself, to its shareholders, to prospective investors and to analysts.

As you read any company's report, be very aware of the need to question and check everything:

(a) Are any of the figures in the accounts not clear? Is there an explanation in the Chairman's Statement or the Directors' Report? Do the notes help?
(b) Is the chairman expressing over-optimistic hopes in his statement? Do they look as though they can be supported by the company's current financial position? Do they look sensible in the light of the economy here and abroad?

It is unlikely, although not impossible, that you would find a direct lie in a company's report, but you should always look at the information critically to see whether a particular proposal or intention looks as if it can be justified.

Some of the items in a report are included because they must be, while some are included because the company wants to include them. The following must be included in any public company's report:

(a) Directors' Report.
(b) Auditors' Report.
(c) Balance Sheet – company and group.
(d) Profit and Loss Account – company or, if there is a group, then group only.
(e) Cash Flow Statement – company or, if there is a group, then group only.
(f) Notes giving the required information.
(g) Details of directors' interests.

Other items are optional, but you would generally be surprised if the following were not there in some form:

(a) Chairman's Statement. What is there to hide?
(b) Ten-year record missing? Has the company not been performing consistently in the long term?

In a sense, reading a company report is something that lawyers are well trained to do – you check and question everything before accepting it as true.

Remember, when you are reading the report, that there are other sources of information as well. Keep an eye on newspaper reports, television news, etc.

### 9.4.2 Partnerships and sole practitioners

There will be no published accounts for partnerships and sole practitioners. Even so, you should get copies of the accounts they produce and study them.

Be aware that the requirements as to the format and content of reports which apply to companies do not apply to unincorporated bodies to anywhere near the same extent.

In these circumstances, you must get as much information about the business as you can. Find out the following:

(a) Are its premises in a suitable area?
(b) Does it seem to be busy?
(c) Is it dealing in something which is going to provide an income in the long term?
(d) What sort of reputation does it have locally?
(e) What can you find out about the proprietors?

You can then look at the accounts in the light of that information. When your analysis raises further questions, you can get down to detailed discussions of the problems with the proprietors or their advisers.

Obviously, the amount of information you can get will depend on what your relationship is, or is to be, with the business.

## 9.5 Preliminary steps

As well as obtaining as much general information about the business as you can, there are a number of preliminary steps you should take before launching into a detailed analysis of the accounts. These involve, in part, checking the accuracy and reliability of the figures presented and, in part, building up a general picture of the business and the market in which it operates, so that the information extracted can be considered in a proper context. What might be normal for a small business might be very unusual for a large one. A particular level of profitability may be commendable in a time of recession but disappointing in a period when business generally is 'booming'.

Common preliminary steps are as follows.

(1) *Obtain the accounts for several years.* If you are going to make a realistic assessment of a business, it is important that you obtain its accounts for several years rather than for the previous year alone. One year's accounts will reveal important information – the extent of borrowings, the value of fixed assets, the amount of unpaid bills, the value of stock in hand – but it is difficult to reach reliable conclusions without making comparisons with earlier years.

(2) *Check the date of the Balance Sheet.* A business can choose a Balance Sheet date to suit itself. If the business is seasonal, then a Balance Sheet drawn up at one date could include figures which would show the business in a much more favourable light than a Balance Sheet drawn up at another date.

> Example
>
> A business manufactures Christmas decorations. It sells the decorations to department stores in September. A Balance Sheet drawn up in September would show a healthy cash balance and probably substantial debtors. By contrast, a Balance Sheet drawn up in July would show substantial stock, a high creditors figure and, probably, a large overdraft.

Always consider whether you have to take the date of the Balance Sheet into account when you are analysing the figures.

(a) Check the method of valuing fixed assets.

(b) When were the assets last valued? Freehold premises purchased 20 years earlier for £5,000 may still be shown in the Balance Sheet at that value. Their current value will probably be quite different.

(c) Has provision been made for depreciation? If so, what method has been used?

In the case of a company, you will be looking for the answers to these and other questions in the notes and the statement of accounting policies included in the company's published accounts. If you are dealing with a partnership or sole trader, you should ask for that information from the partners or proprietor.

> Exercise 9A
>
> What will be the effect on the Profit and Loss Account and on the Balance Sheet if values for fixed assets and depreciation are inaccurate?

(3) *Check how the closing stock is valued.* The normal method is to value stock at the lower of cost or current market value. If you want to do the job thoroughly, you should inspect the stock. It may be that it includes items which are no longer readily saleable. For example, in the fashion trade, a business may have purchased items some months ago, which are now out of fashion. They could still be appearing in the accounts under 'Stock' at cost price, when in fact their current market value is little or nothing.

Exercise 9B

How will the Profit and Loss Account and the Balance Sheet be affected if the figure for stock is overstated?

(4) *Analyse the figure given for debtors.* Will all the debts really be paid? Has a provision been made for bad debts? It is quite possible for a business not to write off bad debts so that the debtors figure appears larger than the amount of cash which the business can readily expect to receive.

Exercise 9C

Why might a business prefer not to write off bad debts? What else is affected apart from the Balance Sheet?

Are there any dangers in a business having a large number of debtors?

(5) *Look for unusual or exceptional items or major changes.* The picture given by the Profit and Loss Account and Balance Sheet for a particular year can sometimes be distorted because of some exceptional event or major change either in circumstances or in accounting policy.

Example

A business may have borrowed a substantial amount to invest in new plant or machinery. In the short term, profit may be reduced because there has been no time to use the new machinery to increase profits, yet interest charges will already have been incurred. However, in the long term, there may be prospects of rapid growth in future years.

Fixed assets such as land and buildings may have been revalued for the first time in many years. This will make the Balance Sheet look quite different, but in reality nothing has changed.

You will have to take all these matters into account, particularly if you are going to make comparisons with previous years.

## 9.6 Some general considerations

### 9.6.1 Profitability, solvency and liquidity

The two main questions which people ask when reading the accounts of a business are:

(a) Is the business profitable?

(b) Is the business solvent?

Profitability is not the same as solvency. The Profit and Loss Account shows whether the business has made a profit. The Balance Sheet shows whether it is solvent (ie, whether its assets exceed its liabilities).

The fact that the accounts reveal that a profit has been made does not necessarily mean that the money is in the bank.

The Trading and Profit and Loss Accounts of a business will record sales or levels of professional charges which in turn will determine the amount of profit, but, although the goods may have been sold or bills issued, payment may not yet have been received. Thus, although the Profit and Loss Account may show a large profit, the Balance Sheet may record a high figure under debtors and there may be no cash in the bank.

Alternatively, the business may have sold goods or delivered bills and been paid; however, it may have purchased expensive new premises paying cash. The result is that while the Profit and Loss Account will show a profit, there is no money in the bank.

In either example, if the proprietors relied on the Profit and Loss Account to try to withdraw large amounts of cash, they would find they could not because there was no money in the bank.

It is therefore a misconception to think that if a business is profitable it must be solvent (ie, able to pay its debts). This is not so. Obviously, a business which is unprofitable is not likely to be solvent for long, but just because a business is profitable does not necessarily mean that it is able to pay its debts at once. A profitable business may be driven into liquidation if it is unable to pay its debts as they fall due.

> Exercise 9D
>
> The accounts of a business show that it has made a large profit, but that it has no cash. In fact it has a large overdraft. How many possible factors can you think of to account for the lack of cash?

Liquidity is an even more important issue for a business. A business can only use current assets to meet its liabilities if it is to continue in business. If it has to sell fixed assets to meet liabilities, it will eventually be unable to continue trading. It is, therefore, important that the business does not run short of current assets. Cash is the most liquid of current assets. Debtors are also liquid as, even if they are not yet due for payment, the business can always turn them into cash quickly by selling them on to someone else to collect. Stock is less liquid as it may be difficult to sell quickly. Some items can only be sold at certain times of year.

### 9.6.2 Treatment of bank overdrafts

It is necessary to decide how to deal with a bank overdraft, particularly if this is substantial. It will normally appear in the Balance Sheet as a current liability because, in theory at least, it is repayable on demand. The reality may be quite different. The business may maintain a high overdraft indefinitely and finance its activities from it. Unless the business runs into difficulties, the bank will not take steps to call in the money owing.

As a current liability, the bank overdraft will not appear as part of the capital employed in the business. Instead, it will be deducted from the current assets. If, however, it is a source of long-term finance, it should be treated as such in calculating the return on capital which the business is achieving. Again, in calculating whether a business can pay its debts by examining the ratio of current or liquid assets to current liabilities, a totally misleading picture may emerge if no distinction is made between the bank overdraft and ordinary trade creditors.

### 9.6.3 The impact of inflation

It is necessary to make allowance for the impact of inflation. If profits are increasing at the rate of 2% pa when inflation is running at 4% pa, then in real terms profits are falling.

## 9.7 Ratio analysis

### 9.7.1 Why use ratio analysis?

Ratio analysis relates two figures together. The result can be expressed as a percentage or as a ratio. Once you have a percentage or ratio, it is easy to compare the results of different years or of different businesses. You can use ratio analysis to check the profitability and efficiency of a business and also the liquidity.

### 9.7.2 Profitability and efficiency

#### 9.7.2.1 Return on capital

When looking at a set of accounts, the first thing you are likely to want to know is whether or not the business is making a profit. However, you will then want answers to some further questions:

(a) Is the amount of profit made satisfactory when compared to the amount of capital invested in the business?

(b) Is it more or less than the amount of profit similar businesses make from their capital?

To answer these questions, you need to relate the amount of profit produced to the amount of capital used to produce it. This is referred to as the 'return on capital'. It is normally expressed as a percentage:

$$\frac{\text{Net Profit}}{\text{Capital}} \times 100 = \%$$

You can calculate the return on the amount of capital the proprietor has invested or the amount of capital provided from all sources (for example, from bank loans). A proprietor will consider whether the return on capital is satisfactory by reference to the return that could be obtained on other investments.

When calculating the return, you may choose to take the capital figure at the start of the year, the end of the year or an average figure. It is normally easiest to take the figure at the end of the year, although arguably it is more accurate to take the figure at the start of the year as that was the amount invested during the relevant trading period.

**Example**

The balance on the proprietor's capital account at the end of the accounting period is £200,000; net profit for the accounting period was £40,000. The return on capital is:

$$\frac{\text{£}40{,}000}{\text{£}200{,}000} \times 100 = 20\%$$

This compares very favourably with putting the money in a bank or building society account. How does it compare with other similar businesses?

#### 9.7.2.2 Net profit percentage

If the return on capital is unsatisfactory, a proprietor may want to increase net profit. There are only two ways to make more profit. You can increase income or reduce expenses. To increase income you can either sell more items or make more profit on each item sold. The 'net profit percentage' shows the amount of profit made on each item sold.

$$\frac{\text{Net Profit}}{\text{Sales}} \times 100 = \%$$

A business can improve profit by putting up prices. However, a business will usually try to avoid putting up prices as this may drive away customers. It will prefer to reduce expenses or sell more items.

> Example
>
> A business has sales of £400,000 and a net profit of £40,000. The net profit percentage is:
>
> $$\frac{£40{,}000}{£400{,}000} \times 100 = 10\%$$
>
> This means that out of every £1 of sales, 90p goes in expenses and 10p is profit. We would need figures from comparable businesses to decide whether or not the business was performing satisfactorily.

## 9.7.3 Liquidity tests

### 9.7.3.1 Current ratio

The current ratio compares current assets with current liabilities. The result is normally expressed as a ratio.

$$\frac{\text{Current assets}}{\text{Current liabilities}} = \quad :1$$

A cautious business will want a current ratio of at least 1.5:1. However, many retail businesses manage with current ratios which are much lower. This is because they buy goods on credit but sell mainly for cash. Each day, they know that large amounts of cash will be injected. In general, therefore, they can meet liabilities due on a particular day from cash received on that day and need only a small amount of additional liquid funds in reserve.

### 9.7.3.2 Acid test

As we saw earlier, stock may not be quickly saleable. Also, there may be doubts as to whether it is saleable at all. Changes in fashion and technology may make stock obsolete. The acid test is the ratio between current liabilities and current assets excluding stock. (In a non-trading business, we would exclude work in progress as it is uncertain how quickly it can be turned into cash.) These assets are referred to as 'liquid assets':

$$\frac{\text{Liquid assets}}{\text{Current liabilities}} = \quad :1$$

An acid test of 1:1 means that the business has £1 of liquid assets for every £1 of current liabilities. The lower the ratio, the greater the risk of the business being unable to meet its debts as they fall due.

**Example**

The following is an extract from a Balance Sheet:

| | | |
|---|---|---|
| Current Assets | | |
| Stock | 65,000 | |
| Debtors | 50,000 | |
| Cash | 4,000 | |
| Prepayments | 1,000 | |
| | | 120,000 |
| Current Liabilities | | |
| Creditors | (40,000) | |
| Accruals | (10,000) | |
| | | (50,000) |
| Net Current Assets | | 70,000 |

The current ratio is:

$$\frac{£120,000}{£50,000} = 2.4:1$$

The acid test is

$$\frac{£55,000}{£50,000} = 1.1:1$$

There are an enormous number of other ratios which can be applied to a set of accounts. However, these are sufficient to show the way in which ratio analysis can give insight into the true position of a business.

## 9.8 Solutions

Exercise 9A

**Effect on Profit and Loss Account:**

Depreciation is charged as an expense on the Profit and Loss Account. If the depreciation is understated, the profit will be artificially high.

The reverse will be true if the depreciation is overstated.

**Effect on Balance Sheet:**

*Depreciation*

The figure for fixed assets will be unreliable if depreciation is inaccurate. The figure for capital owing to the proprietors will also be unreliable as it is increased by the profit calculated on the Profit and Loss Account.

*Fixed assets*

If assets are overstated, the Balance Sheet will appear healthier than it really is. Fixed assets and capital will both be higher than they should be. If assets are understated, the business may appear to be producing a high profit from its capital, but since capital is understated this will be misleading. If the business is a company, understating its assets will make it vulnerable to takeover.

Exercise 9B

**Effect on Profit and Loss Account:**

Closing stock reduces the figure for cost of goods sold. If cost of goods sold is low, then gross and net profit will appear to be high.

Thus, an overstated closing figure increases profit figures.

**Effect on Balance Sheet:**

Closing stock will be shown as a current asset. An inaccurate figure will increase the balance between current assets and current liabilities.

Exercise 9C

Debtors are shown in the Balance Sheet as current assets. A high debtors figure will increase the apparent value of the assets. It will affect the balance between current assets and current liabilities.

Bad debts are written off in Profit and Loss as expenses. The profit figure will be overstated if insufficient debts are written off as bad.

The business could have cash flow problems if the debtors do not pay. The business could be particularly vulnerable if a large proportion of the debts are owed by a single debtor, as that debtor may become insolvent and unable to pay.

Exercise 9D

You should have considered at least the following:

(a) excessive drawings by proprietors/dividends paid to shareholders;

(b) purchases of fixed assets out of cash received;

(c) failure to collect debts;

(d) excessive stock levels;

(e) dishonesty of staff.

# Part II

# ACCOUNTS FOR A SOLICITOR'S PRACTICE

# Chapter 10

# The Solicitors' Accounts Rules



## 10.1 Introduction

While reading this chapter, you should refer to the Solicitors' Accounts Rules 1998 (the 'Rules'). These replace the Solicitors' Accounts Rules 1991 and incorporate the Accountants' Report Rules 1991.

The Rules are divided into seven sections and include explanatory notes. These notes are part of the Rules.

## 10.2 Principles

The main principles of the Rules are set out in Rule 1. They include the following:

(a) to keep other people's money separate from money of the solicitor or the practice;

(b) to keep other people's money safe in a bank or building society account identifiable as a client bank account;

(c) to use each client's money for that client's matters only;

(d) to keep proper accounting records to show accurately the position with regard to the money held for each client;

(e) to account for interest on other people's money.

In this chapter, we will look at the way in which the Rules put these principles into practice.

The existence and enforcement of the Rules reduces the risk of accidental or deliberate misuse of client money. However, the Rules also demonstrate to the public that the profession is determined to police itself and to protect clients from the risks of accidental or deliberate mishandling of their money.

## 10.3 Who is bound by the Rules?

The Rules apply to sole practitioners, partners, assistant solicitors, in-house solicitors, directors of companies recognised by The Law Society under the Administration of Justice Act 1985 and registered foreign lawyers. In practical terms, they also bind anyone else working in a practice, such as cashiers and non-solicitor fee earners. Non-compliance by any member of staff will lead to the principals being in breach of the Rules, since the principals of a practice are required by Rule 6 to ensure compliance.

The case of *Weston v The Law Society* (1998) *The Times*, July 15 is a salutary reminder of how careful a partner in a firm must be. The Court of Appeal confirmed that it was appropriate to strike off a solicitor where no dishonesty was alleged. The solicitor in question was liable for breaches of the Rules committed by his partners even though he had been unaware of them. A partner is responsible for all breaches committed.

Lord Bingham of Cornhill referred to the 'duty of anyone holding anyone else's money to exercise a proper stewardship in relation to it'.

The Rules do not apply to solicitors employed by bodies such as local authorities or when carrying out judicial functions, such as acting as a coroner (Rule 5).

The 1998 Rules for the first time extend the application of the Rules (though only to a limited extent) to solicitors acting as:

(a) liquidators;
(b) trustees in bankruptcy;
(c) Court of Protection receivers;
(d) trustees of occupational pension schemes;

and to solicitors who hold client money jointly with a client, another solicitors' practice or a third party. Solicitors acting in such capacities are bound by some of the record-keeping requirements contained in Rules 32 and 33.

## 10.4 Categories of money

### 10.4.1 Three categories

Rule 13 divides money into one of three categories:

(a) client money;
(b) controlled trust money;
(c) office money.

### 10.4.2 Client money

A client is a person for whom the solicitor acts.

Client money is money held or received for a client *plus* all other money which is not controlled trust money or office money.

Note that the definition of client money goes beyond holding money for 'a client'. If the solicitor holds money for someone who is not a client, for example as stakeholder, bailee, agent, donee of a power of attorney, liquidator, trustee in bankruptcy or Court of Protection receiver, the money is client money.

Client money includes money received as 'an advance' or 'generally on account of costs', but not money received for costs in payment of a bill or agreed fee. This is an important distinction.

Exercise 10A

(a) Solicitor issues a bill to Client A for professional charges of £460. The client sends the solicitor a cheque for £460.
**Is the £460 client money or office money?**

(b) Solicitor asks Client B for £200 generally on account of costs. The client sends the solicitor a cheque for £200.
**Is the £200 client money or office money?**

Where a solicitor receives money to cover disbursements which have not yet been paid, the money will normally be client money. (There is a limited exception to this; see **10.6.1**.)

### 10.4.3 Controlled trust money

Controlled trust money is money held or received for a controlled trust. A controlled trust arises when a solicitor is the sole trustee of a trust or a co-trustee only with one or more of his partners or employees (see Rule 2(2)(h)). There is no outside trustee to scrutinise such trusts and so they are singled out for special treatment. Money held for a trust which is not a controlled trust will be client money.

### 10.4.4 Office money

Office money is money which belongs to the solicitor or the practice. It includes the following:

(a) interest earned on client money placed on a general deposit (under the Solicitors Act 1974, solicitors are entitled to keep such interest, although they will probably have to compensate the client – see below);

(b) money received for profit costs and VAT where a bill has been sent or a fee agreed (Rule 19(2) and (5));

(c) money received to reimburse the solicitor for disbursements already paid on behalf of clients;

(d) money received for disbursements which the solicitor has not yet paid but for which the solicitor has incurred liability, for example where a solicitor has an account at the Land Registry and pays monthly for searches.

However, money received for unpaid 'professional' disbursements is not office money. Professional disbursements according to Rule 2 are fees of counsel, experts, interpreters, translators, process servers, surveyors, estate agents, etc. Money received in advance for such payments is classified as client money.

The reason for the distinction between the types of unpaid disbursements is that professional disbursements often amount to large sums of money, whereas items such as search fees are normally small. It would not be right for solicitors to be allowed to keep large sums in the office bank account which are actually due to other people.

**Example**

A solicitor acts for a client in connection with a land dispute. The solicitor carries out a Land Registry search. The Land Registry charges the price of the search to the solicitor's account. The solicitor also instructs counsel to advise and receives counsel's invoice for the advice.

The solicitor then sends the client a bill showing the solicitor's profit costs, the Land Registry search fee and counsel's fee. The client sends a cheque in payment.

The amount representing the profit costs and the unpaid Land Registry search fee is office money, but the amount representing the unpaid counsel's fee is client money.

*Note:* A solicitor cannot be his own client for the purposes of the Rules (see Note (xii) to Rule 13) so, if the practice conducts a transaction for a partner, any money received is office money. However, if the money is held for the partner *and another person* (eg, a spouse), it will be client money.

> Exercise 10B
>
> Gibson and Weldon are solicitors in partnership together.
>
> (a) Gibson asks Weldon to deal with the purchase of a house for her. Shortly before completion, Gibson gives Weldon the balance of the purchase price required for completion. Is the firm holding client money?
>
> (b) Gibson is selling her house. Weldon is acting. The buyer pays a deposit to the firm to hold as stakeholders. Is the deposit client money?

## 10.5 Use of the client bank account

### 10.5.1 Requirement for client bank account

Rule 14(1) requires a solicitor to keep at least one client bank account. The account must be in the name of the firm and include the word 'client' in the title. It must be kept at a bank or building society in England and Wales. A firm need only have one client bank account but will often choose to have more than one (eg, a current account and one or more deposit accounts).

### 10.5.2 Use of client bank account(s)

The primary rule relating to the use of the client bank account is Rule 15. It states that, *except as provided otherwise:*

(1) client money and controlled trust money *must* without delay be paid into the client bank account;

(2) *only* client money or controlled trust money may be paid into a client bank account.

*Note:* 'Without delay' is defined by Rule 2(2)(z) as on the day of receipt or on the next working day.

### 10.5.3 Use of client bank account for other money

Rule 15(2)(a) allows a solicitor to use office money to open a client bank account or to maintain it at an agreed level.

> Examples
>
> (1) Smith and Brown are about to start practising in a partnership. As a preliminary, they need to open a client bank account and an office bank account. As yet, they are holding no client money, so they are allowed to use their own office money to open a client bank account.
>
> (2) Smith and Brown have agreed with the bank that the balance on the client bank account will not be allowed to fall below £10,000. They will be allowed to pay in office money as and when required to maintain that balance.
>
> A bank might impose such a condition in return for allowing the firm to operate an overdraft on its office bank account.

Rule 15(2)(b) allows a solicitor to advance money to a client or controlled trust where the firm holds insufficient money in the client bank account and needs to make a payment for that client. The money advanced becomes client money or controlled trust money and subject to the ordinary rules applying to such money. (This is not really an example of using the client bank account for other money, as the money advanced becomes client or controlled trust money.)

Rule 15(2)(c) allows a solicitor to pay office money into the client bank account to replace money withdrawn improperly.

> **Example**
>
> A junior employee withdraws money from the bank account for a client, not realising that the firm is holding no money for that client.
>
> As soon as the mistake is discovered, the firm should rectify it by paying office money into the client bank account.
>
> *Note:* An efficient firm will organise a system which makes such a mistake impossible.

Rule 15(2)(d) allows a solicitor to pay office money into the client bank account in lieu of interest which could have been earned on client or trust money had the money of the client or controlled trust been placed on special deposit.

Solicitors often receive cheques from clients containing a mixture of office and client money or controlled trust money.

Rule 20 provides that the money can be 'split' between the office and client bank account. Alternatively, the whole amount can be paid into the client bank account. Although the Rules allow a cheque to be split between two bank accounts, it is rare for banks to agree to do this. Splitting cheques is, therefore, done only rarely.

> **Example**
>
> Client X sends a cheque made up of £235 in payment of the solicitor's professional charges and VAT and £12,000 required to complete the purchase of her house. The whole £12,235 can be paid into the client bank account. The £235 can then be transferred from the client bank account to the office bank account at a later stage.
>
> *Note:* It would be a breach of the Rules to pay the £12,000 of client money into the office bank account.
>
> Alternatively, it would be permissible to 'split' the cheque and pay £235 into the office bank account and £12,000 into the client bank account.

Where the cheque is not split, the office money element must be transferred out within 14 days of receipt.

*Note:* Rules 19 and 21 provide further ways of dealing with some types of mixed payments (see **10.6**).

### 10.5.4 Situations where client money can be withheld from the client bank account (1)

(1) Rule 16(1)(a) provides that client money can be held outside the client bank account (eg, in the solicitor's safe or in a non-client bank account), but only where the client gives written instructions to the solicitor or where the solicitor confirms the client's instructions in writing.

*Note:* The money is client money and the record-keeping requirements of Rule 32 must be complied with.

(2) Under Rule 16(1)(b), the client may instruct the solicitor to place the money in a bank or building society account opened in the name of the client or some other person designated by the client. The instruction must be in writing or acknowledged in writing.

*Note:* Once the money is paid into such an account, it ceases to be client money and is not subject to the record-keeping requirements of Rule 32.

(3) Rule 17 provides that client money can be withheld in the following circumstances:

(a) cash is received and is paid without delay in the ordinary course of business to the client or, on the client's behalf, to a third party;

(b) a cheque or draft is received and is endorsed over in the ordinary course of business to the client or, on the client's behalf, to a third party;

(c) money is withheld on instructions under Rule 16;

(d) money is received for unpaid professional disbursements and is dealt with under Rule 19(1)(b) (see below);

(e) money is received for unpaid professional disbursements from the Legal Services Commission and is dealt with under Rule 21 (see below);

(f) money is withheld on the written authorisation of The Law Society (only rarely will such authorisation be given and the Society is able to impose a condition that the solicitor pay the money to a charity which gives an indemnity against any later legitimate claims to the money).

*Note:* Even though client money is withheld from the client bank account, dealings with it must be recorded in accordance with Rule 32.

### 10.5.5 Situations in which controlled trust money can be withheld from the client bank account

Rule 18 provides that controlled trust money can be withheld from the client bank account in the following circumstances:

(a) where cash is received and without delay paid in cash in the execution of the trust to a beneficiary or third party;

(b) where a cheque or draft is received and without delay is endorsed over in the execution of the trust to a beneficiary or third party;

(c) where a trustee in accordance with the trustee's powers pays the money into an account of the trustee which is a non-client bank account or properly retains cash;

(d) where (as in Rule 17(f)) The Law Society gives written authorisation.

*Note:* In situations (a)–(c), the record-keeping requirements of Rule 32 must be complied with.

### 10.5.6 When can money be taken out of the client bank account? (Rule 22)

#### 10.5.6.1 How much can be spent?

The solicitor must not withdraw more money from the client bank account than is being held there for a particular client (or controlled trust) (Rule 22(5)). For example, if a solicitor holds £500 for Client A and £300 for Client B in the client bank account, the solicitor can spend only £300 from the client bank account for Client B.

There is one limited exception provided by Rule 22(6). This allows the solicitor to make an excessive payment from the client bank account for a particular client or controlled trust *but only where* the solicitor holds sufficient money in a separate designated client bank account and immediately transfers sufficient money from the separate designated client bank account to the general client bank account.

Rule 22(8) states that a client bank account must not be overdrawn except in limited circumstances, the most important of which is where a controlled trustee overdraws a separate designated client account for a controlled trust by making payments (eg, for inheritance tax) before selling sufficient trust assets to cover the payments.

### 10.5.6.2 For what purposes can money be withdrawn from the client bank account?

*Client money* can be withdrawn where it is:

(a) properly required for a payment to or on behalf of the client (or person for whom the money is held);
(b) properly required for payment of a disbursement on behalf of the client;
(c) properly required in full or partial reimbursement of money spent by the solicitor on behalf of the client – money is 'spent' when a cheque is dispatched or where liabilities dealt with by an account are incurred (eg, search fees, taxi fares);
(d) transferred to another client account (eg, a separate designated account);
(e) withdrawn on the client's instructions: the instructions must be in writing or be confirmed by the solicitor in writing;
(f) a repayment to the solicitor of money advanced by the solicitor to the client to fund a payment (under Rule 15(2)(6));
(g) money which has been paid into the account in error – it must be withdrawn 'promptly' (Rule 22(4));
(h) money withdrawn on the written authorisation of The Law Society.

*Controlled trust money* can be withdrawn in similar circumstances.

*Office money* can be withdrawn where it:

(a) was paid in to open or maintain an account and is no longer required;
(b) is properly required to pay a solicitor's 'costs' and the solicitor has sent a bill or other written notification;
(c) was paid into the client bank account under Rule 19(1)(c) and needs to be withdrawn within 14 days (see below);
(d) was part of an unsplit cheque;
(e) was paid into the account in breach of Rules – it must be withdrawn 'promptly' (Rule 22(4)).

*Note:* Where a solicitor wants to transfer money from the client bank account for the firm's own costs, the solicitor must send a bill or other written notification. It must transfer the money (which becomes office money after the issue of the bill) within 14 days (Rule 19(2) and (3)).

### 10.5.6.3 How is the money withdrawn?

A withdrawal must be authorised by a suitable person, for example a solicitor with a current practising certificate (see Rule 23(1)).

If the money is withdrawn in favour of the solicitor, the payment from the client bank account must be by cheque in favour of the solicitor or by transfer into the office bank account. The payment must not be in cash or a cheque in favour of a third party. This is to ensure that it is easy to see the amount of client money taken by the firm.

> Example
>
> A solicitor is owed £100 in profit costs by Client A and owes £100 to a tradesman. The solicitor is holding £500 of A's money in the client bank account.
>
> Provided the solicitor delivers a bill or other written confirmation of costs, the solicitor can withdraw £100 of the money held for A from the client bank account.
>
> However, it cannot be withdrawn in cash or by way of a cheque in favour of the tradesman. It must either be a cheque in favour of the solicitor or a transfer to the office bank account.

## 10.6 Special rules on dealing with money received in payment of a bill (Rules 19 and 21)

Rule 19 is quite complicated and you need to study it carefully.

When a solicitor receives money in payment of a bill or other written intimation of costs, the solicitor has various options. These are set out below.

### 10.6.1 Determine the composition of the receipt without delay and deal with it appropriately (Rule 19(1)(a))

You need to remember Rule 13, which sets out the Rules on classification of money.

(a) In particular, remember that *money* received to *repay* the solicitor for disbursements already paid is *office money*.

(b) Money received to cover the cost of *unpaid disbursements* where the solicitor has incurred liability to pay is *office money*, unless the disbursements are '*professional disbursements*'.

(c) Money received for *unpaid professional disbursements*, even where the solicitor has incurred liability to pay, is *client money*.

When a solicitor is proceeding under Rule 19(1)(a), a receipt which is entirely office money will be paid into the office bank account.

A receipt which is entirely client money (eg, money for unpaid professional disbursements) will be paid into the client bank account.

A receipt which is a mixture of office and client money will be split or all paid into the client bank account.

Rule 19(1)(b)–(d) goes on to give alternatives.

### 10.6.2 Receipts consisting of office money and client money in the form of unpaid professional disbursements for which the solicitor is liable (Rule 19(1)(b))

The solicitor can place the entire amount in the office bank account *provided*, by the end of the second working day following receipt, the solicitor either pays the professional disbursements or transfers the amount required for the disbursement to the client bank account.

The effect of this option is to make life a little easier for solicitors. Where a receipt consists only of these two elements, the whole amount can be paid into the office bank account. This reduces the number of transfers made between client and office bank account.

*Note:* This option cannot be used if liability for professional disbursements has not yet been incurred, nor where the receipt includes other types of client money.

### 10.6.3 Any receipt irrespective of its composition (Rule 19(1)(c))

A solicitor can always elect to pay any receipt irrespective of its composition into the client bank account. Any office money element *must* be transferred out of the client bank account within 14 days of receipt.

### 10.6.4 Receipts from the Legal Services Commission (Rule 19(1)(d))

These can be dealt with under Rule 21, which provides two special dispensations for payments made by the Legal Services Commission (LSC):

(a) A payment on account by the LSC in anticipation of work to be carried out can be placed in the office bank account provided the LSC gives written instructions that it should be done.

(b) A payment by the LSC for profit costs can be placed in the office bank account even when it is mixed with client money for unpaid disbursements or professional disbursements provided the disbursements are paid or the money for them transferred to the client bank account within 14 days of receipt.

Exercise 10C

A firm issues a bill which consists of the following items:

| | £ |
|---|---|
| Firm's Professional Charges | 200 |
| VAT | 35 |
| Court Fees (Paid) | 80 |
| Land Charges Search (unpaid)[1] | 20 |
| Counsel's Fees (unpaid)[1] | 470 |
| | 805 |

[1]The solicitor has incurred liability for these items.

What options are available to the firm when dealing with the receipt of £805?

## 10.7 Deposit interest

### 10.7.1 When must interest be paid?

Rule 24(1) provides that, where a solicitor has chosen to open a separate deposit bank account designated with the name of the client (or controlled trust), any interest earned on that account must be accounted for to the client.

Rule 24(2) provides that, where a solicitor has chosen to hold client money in the general client bank account, the solicitor must account for a sum in lieu of interest calculated in accordance with Rule 25 (see below) *unless* one of the conditions set out in Rule 24(3) is met.

The conditions set out in Rule 24(3) are:

(a) The amount of interest calculated is £20 or less.

(b) The amount held and the period for which it is held falls into the de minimis table set out below:

| *Amount not exceeding* | *Time not exceeding* |
|---|---|
| *£* | *weeks* |
| 1,000 | 8 |
| 2,000 | 4 |
| 10,000 | 2 |
| 20,000 | 1 |

*Note:* If the solicitor holds an amount exceeding £20,000 for one week or less, it may still be fair and reasonable for interest to be paid.

(c) The money is held for counsel's fees and counsel has requested a delay in settlement.

(d) The money is held for the Legal Services Commission.

(e) The money held in the client bank account represents a sum advanced by the solicitor under Rule 15(2)(b) to cover a disbursement for which there was insufficient client money available.

(f) There is an agreement that interest shall not be paid.

### 10.7.2 How is interest calculated?

Solicitors must aim to obtain a reasonable rate of interest on separate designated deposit accounts and must account for a fair sum in lieu of interest on money held in a general client bank account. The sum in lieu of interest need not reflect the highest rate of interest available, but it is not acceptable to look only at the lowest rate of interest available. It should be calculated at a rate not less than the higher of:

(a) the rate payable on a separate designated client account for the amount held;

(b) the rate payable on the relevant amount if placed on deposit on similar terms by a member of the business community.

### 10.7.3 Factors affecting choice of method

When the solicitor opens a separate designated deposit bank account, the bank calculates the amount and pays the amount of interest earned. When one is not opened, the solicitor has to calculate the appropriate amount and pay it from the office bank account. It might seem, therefore, that it is always preferable to open a separate designated deposit account. However, this is not so.

A solicitor who opened a separate designated deposit bank account for every client for whom money was held would end up with an enormous number of different bank accounts, and this would be administratively inconvenient.

Moreover, a solicitor is allowed under the Solicitors Act 1974 to put client money held in a general client bank account on deposit and keep any interest earned over and above what is required to be paid under the Rules. In general, the more money placed in a deposit account, the higher the rate of interest the solicitor is able to earn. The solicitor only has to pay the client the rate the amount held *for that client* would have earned. The result is that the solicitor may earn more interest than is paid out. This is likely to encourage the solicitor to use the second method.

### 10.7.4 Money of controlled trusts

The rules on interest do not apply to controlled trusts. The general law requires a solicitor to act in the best interests of a trust and not to profit from his position as a trustee. Thus, a solicitor should obtain the best rate of interest possible for a controlled trust and account to the trust for all interest earned. The options are therefore either:

(a) to put the money of a controlled trust into a separate designated deposit account; or

(b) to set up a general client bank account just for money of controlled trusts. The interest earned is office money and will be paid into the office bank account in the ordinary way, but the solicitor must then allocate it to each controlled trust without delay.

The solicitor must be careful not to obtain an indirect benefit from the controlled trust money, for example by getting a higher rate of interest on other money because of the addition of the trust money.

## 10.8 What records must a solicitor keep?

### 10.8.1 Importance of records

The Law Society is just as concerned that solicitors should keep the correct records as that they should do the correct things. It is impossible to check what is happening if records are inadequate.

### 10.8.2 The basic records

Rule 32 sets out the basic requirements for everyday transactions:

(1) A solicitor must at all times keep properly written-up records to show dealings with:

  (a) client money held or paid by the solicitor; and

  [*Note:* This includes money withheld from the client bank account under Rule 16.]

  (b) controlled trust money held or paid by the solicitor.

  [*Note:* This includes money held in a non-client bank account.]

(2) All dealings with client money (and controlled trust money) must be recorded:

  (a) in a client cash account or in a record of sums transferred from one client ledger account to another; and

  (b) on the client columns of a client ledger account.

(3) If separate designated client accounts are used:

  (a) a combined account must show the total amount held in separate designated client accounts; and

  (b) the amount held for each client must be shown either in the deposit column of a client ledger or on the client columns of a client ledger kept specifically for showing money held in a separate designated client account for each client.

(4) All dealings with office money relating to any client or controlled trust matter must be appropriately recorded in an office cash account and on the office columns of a client ledger account.

## 10.9 Solutions

Exercise 10A

(a) Office money. It is a specific payment of a bill.

(b) Client money. It is generally on account of costs.

Exercise 10B

(a) No. The only person entitled to the money (until completion) is a partner in the firm.

(b) Yes. The partner in the firm is not the only person entitled to the money. Stakeholder money is held jointly for both buyer and seller awaiting the event.

Exercise 10C

First identify the composition of the receipt:

- Professional charges and VAT – office money.
- Paid court fees – office money.
- Unpaid search fee – office money (liability has been incurred).
- Unpaid counsel's fee – client money (professional unpaid disbursements).

(1) Under Rule 19(1)(a) and Rule 20, the receipt can be split. The office money element is paid into the office bank account, the client money element into the client bank account.

(2) Alternatively, the whole amount is paid into the client bank account, but the office money element must be transferred out within 14 days.

(3) The whole amount can be paid into the office bank account under Rule 19(1)(b), provided the counsel's fee is paid or the money required for it is transferred to the client bank account by the end of the second working day following receipt.

# Chapter 11
# Simple Entries for Solicitors



## 11.1 The two sets of accounting records

In order to control dealings with client money, a more sophisticated set of accounts is needed for a firm of solicitors than for most other businesses. It is essential that all the records of 'client money' dealings are clearly separated from the records of the ordinary 'office money' dealings of the firm.

One way of understanding the system is to think of yourself carrying on two separate businesses with two separate sets of accounts. Thus, you would need one set (Set A) for the first business - say the business which handles client money - and another set (Set B) for the second - say the firm's ordinary business accounts. This explains the reason for one of the fundamental bookkeeping rules for solicitors. The two sets of accounts are entirely separate. Thus, you cannot enter a debit on one set of accounts (Set A) and a credit on the other set (Set B).

## 11.2 The format of the accounts

### 11.2.1 Requirements

The rules do not specify any particular type of accounting system, and a solicitor can therefore choose any of the various systems on the market which enable the recording requirements of Rule 32 to be satisfied. These range from a simple card system to sophisticated, computerised systems, but they all have one thing in common - they are based on the principles of double-entry bookkeeping.

### 11.2.2 The dual cash account

Anyone running a business will want to keep a cash account to record dealings with their bank account. A solicitor is *required* by Rule 32(2) to keep a cash account for dealings with the client bank account and by Rule 32(4) to keep a separate cash account for dealings with the office bank account. Thus, the solicitor will need (at least) two separate cash accounts. To ease the administrative burden of actually moving from a cash account in one place to another cash account in a different place and back again, the normal format is to have the two individual cash accounts on the same page next to one another. One set of columns for 'Date' and 'Details' will do for both accounts.

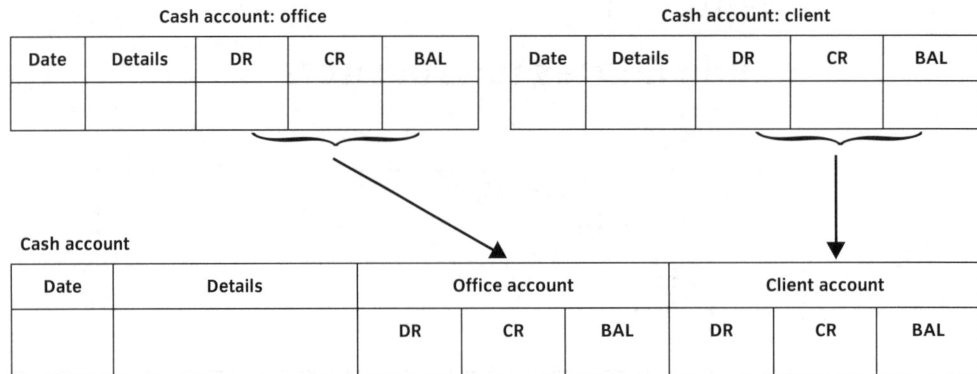


### 11.2.3 The dual ledger account for each client

To comply with Rule 32(2) and (4), there must be one ledger account for each client to show dealings with office money on behalf of that client and another ledger account to show dealings with client money for that client. As with the two cash accounts, it is usual to combine the two ledger accounts to show them side by side.

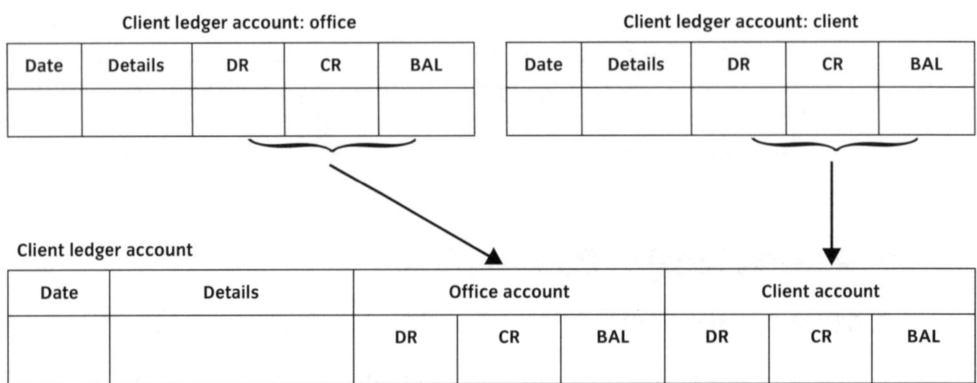


## 11.3 Receipts

First decide whether you are receiving office money or client money. The receipt can then be recorded in the correct section.

The entry in the cash account is a DR entry.

The corresponding CR entry is in the ledger account of the client from whom, or on whose behalf, the money is received.

If the receipt is into the office bank account, it will reduce the amount the client owes the firm (ie, it will reduce the DR balance on the office columns of the client ledger account). If the receipt is into the client bank account, the resulting CR balance on the client columns of the client ledger account will show that the firm 'owes' the client money, ie, the client is *a creditor* of the firm.

Example

Client Jones owes firm £100. (This means there is a DR balance on the office columns of Jones's ledger account.) Solicitor receives £20 from client Jones. Solicitor decides that it is a receipt of office money.

DR Cash account
CR Jones ledger account
} Office section

**Client:** Jones
**Matter:**

| Date | Details | Office account | | | Client account | | |
|---|---|---|---|---|---|---|---|
| | | DR | CR | BAL | DR | CR | BAL |
| | Balance | | | 100DR | | | |
| | Cash | | 20 | 80DR | | | |

**Cash account**

| Date | Details | Office account | | | Client account | | |
|---|---|---|---|---|---|---|---|
| | | DR | CR | BAL | DR | CR | BAL |
| | Balance | | | xxx | | | xxx |
| | Jones | 20 | | xxx | | | |

Example

Solicitor receives £300 from client Brown. Solicitor decides that it is a receipt of client money.

DR Cash account
CR Brown ledger account
} Client section

**Client:** Brown
**Matter:**

| Date | Details | Office account | | | Client account | | |
|---|---|---|---|---|---|---|---|
| | | DR | CR | BAL | DR | CR | BAL |
| | Cash | | | | | 300 | 300CR |

**Cash account**

| Date | Details | Office account | | | Client account | | |
|---|---|---|---|---|---|---|---|
| | | DR | CR | BAL | DR | CR | BAL |
| | Balance | | | | | | xxx |
| | Brown | | | | 300 | | xxx |

## 11.4 Payments

First, decide whether you are making the payment from the office or client bank account so that the payment can be recorded in the appropriate cash account.

The entry on the cash account is a CR entry.

The corresponding double entry is a DR in the ledger account of the client on whose behalf the payment is made.

If the payment is made from the office bank account, the resulting DR balance on the office columns of the client ledger will show that the client owes the firm money, ie, is *a debtor*. If the payment is made from the client bank account, it will reduce the amount held for the client (ie, it will reduce the CR balance on the client columns of the client ledger).

Remember that, under Rule 22(5), a payment must not be made from the client bank account unless the firm is holding sufficient funds in the client bank account for that client.

**Example**

Solicitor pays court fees of £40 on behalf of client Black. The solicitor holds no client money for Black so must make the payment using office money:

CR Cash account
DR Black ledger account } Office section

**Client:** Black
**Matter:**

| Date | Details | Office account | | | Client account | | |
|---|---|---|---|---|---|---|---|
| | | DR | CR | BAL | DR | CR | BAL |
| | Cash | 40 | | 40DR | | | |

**Cash account**

| Date | Details | Office account | | | Client account | | |
|---|---|---|---|---|---|---|---|
| | | DR | CR | BAL | DR | CR | BAL |
| | Balance | | | XXX | | | |
| | Black | | 40 | XXX | | | |

**Example**

Solicitor is holding client money of £500 for client White. Solicitor makes a payment of £500 for client White.

The solicitor holds sufficient client money for White to be able to make the payment using client money.

CR Cash account
DR White ledger account } Client section

**Client:** White
**Matter:**

| Date | Details | Office account | | | Client account | | |
|---|---|---|---|---|---|---|---|
| | | DR | CR | BAL | DR | CR | BAL |
| | Balance | | | | | | 500CR |
| | Cash | | | | 500 | | – |

**Cash account**

| Date | Details | Office account | | | Client account | | |
|---|---|---|---|---|---|---|---|
| | | DR | CR | BAL | DR | CR | BAL |
| | Balance | | | | | | XXX |
| | White | | | | | 500 | XXX |

**Exercise 11A**

You act for Smith. Record the following events on Smith's ledger account and on the cash account.

*Note:* Assume that the balances on the cash account are office £1,000 DR, client £20,000 DR. Assume the balances on Smith's ledger account are zero.

June

1 Smith sends £1,000 generally on account of costs.

*Note:* This is a receipt of client money because it is not in payment of a bill for profit costs nor in reimbursement of an expense.

2 Firm pays £100 on Smith's behalf.

*Note:* This can be paid from the client bank account since sufficient funds are available.

4 Firm pays £900 on Smith's behalf.

*Note:* This can be paid from the client bank account since sufficient funds are available.

6 Firm pays £200 on Smith's behalf.

*Note:* This must be paid from the office bank account since no funds are held for Smith.

8 Firm pays £400 on Smith's behalf.

*Note:* This must be paid from the office bank account since no funds are held for Smith.

10 Smith sends firm £600 in reimbursement of expenses incurred.

*Note:* Subject to Rule 19(1)(c), this must be paid into the office bank account since it is a receipt of office money.

## 11.5 Profit costs

When the solicitor issues a bill to the client, it will include an item for professional charges and VAT on those charges. The solicitor will want to make entries in the accounts to show that the client now owes the firm money.

*Note:* At this stage, there is no movement of cash, so no entry is made in the cash account.

On the client ledger account, the bookkeeper must make DR entries for profit costs and VAT in the office section. The entries must be made in the office section (even if the solicitor holds client money). This is because the purpose of the DR entries is to show that the client has incurred a debt to the firm. You are not yet recording the paying of cash.

The corresponding CR entries are made on the profit costs account and HM Revenue & Customs account respectively.

**Example**

Solicitor issues a bill for £400 profit costs plus £70 VAT to client Smith.

DR Smith ledger account £400
DR Smith ledger account £70

CR Profit costs account £400
CR Revenue & Customs account £70

(See **Chapter 13** for details of VAT.)

**Client:** Smith
**Matter:**

| Date | Details | Office account | | | Client account | | |
|---|---|---|---|---|---|---|---|
| | | DR | CR | BAL | DR | CR | BAL |
| | Costs | 400 | | 400DR | | | |
| | VAT | 70 | | 470 | | | |

**Profit costs**

| Date | Details | DR | CR | BAL |
|---|---|---|---|---|
| | Smith | | 400 | 400CR |

**Revenue & Customs**

| Date | Details | DR | CR | BAL |
|---|---|---|---|---|
| | Smith | | 70 | 70CR |

Exercise 11B

Prepare the cash account and client ledger account for X to record the following events.

Solicitor acts for X in a litigation matter. The balances on the cash account are office £1,000DR, client £1,000DR. The balances on X's ledger account are zero.

June

1 X sends solicitor £200 on account of costs.

*Note:* This is a receipt of client money because it is not in payment of a bill nor in reimbursement of an expense.

2 Solicitor pays court fees £20.

*Note:* This can be paid from the client bank account since sufficient funds are available.

5 Solicitor pays expert witness £180.

*Note:* This can be paid from the client bank account since sufficient funds are available.

7 Solicitor pays another expert witness £150.

*Note:* There is no client money available. The payment must be made from the office bank account.

10 Matter is settled. Solicitor receives a cheque from the defendant for £5,000 in full and final settlement. This cheque is made out to the firm.

*Note:* The firm has received client money. (Had the cheque been made out to the client, the firm would simply have forwarded it to the client. It would not have been possible to pay the cheque into a bank account in the firm's name.) The solicitor could split the cheque and take £150 in reimbursement of the expense incurred. However, we will pay it all into the client bank account.

12 Solicitor sends client a cheque for £5,000.

*Note:* This is a payment of client money.

14 Solicitor sends X a bill. Profit costs £200. VAT £35. Solicitor asks for the amount necessary to reimburse him for expenses incurred.

16 X sends solicitor amount requested on 14 June.

*Note:* X will send £385 (£235 + £150), and this will be a receipt of office money. Subject to Rule 19(1)(c), it must be paid into the office bank account.

## 11.6 Solutions

### Exercise 11A

**Client:** Smith
**Matter:**

| Date | Details | Office account | | | Client account | | |
|---|---|---|---|---|---|---|---|
| | | DR | CR | BAL | DR | CR | BAL |
| June | | | | | | | |
| 1 | Cash. On a/c costs | | | | | 1,000 | 1,000CR |
| 2 | Cash | | | | 100 | | 900 |
| 4 | Cash | | | | 900 | | – |
| 6 | Cash | 200 | | 200DR | | | |
| 8 | Cash | 400 | | 600 | | | |
| 10 | Cash | | 600 | – | | | |

**Cash account**

| Date | Details | Office account | | | Client account | | |
|---|---|---|---|---|---|---|---|
| | | DR | CR | BAL | DR | CR | BAL |
| June | Balances | | | 1,000DR | | | 20,000DR |
| 1 | Smith. On a/c costs | | | | 1,000 | | 21,000 |
| 2 | Smith | | | | | 100 | 20,900 |
| 4 | Smith | | | | | 900 | 20,000 |
| 6 | Smith | | 200 | 800 | | | |
| 8 | Smith | | 400 | 400 | | | |
| 10 | Smith Reimbursement expenses | 600 | | 1,000 | | | |

### Exercise 11B

**Client:** X
**Matter:** Litigation

| Date | Details | Office account | | | Client account | | |
|---|---|---|---|---|---|---|---|
| | | DR | CR | BAL | DR | CR | BAL |
| June | | | | | | | |
| 1 | Cash. On a/c costs | | | | | 200 | 200CR |
| 2 | Cash. Court fees | | | | 20 | | 180 |
| 5 | Cash. Expert witness | | | | 180 | | – |
| 7 | Cash. Expert witness | 150 | | 150DR | | | |
| 10 | Cash. Settlement | | | | | 5,000 | 5,000 |
| 12 | Cash. To client | | | | 5,000 | | – |
| 14 | Costs | 200 | | | | | |
| | VAT | 35 | | 385 | | | |
| 16 | Cash. Amount due | | 385 | – | | | |

**Cash account**

| Date | Details | Office account | | | Client account | | |
|---|---|---|---|---|---|---|---|
| | | DR | CR | BAL | DR | CR | BAL |
| June | Balance | | | 1,000DR | | | 1,000DR |
| 1 | X. On a/c costs | | | | 200 | | 1,200 |
| 2 | X. Court fees | | | | | 20 | 1,180 |
| 5 | X. Expert witness | | | | | 180 | 1,000 |
| 7 | X. Expert witness | | 150 | 850 | | | |
| 10 | X. Settlement | | | | 5,000 | | 6,000 |
| 12 | X. Amount sent | | | | | 5,000 | 1,000 |
| 16 | X. Amount requested | 385 | | 1,235 | | | |

# Chapter 12

# Solicitors' Accounts – Transfers



## 12.1 The two types of transfer

The first type of transfer involves the bank moving money from one bank account to another. It occurs when the solicitor instructs the bank to transfer money from the client bank account to the office bank account, or from the office bank account to the client bank account. The solicitor must make entries on the firm's internal cash accounts and client ledger to record the fact that money has actually moved between bank accounts.

The second type does not involve the bank moving money from one bank account to another. It occurs when a solicitor who is holding money in the client bank account for one client is instructed to stop holding the money to the order of the first client and to start holding it to the order of a second client. This type of transfer is called an inter-client transfer. To comply with the Rules and to keep the solicitor's internal records accurate, the solicitor must make entries on the ledger accounts of the two clients to show how much is held for each. No entries are made on the firm's internal cash account since there has been no movement of cash in the firm's bank accounts.

## 12.2 Transfers between client bank account and office bank account

### 12.2.1 Why might such a transfer occur?

#### 12.2.1.1 Reimbursement of an expense incurred

A solicitor can transfer client money from the client bank account to the office bank account to reimburse the solicitor for money spent by the solicitor on behalf of the client. It is not necessary for the solicitor to issue a bill of costs before making the transfer. Money is 'spent' for this purpose when the solicitor incurs liability for the expense, for example, by charging an amount for taxi fares or search fees to the firm's account.

The money in the client bank account is client money until the solicitor decides to make reimbursement so there is no requirement to make the transfer within 14 days of incurring liability for the expense.

*Note:* Similar Rules apply to controlled trust money.

#### 12.2.1.2 Payment of profit costs

A solicitor can transfer money from the client bank account to the office bank account for the solicitor's own professional fees, including any VAT element, provided a bill has been issued (or a fee agreed in accordance with Rule19(5)).

#### 12.2.1.3 Other

A solicitor can transfer office money to the client bank account in the circumstances set out in Rule 15:

(a) to open or maintain the client bank account;

(b) to advance money to a client or controlled trust where the solicitor needs to make a payment on behalf of the client or trust and insufficient client or trust money is available (once advanced, the money becomes client or controlled trust money);

(c) to replace money withdrawn in error;

(d) in lieu of interest.

### 12.2.2 Recording the transfer from client to office bank account

This is done in two parts, as follows:

(1) The solicitor records the withdrawal of money from the client bank account:

CR cash account<br>DR client's ledger account } Client section

(2) The solicitor records the receipt of money into the office bank account:

DR cash account<br>CR client's ledger account } Office section

**Example**

You act for Green. On 10 April, you receive £800 from Green on account of costs to be incurred. On 26 April, you send Green a bill for £400 plus £70 VAT. On 28 April, you transfer £470 from the client bank account to the office bank account.

Entries are as follows.

(1) The £800 is client money. It will be paid into the client bank account and recorded in Green's ledger account and in the cash account.

**Client:** Green
**Matter:** Miscellaneous

| Date | Details | Office account | | | Client account | | |
|---|---|---|---|---|---|---|---|
| | | DR | CR | BAL | DR | CR | BAL |
| Apr 10 | Cash: From Green. On account | | | | | 800 | 800CR |

**Cash account**

| Date | Details | Office account | | | Client account | | |
|---|---|---|---|---|---|---|---|
| | | DR | CR | BAL | DR | CR | BAL |
| Apr 10 | Green | | | | 800 | | XXX |

(2) When the bill is issued, the entries for costs and VAT will be DR entries on Green's ledger account (remember that costs and VAT are always debited in the *office* section).

The CR entries will be on the costs and Revenue & Customs account which we have not shown.

**Client:** Green
**Matter:** Miscellaneous

| Date | Details | Office account | | | Client account | | |
|---|---|---|---|---|---|---|---|
| | | DR | CR | BAL | DR | CR | BAL |
| Apr | | | | | | | |
| 10 | Cash: From Green. On account | | | | | 800 | 800CR |
| 26 | Costs | **400** | | 400DR | | | |
| | VAT | **70** | | 470 | | | |

**Cash account**

| Date | Details | Office account | | | Client account | | |
|---|---|---|---|---|---|---|---|
| | | DR | CR | BAL | DR | CR | BAL |
| Apr | | | | | | | XXX |
| 10 | Green | | | | 800 | | |

(3) The withdrawal from client account will look like this:

**Client:** Green
**Matter:** Miscellaneous

| Date | Details | Office account | | | Client account | | |
|---|---|---|---|---|---|---|---|
| | | DR | CR | BAL | DR | CR | BAL |
| Apr | | | | | | | |
| 10 | Cash: From Green. On account | | | | | 800 | 800CR |
| 26 | Costs | 400 | | 400DR | | | |
| | VAT | 70 | | 470 | | | |
| 28 | Cash. Transfer from client account | | | | **470** | | 330 |

**Cash account**

| Date | Details | Office account | | | Client account | | |
|---|---|---|---|---|---|---|---|
| | | DR | CR | BAL | DR | CR | BAL |
| Apr | | | | | | | XXX |
| 10 | Green | | | | 800 | | |
| 28 | Green | | | | | **470** | |

(4) The receipt into office account will look like this:

**Client:** Green
**Matter:** Miscellaneous

| Date | Details | Office account | | | Client account | | |
|---|---|---|---|---|---|---|---|
| | | DR | CR | BAL | DR | CR | BAL |
| Apr | | | | | | | |
| 10 | Cash: From Green. On account | | | | | 800 | 800CR |
| 26 | Costs | 400 | | 400DR | | | |
| | VAT | 70 | | 470 | | | |
| 28 | Cash. Transfer from client account | | | | 470 | | 330 |
| | Cash. Transfer to office account | | **470** | – | | | |

| Cash account | | | | | | | |
|---|---|---|---|---|---|---|---|
| Date | Details | Office account | | | Client account | | |
| | | DR | CR | BAL | DR | CR | BAL |
| Apr | | | | | | | XXX |
| 10 | Green | | | | 800 | | |
| 28 | Green | | | | | 470 | |
| | Green | 470 | | | | | |

*Note:* For the sake of convenience, the withdrawal from the client bank account and the receipt into the office bank account are often shown on the same line like this:

| Client: Green<br>Matter: Miscellaneous | | | | | | | |
|---|---|---|---|---|---|---|---|
| Date | Details | Office account | | | Client account | | |
| | | DR | CR | BAL | DR | CR | BAL |
| Apr | | | | | | | |
| 10 | Cash: From Green. On account | | | | | 800 | 800CR |
| 26 | Costs | 400 | | 400DR | | | |
| | VAT | 70 | | 470 | | | |
| 28 | Cash. Transfer from client account to office account | | 470 | – | 470 | | 330 |

| Cash account | | | | | | | |
|---|---|---|---|---|---|---|---|
| Date | Details | Office account | | | Client account | | |
| | | DR | CR | BAL | DR | CR | BAL |
| Apr | | | | | | | XXX |
| 10 | Green | | | | 800 | | |
| 10 | Green. Transfer from client to office account | 470 | | | | 470 | |

## 12.3 Inter-client transfers

### 12.3.1 What is happening?

Sometimes, a solicitor who is holding money in the client bank account for Client A stops holding that money for Client A and starts holding it for Client B. An example would be where A owes B money and asks the solicitor to hold the money for B. No money is taken out of the client bank account. The solicitor is simply complying with the requirement in Rule 1(g) to show accurately the position with regard to the money held for each client. This type of transfer is sometimes referred to as a 'paper' transfer or an 'inter-client' transfer.

### 12.3.2 Requirements

The transfer must comply with Rule 30. This means that the solicitor can make the paper entries only if the money could have been:

(a) withdrawn from the client bank account on the instructions of the first client under Rule 22(1); and

(b) paid into the client bank account on the instructions of the second client under Rule 15.

If the transfer is a 'private loan', the solicitor must have the prior written authority of both clients. This is not necessary if the transfer is for other purposes, for example, a gift or in discharge of a debt. A private loan is any loan other than one provided by an institution which provides loans on standard terms in the normal course of its activities.

### 12.3.3 Recording the transfer

The transfer must be shown in the client ledger accounts of both clients:

DR Client ledger account of first client
CR Client ledger account of second client

In addition, to comply with Rule 32(2), it is necessary to keep a separate record. This will usually be referred to as a 'transfer journal' or a 'transfer sheet'.

**Example**

You are instructed by Anne Brown to collect a debt of £10,000 from White & Co. You write to White & Co requesting payment. On 7 August, you receive a cheque from White & Co for £10,000 in payment of the debt.

You already act for Anne's sister, Jane Brown, who is buying a flat. On 9 August, Anne tells you that she is making a gift of £1,000 to Jane and asks you to hold £1,000 of her money to the order of Jane. You make the necessary inter-client transfer.

Entries are as follows.

(1) When the £10,000 is received, it is client money held to the order of Anne. It will be recorded like this:

**Cash account**

| Date | Details | Office account | | | Client account | | |
|---|---|---|---|---|---|---|---|
| | | DR | CR | BAL | DR | CR | BAL |
| | | | | | | | XXX |
| Aug 7 | Anne Brown | | | | 10,000 | | |

**Client:** Anne Brown
**Matter:** Debt collection

| Date | Details | Office account | | | Client account | | |
|---|---|---|---|---|---|---|---|
| | | DR | CR | BAL | DR | CR | BAL |
| Aug 7 | Cash. From White & Co. Debt | | | | | 10,000 | 10,000CR |

(2) When Anne instructs you to hold £1,000 to the order of Jane, there will be no entry on the cash account. There will be the following entries on the ledger accounts of Anne and Jane:

**Client:** Anne Brown
**Matter:** Debt collection

| Date | Details | Office account | | | Client account | | |
|---|---|---|---|---|---|---|---|
| | | DR | CR | BAL | DR | CR | BAL |
| Aug 7 | Cash. From White & Co. Debt | | | | | 10,000 | 10,000CR |
| 9 | Jane Brown. Transfer (TJ) | | | | 1,000 | | 9,000 |

**Client:** Jane Brown
**Matter:** Litigation

| Date | Details | Office account | | | Client account | | |
|---|---|---|---|---|---|---|---|
| | | DR | CR | BAL | DR | CR | BAL |
| Aug 9 | Anne Brown. Transfer (TJ) | | | | | 1,000 | 1,000CR |

There will be a record on the transfer journal. You can include the initials 'TJ' in the details columns of the client ledger, but this is not essential. It *is* essential to give the name of the ledger account where the other part of the double entry is made.

Exercise 12A

You are a solicitor. The following events occur:

February

1 You receive £800 generally on account of costs from your client, Dean.

4 You pay a court fee of £100 (no VAT) on behalf of your client, Wade.

5 You receive £7,000 on behalf of your client, Will. It is a debt collected.

8 You agree to act for Simon. You ask for £300 generally on account of costs. Dean tells you that he is prepared to lend Simon the money for this. Dean and Simon instruct you in writing to make the necessary transfer.

11 You issue a bill to Will. Your costs are £440 plus £77 VAT. You transfer the costs from the client bank account to the office bank account.

13 You issue a bill to Wade for £200 plus £35 VAT. Will, who is Wade's uncle, instructs you to transfer an amount sufficient to pay Wade's indebtedness to you from the amount you are holding for Will. It is a gift from Will to Wade.

14 You issue Dean a bill for £600 plus £105 VAT. You transfer the remaining money held for him in the client bank account to the office bank account in part payment of the bill.

Explain the application of the Rules to each transaction, and prepare the clients' ledger accounts and the cash account.

## 12.4 Solutions

Exercise 12A

1 February The money is client money. You must pay it into the client bank account (Rule 15).

4 February You are holding no money for Wade, so you must pay the money out of the office bank account (Rule 22(5)).

5 February The money is client money. You must pay it into the client bank account (Rule 15).

8 February Rule 30 applies. Written instructions are needed for a private loan from one client to another (Rule 30(2)). The money could be withdrawn from the client bank account on Dean's instructions (Rule 22(1)) and could be received into the client bank account on Simon's instructions (Rule 15). Thus, Rule 30 is satisfied and the inter-client transfer can be made. A record must be made in the transfer journal (Rule 32(2)).

11 February **The bill** DR Will's ledger account office section with costs and VAT. CR costs account and HM Revenue & Customs ledger account respectively.

**The transfer** The withdrawal from the client bank account and transfer to the office bank account is allowed by Rule 22(3)(b).

13 February **The bill** DR Wade's ledger account office section with costs and VAT. CR costs account and HM Revenue & Customs ledger account respectively.

**The transfer** Rule 30 is not satisfied. The money could be withdrawn from the client bank account on Will's instructions, but it could not be paid into the client bank account on Wade's instructions because it is being received specifically in payment of your bill. This is office money and, as such, should be paid into the office bank account. You must therefore pay the money out of the client bank account on behalf of Will and receive it into the office bank account on behalf of Wade.

14 February **The bill** Entries as above.

**The transfer** Rule 22(3)(b) applies. The entries are the same as those on 11 February.

*Note:* When Dean pays the balance, the money received will be office money and must be paid straight into the office bank account (unless it is dealt with under Rule 19(1)(c)).

The accounts are shown below.

**Client:** Dean
**Matter:** Miscellaneous

| Date | Details | Office account | | | Client account | | |
|---|---|---|---|---|---|---|---|
| | | DR | CR | BAL | DR | CR | BAL |
| Feb | | | | | | | |
| 1 | Cash. From Dean. Generally on account | | | | | 800 | 800CR |
| 8 | Simon. Transfer (TJ) | | | | 300 | | 500 |
| 14 | Costs | 600 | | 600DR | | | |
| | VAT | 105 | | 705 | | | |
| | Cash. Transfer from client to office account | | 500 | 205 | 500 | | – |

**Client:** Wade
**Matter:** Miscellaneous

| Date | Details | Office account | | | Client account | | |
|---|---|---|---|---|---|---|---|
| | | DR | CR | BAL | DR | CR | BAL |
| Feb | | | | | | | |
| 4 | Cash. Court fee | 100 | | 100DR | | | |
| 13 | Costs | 200 | | 300 | | | |
| | VAT | 35 | | 335 | | | |
| | Cash: Transfer from Will | | 335 | – | | | |

**Client:** Will
**Matter:** Miscellaneous

| Date | Details | Office account | | | Client account | | |
|---|---|---|---|---|---|---|---|
| | | DR | CR | BAL | DR | CR | BAL |
| Feb | | | | | | | |
| 5 | Cash. Debt collected | | | | | 7,000 | 7,000CR |
| 11 | Costs | 440 | | 440DR | | | |
| | VAT | 77 | | 517 | | | |
| | Cash. Transfer costs from client to office account | | **517** | – | 517 | | 6,483 |
| 13 | Cash. From client to office account for Wade | | | | 335 | | 6,148 |

**Client:** Simon
**Matter:** Miscellaneous

| Date | Details | Office account | | | Client account | | |
|---|---|---|---|---|---|---|---|
| | | DR | CR | BAL | DR | CR | BAL |
| Feb | | | | | | | |
| 8 | Dean. Transfer (TJ) | | | | | 300 | 300CR |

**Cash account**

| Date | Details | Office account | | | Client account | | |
|---|---|---|---|---|---|---|---|
| | | DR | CR | BAL | DR | CR | BAL |
| Feb | | | | XXX | | | XXX |
| 1 | Dean | | | | 800 | | |
| 4 | Wade | | 100 | | | | |
| 5 | Will | | | | 7,000 | | |
| 11 | Will | 517 | | | | 517 | |
| 13 | Will | | | | | 335 | |
| | Wade | 335 | | | | | |
| 14 | Dean | 500 | | | | 500 | |

# Chapter 13
# Value Added Tax



## 13.1 General principles

VAT involves two distinct aspects: output tax (charged by a business to its customers) and input tax (charged to the business by its suppliers). A business registered for VAT charges its customers output tax and then accounts to HM Revenue & Customs for tax. In other words, it acts as an unpaid tax collector. It will normally be possible for such a business to deduct input tax charged to the business from the amount accounted for to HM Revenue & Customs. See **13.1.2**.

### 13.1.1 Output tax

VAT is chargeable on the supply of goods or services where the supply is a taxable supply and is made by a taxable person in the course or furtherance of a business carried on by him (Value Added Tax Act (VATA) 1994, s 4(1)). Each element of this definition will be considered further below.

The person making the supply is liable to account to the government for the amount of tax which he charges.

#### 13.1.1.1 Supply of goods

This comprises all forms of supply whereby the whole property in goods is transferred, including a gift of goods.

#### 13.1.1.2 Supply of services

This is anything which is not a supply of goods, but is done for a consideration. Note that a gratuitous supply of services is not a supply for VAT purposes, in contrast to a gift of goods.

#### 13.1.1.3 Taxable supply

This means any supply of goods or services other than an exempt supply. Exempt supplies are listed in Sch 9 of the VATA 1994 and include supplies of land (except for commercial purposes), insurance, postal services, finance, health services, and burial and cremation.

Taxable supplies may be divided into two categories:

(a) those which are chargeable at the standard rate of 17.5%; and

(b) those which are chargeable at a zero rate. Zero-rated supplies are listed in Sch 8 of the VATA 1994 and include supplies of food, water, books, international services and transport.

Zero-rated and exempt supplies are similar in that no VAT is actually charged in either case by the supplier to his customer.

However, they must be carefully distinguished since only a person who makes taxable supplies is able to recover input tax, ie, the VAT charged to him by his suppliers.

A solicitor supplying legal services will be making a standard-rated supply. Legal services include profit costs and *some* payments made for clients (see below). A solicitor supplying insurance will be making an exempt supply.

#### 13.1.1.4 Taxable person

A person is a taxable person if he *is* or *is required to be* registered under the Act. A person must register if, broadly, the value of his taxable supplies (*not* his profit) in the preceding 12 months exceeded a figure specified in each year's Budget. A firm of solicitors will virtually always have to be registered.

Notice that voluntary registration is permitted. A person may register voluntarily in order to recover input tax charged to him.

#### 13.1.1.5 Business

VAT is chargeable by a taxable person only on taxable supplies made in the course or furtherance of a business carried on by him.

'Business' includes any trade, profession or vocation, but the term is not limited to these activities since it also covers, for example, the provision by certain clubs and associations of facilities to members.

Furthermore, although the services of an employee are not generally taxable, the Act provides that, where a person, in the course of carrying on a trade, profession or vocation, accepts any office, any services supplied by him as holder of the office shall be treated as supplied in the course of a business carried on by him and are therefore chargeable with VAT.

A solicitor who is a taxable person must charge VAT not only on his supplies of legal services but also on any other supplies he makes in the course of his business, eg, the sale of redundant office equipment.

### 13.1.2 Input tax

Where VAT is charged on the supply to a taxable person of any goods or services for the purposes of his business, he may generally deduct such tax from the amount of output tax for which he is liable to account to HM Revenue & Customs (s 25(2)). Since input tax charged to a taxable person is recoverable by him, it follows that VAT is not an expense of a person who makes only taxable supplies, whether at the standard or zero rate.

A person who makes only exempt supplies is not a taxable person and so is unable to recover any input tax.

> **Example**
>
> A, an undertaker, and B, a bookseller, each buy stationery for £200 + £35 VAT. The bookseller can recover the VAT; therefore, the expense to be charged to the Profit and Loss Account is only £200. The undertaker cannot recover the VAT and, therefore, the expense to be charged to the Profit and Loss Account is £235.

Where a taxable person makes both taxable and exempt supplies, he is then partly exempt and may only recover a proportion of the input tax charged to him. A solicitor who supplies insurance may find himself in this position.

Where the exempt supplies made by a taxable person fall within certain de minimis limits, they can be ignored, with the result that all his input tax is recoverable.

### 13.1.3 Value of supply

Where a supply is fully taxable, VAT at the rate of 17.5% is payable on the value of the supply. If the consideration is in money, the value of the supply is such amount as, with the addition of the total tax payable, is equal to the consideration (s 19(2)).

If a price or fee is agreed, this will be deemed to include VAT unless expressly stated to be tax exclusive.

> Exercise 13A
>
> A solicitor agrees to provide a legal service for client X for £200. How much will be recorded as profit costs and how much as VAT?

### 13.1.4 Time of supply

The importance of the time of supply (or tax point) is that it decides the quarter at the end of which a taxable person becomes liable to account for output tax on a particular supply. It also determines the quarter in which a taxable person can claim input tax on a taxable supply made to him. The basic tax points are as follows:

(a) *Goods* When the goods are removed or made available to the purchaser (s 6(2)).

(b) *Services* When the services are completed (s 6(3)).

These basic tax points will be varied in the following cases:

(a) If, within 14 days after the basic tax point, the supplier issues a tax invoice, the date of the invoice will become the tax point unless a longer period has been agreed with HM Revenue & Customs (s 6(5) and (6)). In the case of solicitors, there is a general extension of the 14-day period to three months, so that, provided solicitors deliver their bills within three months of completion of their services, the date of each bill will be the tax point.

(b) If, before a basic tax point arises, the supplier issues a tax invoice or receives payment, the supply will, to the extent covered by the invoice or payment, be treated as taking place at the date of the invoice or payment (s 6(4)).

### 13.1.5 Tax invoices

Such invoices are of vital importance to a taxable person since they are evidence of his right to recover the input tax on a supply made to him, ie, without such an invoice, he will generally be unable to claim an input credit, irrespective of whether or not he has made payment to the supplier.

A taxable person making a taxable supply to another taxable person must, within 30 days after the time of supply (or within such longer period as HM Revenue & Customs allow), provide him with a tax invoice, which must state the following particulars:

(a) an identifying number;
(b) the date of the supply, ie, the tax point;
(c) the supplier's name, address and VAT registration number;
(d) the name and address of the person to whom the supply is made;
(e) the type of supply, eg, sale, loan, hire;
(f) the description of the goods or services supplied;
(g) the quantity of goods or the extent of the services and the amount (excluding VAT) payable for each description;
(h) the total amount payable (excluding VAT);
(i) the rate of cash discount;
(j) the rate and amount of tax charged.

### 13.1.6 Collection and accounts

Accounting for VAT will generally be by reference to quarterly accounting periods. Within one month after the end of each quarter, a taxable person must send a completed return form to HM Revenue & Customs, together with a remittance for the tax due. The amount payable, ie, total output tax charged less deductible input tax, is obtained from a statutory VAT account, which is required to be kept by every taxable person for each tax period. Apart from these details of the tax due, the return form must also contain a list of the tax exclusive value of all outputs, and also the total of all inputs exclusive of tax.

There are proposals to move from a quarterly to a yearly accounting system.

Example

(a) During an accounting period, a firm of solicitors sends bills charging total profit costs of £200,000 plus output tax of £35,000. In the same period, the firm buys office equipment for £40,000 plus input tax of £7,000.

The firm accounts to HM Revenue & Customs as follows:

| | £ |
|---|---|
| Output tax charged | 35,000 |
| *less* input tax suffered | (7,000) |
| Payable to HM Revenue & Customs | 28,000 |

(b) During an accounting period, a retailer sells food for £50,000 plus output VAT at the zero rate. In the same period, the retailer buys equipment for £10,000 plus input tax of £1,750.

The retailer accounts to HM Revenue & Customs as follows:

| | £ |
|---|---|
| Output tax charged | 0 |
| *less* input tax suffered | (1,750) |
| Recoverable from HM Revenue & Customs | 1,750 |

*Note:* In both these examples, the supplier can recover the input tax paid because the supplier is making taxable supplies, even though, in the case of the retailer, they are at the zero rate.

(c) A funeral director sends bills for burial and cremation totalling £150,000. No VAT is charged as these are exempt supplies. During the same period, the funeral director buys equipment for £15,000 plus input tax of £2,625.

The funeral director is not a taxable person and so does not account to HM Revenue & Customs. Therefore, the funeral director cannot recover the input tax paid.

## 13.2 VAT and the solicitor

### 13.2.1 Professional charges

Solicitors must charge VAT on their supply of services.

Example

| Bill | £ |
|---|---|
| Professional charges | 100.00 |
| VAT @ 17.5% | 17.50 |
| Total | 117.50 |

Entries: The solicitor will need a ledger account in the name of HM Revenue & Customs as well as a costs account and a ledger account in the name of the client.

CR Costs with professional charges
CR HM Revenue & Customs with VAT
DR Client ledger (office section) with professional charges and VAT as separate amounts

Client:
Matter:

| Date | Details | Office account | | | Client account | | |
|---|---|---|---|---|---|---|---|
| | | DR | CR | BAL | DR | CR | BAL |
| | Costs | 100 | | 100DR | | | |
| | VAT | 17.50 | | 117.50 | | | |

### 13.2.2 What are disbursements?

As a matter of convenience for the client, solicitors frequently pay expenses (eg, court fees) on behalf of the client. Such expenses are often referred to as 'disbursements'. It would be unduly harsh if HM Revenue & Customs treated such items as part of the supply of services and required the solicitor to charge VAT on such expenses. HM Revenue & Customs do not regard 'disbursements' as part of the solicitor's supply of services. However, an item can only be treated as a 'disbursement' if it is what HM Revenue & Customs regard as a disbursement.

Payments may be treated as disbursements if all the following conditions are satisfied:

(a) The solicitor acted as agent for his client when paying the third party.
(b) The client actually received and used the goods or services provided by the third party to the solicitor. (This is the condition which usually prevents the solicitor's own travelling expenses, telephone bills, postage, etc, being treated as disbursements for VAT purposes.)
(c) The client was responsible for paying the third party.
(d) The client authorised the solicitor to make payment on his behalf.
(e) The client knew that the goods or services would be provided by a third party.
(f) The solicitor's outlay must be separately itemised when invoicing the client.
(g) The solicitor must recover only the exact amount paid to the third party.

Thus, it can be seen that many payments made by a solicitor on his client's behalf can be regarded as disbursements for tax purposes.

Items normally and necessarily part of the service rendered by the solicitor to his clients, for example, telephone charges, postage and photocopying charges, are not disbursements; they are overheads of the business, and HM Revenue & Customs require solicitors to charge VAT on them. As a general rule, travelling expenses incurred by a solicitor are not disbursements and must be included as part of the solicitor's overall charge. This view was upheld in the case of *Rowe & Maw (A Firm) v Customs and Excise Commissioners* [1975] 1 WLR 1291. The court held that the cost of fares incurred by the solicitor was incurred for the solicitor, not for the client. Many firms do not include a separate item on the bill for post, fares, photocopying and telephone but include them in the figure charged for profit costs.

In such a case, since VAT is charged on profit costs, VAT will inevitably be charged on the post, fares, photocopying and telephone element. Where a separate mention is made of such elements, the firm must remember to charge VAT on the separate elements.

The Law Society's view is that it is not normally appropriate to make a separate charge for such items, although there may be exceptional cases where it is permissible.

Example

(1) You send a bill to your client, Wright. The following is an extract:

Professional charges...

[Details of the work are set out]

| | £ |
|---|---|
| Profit costs | 800 |
| VAT @ 17.5% | 140 |
| Post, fares and telephone calls | 40 |
| VAT @ 17.5% | 7 |

In Wright's ledger account, it is simplest to DR £840 as profit costs and £147 as VAT.

(2) Alternatively, the bill could have appeared as follows:

Professional charges...

[Details of the work are set out]

| | £ |
|---|---|
| Profit costs | 840 |
| VAT | 147 |

### 13.2.3 The treatment of disbursements

The solicitor simply passes on the cost to the client. The payment may be for an item which is non-taxable or which includes its own VAT.

#### 13.2.3.1 Non-taxable

These are payments for something not subject to VAT, such as exempt supplies and supplies not in the course of business, for example, court fees, stamp duty, land registry fees, search fees, etc.

The solicitor can pay these out of the client bank account if there is sufficient money in the client bank account. Otherwise, they are paid out of the office bank account.

In neither case does the solicitor pay VAT to the supplier or charge the client VAT when obtaining reimbursement.

### 13.2.3.2 Taxable

These are payments made by the solicitor to a taxable person in respect of taxable supplies (eg, counsel, surveyor, accountant, estate agent, etc). The payment made by the solicitor will include a VAT element. That VAT element must be passed on to the client. The solicitor does not charge the client any additional VAT.

There are two methods of passing on the VAT. The choice depends on whether the original supplier addressed the invoice to the solicitor or to the client. If addressed to the solicitor, the '*principal*' method must be used; if addressed to the client, the '*agency*' method must be used.

(1) *Agency method*

If the invoice is addressed to the client, the supply is treated as made to the client. The solicitor simply acts as the agent, handing over the money on behalf of the client. If there is sufficient client money standing to the credit of the client, the payment can be made from the client bank account; otherwise, it must be made from the office bank account.

The solicitor does not separate the fee and VAT on the ledger account or cash account, but instead debits the tax inclusive amount as a global sum. If the payment is made out of office money, then the solicitor will seek reimbursement of the tax inclusive amount, again without separating the fee and the VAT.

The solicitor must, if asked, send the supplier's tax invoice to the client. If the client is registered for VAT and the supply is in the course or furtherance of a business, the invoice can be used by the client to recover the input tax.

**Example**

A solicitor pays an expert witness's bill on behalf of a client. The bill is for £1,000 plus £175 VAT. The invoice is addressed to the client and is paid using the agency method.

The solicitor simply pays the total sum of £1,175 and does not distinguish between the fee and the VAT. Whether the payment was made out of office money or client money, the solicitor will charge the client £1,175, again without distinguishing between fee and VAT.

If the client is registered for VAT, and therefore wants the invoice, the solicitor must send the client the expert's original invoice. The invoice is addressed to the client, and so the client can claim an input if the client is registered for VAT.

(2) *Principal method*

If the invoice is addressed to the solicitor, the supply is treated as made to the solicitor in the first instance. The solicitor, therefore, pays the supplier's fees, together with the input tax charged from the office bank account.

The solicitor then resupplies the item to the client at the VAT exclusive price.

The solicitor will charge output tax on the firm's professional charges *and* on the disbursement.

If the client is entitled to a tax invoice, the solicitor will provide one to cover both the disbursement and the solicitor's own professional charges.

**Example**

A solicitor receives an expert witness's invoice for £200 plus £35 VAT. The solicitor pays:

| | £ |
|---|---|
| Expert's fee | 200 |
| *plus* input tax | 35 |
| | 235 |

The solicitor records the fee and the VAT as separate items on the cash account.

The VAT is recorded on the HM Revenue & Customs account. The tax exclusive amount is recorded on the client ledger account.

When the solicitor later charges the client his own profit costs of £400, the bill will include:

| | £ |
|---|---|
| Expert's fee | 200 |
| Profit costs | 400 |
| *plus* output tax (£35 + £70) | 105 |

The expert's fee and the VAT are separate items on the bill.

*Note*: A disbursement paid on the principal method must be paid out of the office bank account, even if there is client money available. This is because the supply is treated as made to the solicitor and not to the client.

#### 13.2.3.3 A summary

Students generally find principal method disbursements difficult to deal with. The following summary may be helpful:

(1) Identify that the disbursement is to be treated on the principal basis – if the invoice is addressed to the solicitor, it will be treated on the principal basis.

(2) CR the disbursement and the VAT on it to cash account office section – it is common, but not essential, to show the two elements separately.

(3) DR VAT to HM Revenue & Customs ledger.

DR VAT exclusive amount to client ledger office section.

Make a memorandum note in the 'Details' column of the client ledger of the amount of VAT which must be added to the VAT charged to the client when an invoice is issued.

(4) When a bill is issued, add the VAT on the principal method disbursement to the VAT on the profit costs and make the normal entries for delivery of a bill.

DR client ledger office section, with VAT and costs as two separate amounts.

CR the costs account and HM Revenue & Customs account, with costs and VAT respectively.

#### 13.2.3.4 Counsel's fees – concessionary treatment

A concessionary treatment for counsel's fees was agreed between HM Revenue & Customs, The Law Society and the Bar when VAT was first introduced and was published in the *Law Society Gazette*, 4 April 1973.

The agent (usually a solicitor or accountant) may treat counsel's advice as supplied directly to the client and the settlement of the fees as an agency method disbursement. Counsel's VAT invoice may be amended by adding the name and address of the client and inserting 'per' before the agent's own name and address. The fee note from counsel will then be recognised as a valid VAT invoice in the hands of the client. Where the agent considers that the services of counsel, if supplied directly to the client, would be outside the scope of UK VAT, he may certify the counsel's fee note to this effect and pay only the VAT exclusive fee.

Normally, the tax point for counsel's services will be determined by payment and not delivery of a fee note. On payment, counsel's clerk will add the VAT number of counsel and other particulars required under reg 13 of the VAT Regulations 1995 to constitute a document as a VAT invoice so that the receipted fee note is a VAT invoice. This will usually be made out to the solicitor (so that the solicitor can claim input tax credit). However, if the solicitor alters the fee note so that it is addressed to the client (and input tax credit can be taken by his client), the solicitor should keep a photocopy of the VAT invoice, passing the original amended receipted fee note to the client. This is in case the fee note needs to be dealt with in an assessment of costs.

**Exercise 13B**

You act for Barton in connection with a tax dispute. The following events occur:

July

| | |
|---|---|
| 8 | You receive £1,000 from Barton on account of costs to be incurred. |
| 10 | You pay a court fee of £100 out of client money. |
| 22 | You pay an accountant's fee of £400 plus £70 VAT. The invoice was addressed to you. |
| 29 | You pay a surveyor's fee of £600 plus £105 VAT. The invoice was addressed to Barton. |

August

| | |
|---|---|
| 7 | You send Barton a bill and VAT invoice. Your costs are £800 plus appropriate VAT. |
| 9 | You transfer the £195 remaining in the client bank account to the office bank account in part payment of your costs. |
| 11 | You receive from Barton a cheque for the balance of the costs outstanding. |

Prepare the cash account and client ledger account for Barton, together with the relevant entries on the ledger account for HM Revenue & Customs.

**Exercise 13C**

You act for Avis in a boundary dispute. The following events occur:

November

| | |
|---|---|
| 5 | You pay a court fee of £100 on Avis's behalf. |
| 7 | You receive a cheque from Avis for £1,000 on account of costs. You do not split the cheque. |
| 9 | You pay counsel's fee of £400 plus VAT on behalf of Avis. The invoice was addressed to you, but you add the name and address of Avis. |
| 11 | You pay a surveyor's fee of £200 plus VAT. The invoice was addressed to you. |
| 13 | You send Avis a bill. Your profit costs are £600 plus VAT. |
| 15 | You transfer the £530 remaining in the client bank account in part payment of your bill. You receive a cheque from Avis for the balance of £510. |

Comment on the application of the Accounts Rules, and explain what steps you will take to deal with the VAT elements involved in this transaction.

Prepare the cash account and client ledger account for Avis, together with the relevant entries on the ledger account for HM Revenue & Customs.

## 13.3 Solutions

Exercise 13A

The fee is inclusive of VAT. If the profit costs are regarded as 100%, the solicitor can be said to have received 100% plus 17.5% (profit costs plus VAT). To calculate the profit costs, it is therefore necessary to divide by 117.5 to give 1% of the receipt and to multiply by 100 to give 100% of the receipt.

$$\text{Receipt} \times \frac{100}{117.5}$$

$$£200 \times \frac{100}{117.5} = £170.21$$

$$\text{VAT} = £29.79$$

Exercise 13B

*Notes*

July

8 The money is client money. It will be paid into the client bank account in the usual way pursuant to Rule 15.

10 Rule 22(1)(b) permits the payment out of the client bank account. The court fees are exempt from VAT.

22 The invoice was addressed to you, so the disbursement must be paid using the principal method out of office money. Remember that the solicitor is responsible for paying the input tax.

At this stage, the solicitor only debits the fee, not the VAT, to the client. The cash account records the fee and the total paid, ie, the VAT. The solicitor debits the VAT to the HM Revenue & Customs ledger account.

[*Note:* You will see a note in the details column of Barton's ledger account that the solicitor has paid input tax. This is a reminder to the solicitor to charge the client output tax later.]

29 The surveyor's invoice was addressed to Barton and is therefore payable using the agency method.

There is sufficient money in the client bank account, and it is sensible to make the payment out of client's money as permitted by Rule 22(1)(b).

August

7 You debit Barton's ledger account, office section, with costs and VAT. You must consider carefully how much output tax to charge.

The solicitor must charge output tax at the standard rate on the value of his legal services, ie:

(1) the value of the profit costs of £800; plus
(2) the value of any general disbursements – there are none in this case; plus
(3) the value of any taxable disbursements paid on the principal method – in this case the accountant's fee of £400.

Therefore, the solicitor must charge VAT on £800 profit costs plus £400 accountant's fee, which makes a total of £1,200. VAT @ 17.5% is £210.

The double entries for costs and VAT will be in the costs ledger account (not shown) and HM Revenue & Customs ledger account respectively.

[*Note*: There is no entry in the cash account at this point as no movement of money is involved.]

August

9 Rule 22(3)(b) permits the withdrawal from the client bank account for payment of expenses and costs. Rule 23(3) provides that the withdrawal shall be by way of transfer to the office bank account.

11 This money is received from Barton specifically in payment of the outstanding costs and expenses. The money should be paid straight into the office bank account under Rule 19(1)(a) (unless it is paid into the client account in accordance with Rule 9(1)(c)).

The accounts will look like this:

**Client:** Barton
**Matter:** Tax dispute

| Date | Details | Office account | | | Client account | | |
|---|---|---|---|---|---|---|---|
| | | DR | CR | BAL | DR | CR | BAL |
| Jul | | | | | | | |
| 8 | Cash. On account | | | | | 1,000 | 1,000CR |
| 10 | Cash. Court fee | | | | 100 | | 900 |
| 22 | Cash. Accountant's fee [VAT £70 paid] | 400 | | 400DR | | | |
| 29 | Cash. Surveyor's fee | | | | 705 | | 195 |
| Aug | | | | | | | |
| 7 | Costs | 800 | | 1,200 | | | |
| | VAT (£70 + £140) | 210 | | 1,410 | | | |
| 9 | Cash. Transfer from client to office | | 195 | 1,215 | 195 | | – |
| 11 | Cash. From Barton. Balance due | | 1,215 | – | | | |

**Cash account**

| Date | Details | Office account | | | Client account | | |
|---|---|---|---|---|---|---|---|
| | | DR | CR | BAL | DR | CR | BAL |
| Jul | Balance | | | XXX | | | XXX |
| 8 | Barton | | | | 1,000 | | |
| 10 | Barton | | | | | 100 | |
| 22 | Barton | | 400 | | | | |
| | VAT | | 70 | | | | |
| 29 | Barton | | | | | 705 | |
| Aug | | | | | | | |
| 9 | Barton | **195** | | | | 195 | |
| 11 | Barton | **1,215** | | | | | |

**HM Revenue & Customs account**

| Date | Details | Office account | | |
|---|---|---|---|---|
| | | DR | CR | BAL |
| Jul | | | | |
| 22 | Cash. Re Barton | **70** | | 70DR |
| Aug | | | | |
| 7 | Barton | | **210** | 140CR |

The CR balance shown on HM Revenue & Customs ledger account represents the output tax charged to Barton less the input tax paid by the solicitor. The solicitor will have to account to HM Revenue & Customs for this amount.

Exercise 13C

(1) 5 November You are not holding any money for Avis. Therefore, Rule 22(5) applies and the money cannot be paid out of the client account. The payment is made out of the office account.

*Entries:*

DR Avis ledger account<br>CR Cash account } Office section

7 November The money is office and client money. You pay it into the client account – Rule 20(2)(b).

*Entries:*

CR Avis ledger account<br>DR Cash account } Client section

9 November The invoice is now treated addressed to Avis, so the payment is made using the agency method. You pay an inclusive sum of £470 with no separate record of VAT. There is sufficient money in the client bank account, so make the payment out of the client bank account – Rule 22(1)(b).

*Entries:*

DR Avis ledger account<br>CR Cash account } Client section

11 November This invoice was addressed to you, so you must pay it using the principal method. You record the fee and VAT separately. You DR the fee to Avis and the VAT to HM Revenue & Customs.

Even though there is enough money in the client bank account, you must make a payment on the principal method out of the office bank account.

*Entries:*

Fee DR Avis ledger account<br>CR Cash account } Office section

VAT DR Revenue & Customs ledger account<br>CR Cash account } Office section

13 November You make entries for costs and VAT separately. The DR entry in the client's ledger account is in the *office* section.

You calculate VAT on the total of profit costs, general disbursements (none in this case) and taxable disbursements paid on the principal method. The surveyor's fee was paid on the principal method. VAT is therefore charged on £600 profit costs plus £200 surveyor's fee, making a total of £800. VAT will be £140.

*Entries:*

Costs DR Avis ledger account / CR Costs account } Office section

VAT DR Avis ledger account / CR Revenue & Customs account } Office section

15 November You have £530 remaining in the client bank account. Avis owes you £1,040. You will transfer the £530 and receive a cheque for £510 from Avis.

Rule 22(3)(b) allows the withdrawal of £530 from the client bank account in payment of your expenses and costs respectively.

The money has been received to repay the disbursements and to pay your costs where a bill has been sent. Subject to Rule 19(1)(c), the money must not be paid into the client bank account. It is paid straight away into the office bank account.

*Entries:*

For transfer

Withdrawal from client account

DR Avis ledger account / CR Cash account } Client section

Receipt into office account

CR Avis ledger account / DR Cash account } Office section

For receipt of money from Avis into office account

CR Avis ledger account / DR Cash account } Office section

**Client:** Avis
**Matter:** Boundary dispute

| Date | Details | Office account | | | Client account | | |
|---|---|---|---|---|---|---|---|
| | | DR | CR | BAL | DR | CR | BAL |
| Jul | | | | | | | |
| 5 | Cash. Court fee | 100 | | 100DR | | | |
| 7 | Cash. From Avis. On account of costs | | | | | 1,000 | 1,000CR |
| 9 | Cash. Counsel's fee | | | | 470 | | 530 |
| 11 | Cash. Surveyor's fee [VAT £35 paid] | 200 | | 300 | | | |
| 13 | Costs | 600 | | 900 | | | |
| | VAT (£105 + £35) | 140 | | 1,040 | | | |
| 15 | Cash. Transfer from client to office account | | 530 | 510 | 530 | | – |
| | Cash. From Avis. Balance due | | 510 | – | | | |

| Cash account | | | | | | | |
|---|---|---|---|---|---|---|---|
| **Date** | **Details** | **Office account** | | | **Client account** | | |
| | | **DR** | **CR** | **BAL** | **DR** | **CR** | **BAL** |
| Nov | Balance | | | XXX | | | XXX |
| 5 | Avis | | 100 | | | | |
| 7 | Avis | | | | 1,000 | | |
| 9 | Avis | | | | | 470 | |
| 11 | Avis | | 200 | | | | |
| | C&E | | 35 | | | | |
| 15 | Avis | 530 | | | | 530 | |
| | Avis | 510 | | | | | |

| HM Revenue & Customs account | | | | |
|---|---|---|---|---|
| **Date** | **Details** | **Office account** | | |
| | | **DR** | **CR** | **BAL** |
| Nov | | | | |
| 11 | Cash. Re Avis | 35 | | 35DR |
| 13 | Avis. VAT | | 140 | 105CR |

# Chapter 14

# Splitting Cheques and Receiving Cheques in Payment of a Bill



## 14.1 Rule 20

### 14.1.1 Receipts partly of office and partly of client money (Rule 20)

A solicitor often receives a cheque which is made up partly of office money and partly of client money.

> **Example**
>
> You act for Carollo Ltd. You have paid £40 out of the office bank account on its behalf. In response to a request by you, it sends a cheque for £100, partly to pay back the £40 and partly to cover future disbursements. The £40 is office money and the £60 is client money.

Under Rule 20(2)(a), you can 'split' the cheque. This means paying the different parts of the cheque into different bank accounts. Thus, you could pay the £40 into the office bank account and the £60 into the client bank account.

On splitting the cheque the entries are:

| | |
|---|---|
| DR Office portion to Cash account | Office section |
| DR Client portion to Cash account | Client section |

| | |
|---|---|
| CR Office portion to Client ledger | Office section |
| CR Client portion to Client ledger | Client section |

### 14.1.2 Unsplit cheque

If you do not split the cheque, you must pay it all into the client bank account under Rule 20(2)(b). You will then need to transfer the 'office' portion (ie, the £40) to the office bank account within 14 days of receipt (Rule 20(3)). It is more common to deal with 'mixed' cheques in this way than it is to split them; banks are usually unwilling to split cheques in practice as it creates administrative problems for them.

You must not pay the whole cheque into the office bank account and transfer the client portion to the client bank account. This would be a breach of the Rules.

If not splitting the cheque, the entries are:

| | |
|---|---|
| DR whole amount to Cash account<br>CR whole amount to Client ledger | Client section |

When later transferring office portion:

| | |
|---|---|
| CR Cash account<br>DR Client ledger | Client section |
| DR Cash account<br>CR Client ledger | Office section |

*Entries (if cheque split):*

| Client: Carollo Ltd<br>Matter: | | | | | | | | |
|---|---|---|---|---|---|---|---|---|
| **Date** | **Details** | **Office account** | | | **Client account** | | | |
| Feb | | **DR** | **CR** | **BAL** | **DR** | **CR** | **BAL** |
| 1 | Cash | 40 | | 40DR | | | |
| 10 | Cash | | **40** | – | | **60** | 60CR |

| Cash account | | | | | | | |
|---|---|---|---|---|---|---|---|
| **Date** | **Details** | **Office account** | | | **Client account** | | |
| Feb | | **DR** | **CR** | **BAL** | **DR** | **CR** | **BAL** |
| | | | | | | | XXX |
| 1 | Carollo | | 40 | | | | |
| 10 | Carollo | **40** | | | **60** | | |

*Entries (if cheque* not *split and a transfer is later made of the office money element):*

| Client: Carollo Ltd<br>Matter: | | | | | | | |
|---|---|---|---|---|---|---|---|
| **Date** | **Details** | **Office account** | | | **Client account** | | |
| Feb | | **DR** | **CR** | **BAL** | **DR** | **CR** | **BAL** |
| 1 | Cash | 40 | | 40DR | | | |
| 10 | Cash | | | | | **100** | 100CR |
| | Cash transfer | | **40** | – | **40** | | 60 |

| Cash account | | | | | | | |
|---|---|---|---|---|---|---|---|
| **Date** | **Details** | **Office account** | | | **Client account** | | |
| Feb | | **DR** | **CR** | **BAL** | **DR** | **CR** | **BAL** |
| | | | | XXX | | | XXX |
| 1 | Carollo | | 40 | | | | |
| 10 | Carollo | | | | **100** | | |
| | Carollo transfer | **40** | | | | **40** | |

**Exercise 14A**

You act for Brian.

March

| | |
|---|---|
| 7 | Pay £30 by cheque on Brian's behalf. |
| 15 | You have an interview with Brian. You ask him to reimburse you for the £30 and to give you another £70 in respect of future items. He gives you a cheque for £100. You split the cheque. |
| 21 | Pay £50 by cheque on Brian's behalf. |
| 31 | Brian instructs you to hold the balance on behalf of Christine and you receive confirmation from Christine to hold this sum for her. |

## 14.2 Rule 19

### 14.2.1 Cheques received in full or part payment of a bill

As we saw in **Chapter 10**, Rule 19(1) gives various options for dealing with a cheque received in full or part payment of a bill:

(a) The money can be dealt with in accordance with its nature. Thus, an office money cheque will be paid into the office bank account, a client money cheque will be paid into the client bank account and a mixed cheque will be dealt with under Rule 20.

(b) Where the cheque is office money plus client money in the form of unpaid professional disbursements for which the solicitor has incurred liability, the entire receipt can be paid into the office bank account. However, by the end of the second working day following receipt, the solicitor must either pay the disbursement or transfer the money for it to the client bank account.

*Note:* This option is not available if the cheque received contains client money of any other kind.

(c) The cheque, whatever its nature, can be paid into the client bank account. However, any office money must be transferred out of the client bank account within 14 days of receipt. This option means that a firm can give its clients one bank account number which they can use for direct payments into the firm's account.

(d) Where the cheque is a receipt from the Legal Services Commission, it can always be paid into the office bank account even if it consists entirely of client money for unpaid professional disbursements. However, the solicitor must either pay the disbursement or transfer the money for it to the client bank account within 14 days of receipt.

### 14.2.2 Money received for an agreed fee

An agreed fee is a fixed fee which cannot be varied upwards and which does not depend on the transaction being completed. It must be evidenced in writing. It is not necessary under the Solicitors' Accounts Rules to send a bill provided there is written evidence. However, a solicitor will often choose to send a bill even where a fee has been agreed so as to have a record for VAT purposes.

Money received for an agreed fee is office money and should be paid into the office bank account.

## 14.3 Revision of material in Chapters 10–14

Exercise 14B

(1) **Which one of the following receipts is entirely office money?**

(a) Client A sends you £100 on account of costs.

(b) A deposit received as stakeholder on the sale of a house by Fred, a partner in the firm, to Joe, an assistant solicitor.

(c) Solicitor delivers a bill to Client C for profit costs of £200 + VAT of £35 and £10 for land charges for which liability is incurred but which are not yet paid. Client C sends the solicitor £245.

(d) None of the above.

(2) **Which one of the following cannot be paid into the client bank account?**

(a) Controlled trust money.

(b) Office money to open the client bank account.

(c) A cheque for £235 in settlement of the solicitor's bill for costs of £200 and VAT of £35.

(d) A cheque for £500 received from Client A with a written request that the money should not be paid in until the client gives the solicitor instructions.

(3) **Client X gives a solicitor a cheque for £100 on account of costs. The solicitor endorses the cheque over to an expert witness on X's behalf. Which one of the following statements is correct?**

(a) Rule 17(b) permits the solicitor not to pay the cheque into the client bank account so no entries need be made in the solicitor's accounts.

(b) Rule 32(2) requires the solicitor to record the receipt and payment on the cash account.

(c) Rule 32(2) requires the solicitor to record the receipt and payment on the cash account and client ledger account for X.

(d) Rule 17(b) provides that the solicitor must not pay the cheque into the client bank account.

(4) **Client X sends a solicitor a cheque for £235 in satisfaction of the solicitor's bill for profit costs and VAT. Which one of the following statements is correct?**

(a) The cheque is client money and must be paid into the client bank account without delay.

(b) The cheque is office money and must be paid into the client bank account.

(c) The cheque is office money and must not be paid into the client bank account.

(d) The cheque is office money and can be paid into the client bank account.

(5) **A solicitor is holding £1,000 for Client A. Client A instructs the solicitor to hold £300 of that money to the order of Client B, to whom A owes money. Which one of the following statements is correct?**

(a) A client bank account cheque for £300 must be sent to B.

(b) No entries need be made.

(c) A client bank account cheque for £300 must be drawn, and then the cheque must be paid into the client bank account on B's behalf.

(d) Entries must be made on the client ledger accounts of A and B and on a record of sums transferred from one ledger account to another.

(6) **Brown is a bookseller. He sells only books. He does not charge his customers VAT. Is this because:**

(a) His turnover does not exceed the limit for compulsory registration?

(b) He makes only exempt supplies?

(c) He is not carrying on a 'business' for the purposes of the VATA 1994?

(d) He makes only zero-rated supplies?

(7) **A solicitor (registered for VAT) agrees to draft a will for Client X for £100. Which of the following statements is correct?**

(a) He must charge £17.50 VAT on top of the fee.

(b) He must not charge VAT.

(c) The client will pay him £100 plus VAT.

(d) The client will pay him £100.

(8) **A solicitor completes the administration of an estate on 31 March and sends a bill on 2 April. When is the tax point?**

(a) 31 March.

(b) 2 April.

(c) 14 April.

(d) 30 June.

(9) **A solicitor receives an invoice from an expert witness for £200 + VAT in respect of litigation being conducted for Client X. The invoice is addressed to the solicitor's firm. The solicitor holds £1,000 in the client bank account for X generally on account of costs. Which one of the following statements is correct?**

(a) The solicitor can pay the invoice from the client bank account.

(b) The solicitor must pay the invoice from the office bank account.

(c) The solicitor must debit the client ledger account immediately with £235.

(d) All of the above statements are incorrect.

(10) **You receive a cheque from the client made up partly of office money and partly of client money. Which one of the following statements is correct?**

(a) You must split the cheque.

(b) You may split the cheque.

(c) You must pay the cheque into the client bank account.

(d) You must pay the cheque into the office bank account.

## 14.4 Solutions

Exercise 14A

*Notes*

7 March No client money, so office money must be used.

15 March This cheque includes office and client money, so can be split under Rule 20. If split, you must record two separate receipts, one for client money and one for office money. If not split, it must be paid into the client bank account.

21 March Client money is available and can be used.

31 March This is an inter-client transfer. No entry is made on the cash account although a note must be made in the Transfer Journal.

DR Brian ledger
CR Christine ledger } Client section

**Client:** Brian
**Matter:**

| Date | Details | Office account | | | Client account | | |
|---|---|---|---|---|---|---|---|
| | | DR | CR | BAL | DR | CR | BAL |
| March | | | | | | | XXX |
| 7 | Cash. Payment | 30 | | 30DR | | | |
| 15 | Cash. From you | | 30 | – | | 70 | 70CR |
| 21 | Cash. Payment | | | | 50 | | 20 |
| 31 | Christine. Transfer | | | | 20 | | – |

**Client:** Christine
**Matter:**

| Date | Details | Office account | | | Client account | | |
|---|---|---|---|---|---|---|---|
| | | DR | CR | BAL | DR | CR | BAL |
| March | | | | | | | |
| 31 | Brian. Transfer | | | | | 20 | 20CR |

**Cash account**

| Date | Details | Office account | | | Client account | | |
|---|---|---|---|---|---|---|---|
| | | DR | CR | BAL | DR | CR | BAL |
| March | | | | XXX | | | XXX |
| 7 | Brian. Payment | | 30 | | | | |
| 15 | Brian. Amount from Brian | 30 | | | 70 | | |
| 21 | Brian. Payment | | | | | 50 | |

Exercise 14B

(1) (c) The money is received partly in payment of professional charges and partly for a disbursement for which liability has been incurred, a bill having been received. In (b), the money is held for a partner in the firm *and someone else*. Therefore, the money is client money.

(2) (d) Note that, although the receipt in (c) is office money, it can be paid into the client bank account under Rule 19(1)(c). However, it must not be left longer than 14 days.

(3) (c) See Rule 32(2).

(4) (d) See Rule 19(1)(c).

(5) (d) See Rule 32.

(6) (d)

(7) (d) The solicitor must apportion the fee between the VAT and the VAT exclusive element.

(8) (b) The tax point is the date the bill is isued.

(9) (b) It must be treated on the principal basis and, therefore, must be paid from the office bank account.

(10) (b)

# Chapter 15
# Miscellaneous Matters



## 15.1 Receipt of a cheque made out to the client or a third party

A solicitor who receives a cheque made out not to the firm but to the client (or a third party) *cannot* pay that cheque into a firm bank account. The firm is not the payee.

The solicitor's obligation is only to forward the cheque to the payee without delay. The solicitor has not dealt with client money because the cheque is not 'money' as far as the solicitor is concerned; it is a piece of paper which the solicitor cannot turn into cash. As the solicitor has not dealt with *client money*, there is no obligation under Rule 32 to record the event on the client ledger account and cash account. However, the solicitor will want to keep a written record on the correspondence file.

Many firms will have a special control account where all cheques received by the firm will be recorded irrespective of the payee. This is not required by the Rules but is a useful precaution to prevent cheques being overlooked.

## 15.2 Endorsed cheques

A solicitor may receive a cheque made out to the firm on behalf of a client. Instead of paying the cheque into the client bank account, the solicitor is free under Rule 17(b) (assuming the cheque is endorsable) to endorse the cheque to the client or to a third party on behalf of the client. However, as this is a *dealing* with client's money, it must be recorded under Rule 32 at the time of receipt on the client ledger account and cash account as a receipt and payment of client money. As the cheque passes through the solicitor's hands, having no effect on the balances of the accounts, it is common to make the entries for receipt and payment on the same line.

Example

A solicitor acting for Brown in a debt collection receives a cheque for £1,000 made out to the firm in settlement of a debt due to Brown. The solicitor endorses the cheque to Brown.

| **Client:** Brown | | | | | | | |
|---|---|---|---|---|---|---|---|
| **Date** | **Details** | **Office account** | | | **Client account** | | |
| | | **DR** | **CR** | **BAL** | **DR** | **CR** | **BAL** |
| | Cash. From debtor<br>Cheque endorsed | | | | 1,000 | 1,000 | – |

| Cash account | | | | | | | |
|---|---|---|---|---|---|---|---|
| Date | Details | Office account | | | Client account | | |
| | | DR | CR | BAL | DR | CR | BAL |
| | | | | | | | XXX |
| | Brown. From debtor Cheque endorsed to Brown | | | | 1,000 | 1,000 | |

## 15.3 Returned cheques

There is nothing in the rules to prevent a solicitor drawing against a cheque which has been paid into the client bank account but which has not yet been cleared. However, if that cheque is then dishonoured, there will be a breach of Rule 22, and the solicitor will have to transfer money from the office bank account to the client bank account to make up the deficiency.

Example

On 1 March, you receive £500 on account of costs from your client, Smith.

On 2 March, you pay a court fee of £100 out of the client bank account on behalf of Smith.

On 4 March, Smith's cheque is returned by the bank marked 'Return to Drawer'.

On 7 March, Smith tells you that there has been a mistake and that the cheque should have been met. He asks you to re-present it. You do so on 7 March and it is met.

Because it turns out that you had no money for Smith, you must have used £100 belonging to another client for the benefit of Smith. You must, therefore, transfer £100 from the office bank account to the client bank account to remedy your breach of the rules.

When you re-present the cheque, you can either split it or pay the whole amount into the client bank account and transfer the £100 to the office bank account at a later stage.

*Notes:*

March

1 The money is client money and is paid into the client bank account (Rule 13).

*Entries:*

CR Smith ledger account
DR Cash account } Client section

2 Rule 22 allows the money to be paid out of the client bank account even though the cheque from Smith has not yet been cleared.

*Entries:*

DR Smith ledger account
CR Cash account } Client section

4 You must make entries reversing those made when you received the cheque.

*Entries:*

DR Smith ledger account
CR Cash account } Client section

This results in a DR balance of £100 on Smith's ledger account and you are in breach of Rule 22(5). Effectively, you have used client money on behalf of a client for whom you were not holding any.

4 You must make an *immediate* transfer of £100 from the office bank account to the client bank account to rectify the breach.

*Entries:*

Withdrawal from office account

DR Smith ledger account
CR Cash account } Office section

Receipt into client account

CR Smith ledger account
DR Cash account } Client section

7 When the cheque is re-presented you can, under Rule 20, either pay the whole amount into the client bank account, or, as in this example, split it so that £100 goes into the office bank account and £400 into the client bank account.

*Entries if split:*

£100 Office money

CR Smith ledger account
DR Cash account } Office section

£400 Client money

CR Smith ledger account
DR Cash account } Client section

The accounts look like this:

**Client:** Smith
**Matter:** Miscellaneous

| Date | Details | Office account | | | Client account | | |
|---|---|---|---|---|---|---|---|
| | | DR | CR | BAL | DR | CR | BAL |
| March | | | | | | | |
| 1 | Cash. From Smith On account | | | | | 500 | 500CR |
| 2 | Cash. Court fee | | | | 100 | | 400 |
| 4 | Cash. Smith's cheque – returned | | | | 500 | | 100DR |
| | Cash. Transfer from office account to rectify breach | 100 | | 100DR | | 100 | – |
| 7 | Cash. Smith's cheque re-presented | | 100 | – | | 400 | 400CR |

**Cash account**

| Date | Details | Office account | | | Client account | | |
|---|---|---|---|---|---|---|---|
| | | DR | CR | BAL | DR | CR | BAL |
| March | | | | | | | XXX |
| 1 | Smith | | | | 500 | | |
| 2 | Smith | | | | | 100 | |
| 4 | Smith | | | | | 500 | |
| | Smith | | 100 | | 100 | | |
| 7 | Smith | 100 | | | 400 | | |

A well-run firm will operate a system which makes it impossible to draw against a client bank cheque before it has cleared.

## 15.4 Abatements

Clients frequently complain that the amount of their bill is too high. Sometimes, the solicitor may decide to reduce, or abate, the costs. HM Revenue & Customs allows the output tax to be reduced proportionately.

In order to record the abatement, you simply reverse the entries made when the bill was delivered. You also send the client a VAT credit note.

*Entries:*

DR Costs
DR HM Revenue & Customs } with the reduction

CR Client ledger (office section) with the reduction in costs and VAT.

**Example**

You send your client Jones a bill for £600 plus VAT on 4 May. On 6 May, after discussion with Jones, you agree to reduce the bill by £80 plus VAT.

The accounts will look like this:

**Client:** Jones
**Matter:** Miscellaneous

| Date | Details | Office account | | | Client account | | |
|---|---|---|---|---|---|---|---|
| | | DR | CR | BAL | DR | CR | BAL |
| May | | | | | | | |
| 4 | Costs | 600 | | 600DR | | | |
| | VAT | 105 | | 705 | | | |
| 6 | Costs – Abatement | | 80 | 625 | | | |
| | VAT – Abatement | | 14 | 611 | | | |

**Costs account**

| Date | Details | Office account | | |
|---|---|---|---|---|
| | | DR | CR | BAL |
| May | | | | |
| 4 | Jones | | 600 | 600CR |
| 6 | Jones | 80 | | 520 |

**HM Revenue & Customs account**

| Date | Details | Office account | | |
|---|---|---|---|---|
| | | DR | CR | BAL |
| May | | | | |
| 4 | Jones | | 105 | 105CR |
| 6 | Jones | 14 | | 91 |

If preferred, the firm can debit abatements to a separate abatements account. At the end of the accounting period, the debit balance on the abatements account is transferred to the debit side of the costs account.

## 15.5 Bad debts

### 15.5.1 The general rule

From time to time, a solicitor will realise that a client is not going to pay the amount owing to the firm. The solicitor will have to write off the amount owing for profit costs and VAT and for any disbursements paid from the office bank account. The general rule for VAT used to be that there was no VAT relief, and VAT had to be accounted for to HM Revenue & Customs even if the debt was written off. Thus, the VAT was an additional element of the bad debt and increased the amount which had to be written off.

*Entries:*

CR Client's ledger account, office section } with the whole amount
DR Bad debts account

### 15.5.2 VAT relief

However, VAT relief is now available if the debt has been outstanding for at least six months since the date payment was due. In this case, the solicitor will be entitled to a refund from HM Revenue & Customs.

*Entries:*

When debt is written off:
CR Client's ledger account, office section, with the full amount owing
DR Bad debts account with the full amount owing

When VAT relief becomes available:
CR Bad debts account with amount of VAT
DR HM Revenue & Customs with amount of VAT

Example

On 9 April, you send Green a bill for £400 plus VAT. On 6 June, you write off Green's debt.

Six months after the due date of payment of Green's bill (31 October), you become entitled to VAT bad debt relief.

The accounts will look like this:

**Client:** Green
**Matter:** Miscellaneous

| Date | Details | Office account | | | Client account | | |
|---|---|---|---|---|---|---|---|
| | | DR | CR | BAL | DR | CR | BAL |
| Apr 9 | Costs | 400 | | 400DR | | | |
| | VAT | 70 | | 470 | | | |
| June 6 | **Bad debts** | | 470 | – | | | |

**Profit costs account**

| Date | Details | Office account | | |
|---|---|---|---|---|
| | | DR | CR | BAL |
| Apr 9 | Green | | 400 | 400CR |

| HM Revenue & Customs account | | | | |
|---|---|---|---|---|
| Date | Details | Office account | | |
| | | DR | CR | BAL |
| Apr<br>9 | Green | | 70 | 70CR |
| Oct<br>31 | VAT relief | 70 | | – |

| Bad debts account | | | | |
|---|---|---|---|---|
| Date | Details | Office account | | |
| | | DR | CR | BAL |
| June<br>6 | Green | 470 | | 470DR |
| Oct<br>31 | VAT relief | | 70 | 400 |

## 15.6 Petty cash

### 15.6.1 Need for petty cash account

Any firm will need some petty cash on the premises to meet small cash payments. When cash is withdrawn from the bank for petty cash, the entries will be:

CR Cash – office section
DR Petty cash account

When a payment is made, for example a roll of sticky tape is bought, the entries will be:

CR Petty cash account
DR appropriate ledger account, for example Sundries

### 15.6.2 Petty cash payments for clients

A solicitor will sometimes make a payment from petty cash on behalf of a client. The CR entry will be made on the petty cash account, not on the main cash account. The solicitor will want to DR the client ledger account to show that the client now owes the solicitor for the expense incurred. The DR entry must be made on the office section of the client ledger even if client money is held for the client. This is because petty cash is office money. Thus, by deciding to use petty cash, the solicitor has elected to use office money on behalf of the client.

Example

Solicitor holds £200 in the client bank account for Smith. Solicitor pays £20 expenses to an expert witness from petty cash.

Smith's client ledger account will look like this:

| **Client:** Smith<br>**Matter:** | | | | | | | |
|---|---|---|---|---|---|---|---|
| Date | Details | Office account | | | Client account | | |
| | | DR | CR | BAL | DR | CR | BAL |
| | Cash. Received on account | | | | | 200 | 200CR |
| | **Petty cash. Expert witness** | 20 | | 20DR | | | |

The corresponding credit entry will be on the petty cash account, not on the cash account. Notice that the 'Details' section of Smith's ledger account refers to 'petty cash' not to cash.

## 15.7 Insurance commission

Solicitors sometimes act as agent for an insurance company and collect premiums from the company's customers. The solicitor will be entitled to a commission from the company and will normally account to the company for the premiums collected, less the commission due.

The commission is charged to the company in much the same way as costs are charged to any other client.

However, because commission is an exempt item for VAT purposes, no VAT is charged. An insurance commission account similar to the profit costs account will be required. On charging commission, DR insurance company ledger account, office section, and CR insurance commission ledger account.

If the commission exceeds £20, then Rule 2.05 of The Law Society's Code of Conduct applies (solicitors must account to their clients unless they have the client's agreement to retain commission).

Firms that wish to take advantage of the exemption for professional firms to avoid regulation by the Financial Services Authority in relation to investment business must account for all commission to clients.

**Example**

You hold £300 client's money for Black. On 1 May, Black asks you to make £100 available to ABC Insurance Company in payment of an insurance premium. On 2 May, Brown, a client for whom you arranged insurance with ABC Insurance Company, sends you this year's premium of £200. You act for ABC Insurance Company, which allows you 10% commission on premiums collected for it.

Both Black and Brown have authorised you to retain the commission. On 4 May, you deduct your commission and send ABC the net amount due.

*Notes:*

May

1 You must do an inter-client transfer to show that £100 of the money previously held for Black is now held for the insurance company.

2 You receive £200 *for* the ABC Insurance Company. You never hold it for Brown, so you will credit the money straight to the insurance company's ledger account.

4 You must make a DR entry on the insurance company's ledger account to show that the insurance company owes your firm commission. The CR entry will be on an insurance commission received ledger account.

4 You will record the payment of the net premium to the insurance company.

4 The £30 remaining in the client bank account will be transferred to the office bank account.

**Client:** Black
**Matter:** Miscellaneous

| Date | Details | Office account | | | Client account | | |
|---|---|---|---|---|---|---|---|
| | | DR | CR | BAL | DR | CR | BAL |
| May 1 | Balance | | | | | | 300CR |
| | ABC Insurance Co Transfer of Premium | | | | 100 | | 200 |

**Cash**

| Date | Details | Office account | | | Client account | | |
|---|---|---|---|---|---|---|---|
| | | DR | CR | BAL | DR | CR | BAL |
| May | | | | | | | XXX |
| 2 | ABC Insurance Co. Net premium from Brown | | | | 200 | | |
| 2 | ABC Insurance Co. Net premium | | | | | 270 | |
| 4 | ABC Insurance Co. Transfer commission | 30 | | | | 30 | |

**Client:** ABC Insurance Company
**Matter:**

| Date | Details | Office account | | | Client account | | |
|---|---|---|---|---|---|---|---|
| | | DR | CR | BAL | DR | CR | BAL |
| May | | | | | | | |
| 1 | Black. Premium | | | | | 100 | 100CR |
| 2 | Cash. Premium | | | | | 200 | 200 |
| 4 | Insurance commission due | 30 | | 30DR | | | |
| 4 | Cash. Net premium. To ABC Co | | | | 270 | | 30 |
| 4 | Cash. Transfer commission | | 30 | – | 30 | | – |

Exercise 15A

You act for Forsyth.

March

| | |
|---|---|
| 1 | Forsyth sends £100 on account of costs. |
| 2 | You pay court fees of £40 from the client bank account. |
| 3 | The bank informs you that Forsyth's cheque has been dishonoured. |
| 15 | You re-present the cheque, instructing the bank that, assuming the cheque is honoured, you want £40 to be paid into the office bank account and £60 into the client bank account. |
| 16 | You pay counsel's fee of £200 plus £35 VAT. The invoice is addressed to your client. |
| 18 | You issue a bill for £440 plus £77 VAT. |
| 19 | The client complains, and you reduce the bill by £40 plus £7 VAT. |
| 31 | You write off Forsyth's debt as bad, having transferred any balance in the client bank account to the office bank account. |

Make the necessary entries in Forsyth's client ledger account and the cash account. The balances on the cash account were office £1,000 (DR), client £10,000 (DR).

## 15.8 Solution

Exercise 15A

*Notes:*

March

1 This was received generally on account of costs and is client money.

2 You have client money available and so can make the payment from the client bank account.

3 Drawing against an uncleared cheque is not in itself a breach of rules. However, as the cheque has been dishonoured, there has been a breach which must be remedied by transferring £40 from the office to the client bank account.

15 The re-presented cheque is split between the office and the client bank account. The portion representing reimbursement of the expense incurred for court fees is office money; the balance is client's money.

16 As the invoice is addressed to the client, the agency basis is used.

19 This is an abatement. Simply make the opposite entries you would make if delivering a bill.

31 There is £60 in the client bank account which can be transferred to the office bank account. The rest of Forsyth's indebtedness, including VAT, must be written off as a bad debt.

No VAT relief is available at present. The debt has not been outstanding for six months since the due date for payment.

**Client:** Forsyth
**Matter:**

| Date | Details | Office account | | | Client account | | |
|---|---|---|---|---|---|---|---|
| | | **DR** | **CR** | **BAL** | **DR** | **CR** | **BAL** |
| March | | | | | | | |
| 1 | Cash. On account | | | | | 100 | 100CR |
| 2 | Cash. Court fees | | | | 40 | | 60 |
| 3 | Cash. Dishonoured cheque | | | | 100 | | 40DR |
| 3 | Cash. To remedy breach | 40 | | 40DR | | 40 | – |
| 15 | Cash. Re-presented cheque | | 40 | – | | 60 | 60CR |
| 16 | Cash. Counsel | 235 | | 235 | | | |
| 18 | Costs | 440 | | 675 | | | |
| | VAT | 77 | | 752 | | | |
| 19 | Costs – abatement | | 40 | 712 | | | |
| | VAT – abatement | | 7 | 705 | | | |
| 31 | Cash. Transfer | | 60 | 645 | 60 | | – |
| 31 | Bad debts | | 645 | – | | | |

| Cash | | | | | | | |
|---|---|---|---|---|---|---|---|
| Date | Details | Office account | | | Client account | | |
| | | DR | CR | BAL | DR | CR | BAL |
| March | | | | | | | |
| 1 | Balances | | | 1,000DR | | | 10,000DR |
| 1 | Forsyth. On account | | | | 100 | | 10,100 |
| 2 | Forsyth. Court fees | | | | | 40 | 10,060 |
| 3 | Forsyth. Dishonoured cheque | | | | | 100 | 9,960 |
| 3 | Forsyth. To remedy breach | | 40 | 960 | 40 | | 10,000 |
| 15 | Forsyth. Re-presented cheque | 40 | | 1,000 | 60 | | 10,060 |
| 16 | Forsyth. Counsel | | 235 | 765 | | | |
| 31 | Forsyth. Transfer | 60 | | 825 | | 60 | 10,000 |

# Chapter 16

# Accounting to the Client for Interest



## 16.1 When must a solicitor allow interest?

Under Rule 24(1), a solicitor must account to a client for all interest earned on money held in a separate designated deposit bank account.

Under Rule 24(2), a solicitor must pay a client a sum in lieu of interest where client money is not held in a separate designated deposit bank account. The amount is calculated by reference to the amount which the relevant bank or building society would have paid if a separate designated deposit bank account had been opened.

There are some exceptional cases set out in Rule 24(3) where the solicitor need not make any payment to the client, notably:

(a) if the amount calculated is £20 or less;

(b) the amount held and the period for which it is held does not exceed the amounts and periods set out in the table in Rule 24(3).

Rule 24(7) states that Rule 24 does not apply to controlled trust money. Under the general law of trusts, trustees must account to the trust for all interest earned.

For further problems relating to trust money, see **16.3.3**.

## 16.2 Rule 24(1) – separate designated deposit bank account

### 16.2.1 What is involved?

Rule 32(3) provides that, when a solicitor uses separate designated bank accounts, the solicitor must keep a combined deposit cash account to record the total amount of client money held in separate designated accounts.

Rule 14(5) defines a separate designated deposit for this purpose as a deposit account which includes in its title a reference to the identity of the client.

The solicitor simply opens a separate deposit account at the bank designated with the name of the client and pays the client money into it. All interest allowed by the bank belongs to the client.

The disadvantage of this method is that the solicitor loses the opportunity to benefit from interest earned by client money.

### 16.2.2 Accounting entries

The solicitor will instruct the bank to open a deposit bank account - the separate designated deposit bank account - and to transfer the appropriate amount from the (current) client bank account into it. The solicitor will record the receipt into the separate designated deposit bank account by making a DR entry on the combined deposit cash account.

Entries are also needed on the client ledger accounts to show what has happened to the money.

Rule 32(3)(b) requires that, where a solicitor opens a separate designated deposit account, entries must be made in a separate client ledger account. This new ledger account can be presented as an additional 'client-deposit' section on the ordinary client ledger account. When a separate ledger account is used, the office columns are normally redundant as you already have a client ledger account showing dealings with office money. We have, therefore, shaded the office columns to indicate that they will not be used.

When the bank moves money from the current client bank account to the specially designated deposit bank account, the solicitor must make appropriate entries to record the transfer.

(1) To record a payment out of the current client bank account:

*Entries:*

CR Cash
DR Client ledger account (1) } Client section

(2) To record a receipt into the separate designated deposit bank account:

*Entries:*

CR Client ledger account (2)
DR Deposit cash account

The bank will pay interest earned into the separate designated bank account. The solicitor will record the interest as a CR on the client's new ledger account and as a DR on the deposit cash account.

Before returning money to the client, the solicitor must transfer the total sum including interest from the combined designated deposit bank account to the current client bank account so that a cheque can be drawn on the current account.

**Example**

You act for Dash Ltd, which is owed £2,200 by Bingley. You write to Bingley, and you receive a cheque for the money from him on 3 April. On 4 April, Dash Ltd tells you to hold the money for five weeks until 9 May. You put the money on deposit in a separate designated deposit bank account. On 9 May, you tell the bank to close the account. They tell you that they have allowed £18 interest. The £2,218 is transferred to the current bank account. You send Dash Ltd the £2,200 plus the interest of £18.

*Notes:*

April

3 The money is received as client money and paid into the current client bank account.

*Entries:*

CR Dash Ltd (debt collection) ledger account
DR Cash account } Client section

4 The bank will transfer the cash from your ordinary current client bank account to the separate designated deposit bank account. You will need an entry on your combined designated cash account (CDD) to record the additional funds held in separate designated bank accounts, and a new client ledger account (or additional deposit section on the old client ledger) to show that funds are held for Dash in a separate designated deposit account.

*Entries:*

CR Cash account
DR Dash Ltd (debt collection) ledger account } Client section

DR Deposit cash account
CR Dash Ltd (money held on deposit) ledger account

*Note:*

Had you known on 3 April that you would want to put the money on deposit, you could have paid the money straight into the separate designated deposit bank account without passing it through the ordinary current client bank account.

*Entries:*

DR Deposit cash account
CR Dash Ltd (money held on deposit) ledger account

May

9 Deal with the interest first. The interest has been earned on behalf of Dash Ltd and belongs to it. It is client money and the bank will pay it into the deposit bank account.

*Entries:*

DR Deposit cash account with interest
CR Dash Ltd (money held on deposit) ledger account with interest

Then pay out the total from the separate designated deposit bank account.

*Entries:*

CR Deposit cash account
DR Dash Ltd (money held on deposit) ledger account

Then receive the total into the current client bank account.

*Entries:*

DR Cash account
CR Dash Ltd (debt collection) ledger account } Client section

You can now pay Dash Ltd the total sum you are holding on its behalf.

*Entries:*

CR Cash account
DR Dash Ltd (debt collection) ledger account } Client section

The completed accounts look like this:

**Client:** Dash Ltd
**Matter:** Debt collection

| Date | Details | Office account | | | Client account | | |
|---|---|---|---|---|---|---|---|
| | | DR | CR | BAL | DR | CR | BAL |
| April | | | | | | | |
| 3 | Cash. Bingley | | | | | 2,200 | 2,200CR |
| 4 | Cash. On deposit | | | | 2,200 | | – |
| May | | | | | | | |
| 9 | Cash. Off deposit | | | | | 2,218 | 2,218 |
| | Cash. Returned | | | | 2,218 | | – |

**Client:** Dash Ltd
**Matter:** Money held on deposit

| Date | Details | Office account | | | Client account | | |
|---|---|---|---|---|---|---|---|
| | | DR | CR | BAL | DR | CR | BAL |
| April | | | | | | | |
| 4 | Deposit cash | | | | | 2,200 | 2,200CR |
| May | | | | | | | |
| 9 | Deposit cash interest | | | | | 18 | 2,218 |
| 9 | Deposit cash. A/C closed | | | | 2,218 | | – |

**Cash account**

| Date | Details | Office account | | | Client account | | |
|---|---|---|---|---|---|---|---|
| | | DR | CR | BAL | DR | CR | BAL |
| April | | | | XXX | | | XXX |
| 3 | Dash Ltd. (Debt collection) | | | | 2,200 | | |
| 4 | Dash Ltd. (Debt collection) On deposit | | | | | 2,200 | |
| May | | | | | | | |
| 9 | Dash Ltd. (Debt collection) Off deposit | | | | 2,218 | | |
| | Dash Ltd. (Debt collection) Returned to client | | | | | 2,218 | |

**Combined designated deposit cash account**

| Date | Details | Office account | | | Client account | | |
|---|---|---|---|---|---|---|---|
| | | DR | CR | BAL | DR | CR | BAL |
| April | | | | | | | |
| 4 | Dash Ltd (Money on deposit) | | | | 2,200 | | XXX |
| May | | | | | | | |
| 9 | Dash Ltd (Money on deposit) Interest | | | | 18 | | XXX |
| | Dash Ltd (Money on deposit) | | | | | 2,218 | – |

You may choose to have a separate deposit section on the existing client ledger account instead of a separate client ledger account. In this case, the Dash Ltd example would appear as follows.

**Client:** Dash Ltd
**Matter:** Debt collection

| Date | Details | Office | Client | | | Client – Deposit | | |
|---|---|---|---|---|---|---|---|---|
| | | | DR | CR | BAL | DR | CR | BAL |
| April | | | | | | | | |
| 3 | Cash. Bingley | | | 2,200 | 2,200CR | | | |
| 4 | Cash. On deposit | | 2,200 | | | | | |
| 4 | Deposit cash | | | | | | 2,200 | 2,200CR |
| May | | | | | | | | |
| 9 | Deposit cash. Interest | | | | | | 18 | 2,218CR |
| 9 | Deposit cash. A/c closed | | | | | 2,218 | | – |
| 9 | Cash. Off deposit | | | 2,218 | 2,218CR | | | |
| 9 | Cash. Returned | | 2,218 | | – | | | |

**Cash account**

| Date | Details | Office | Client | | |
|---|---|---|---|---|---|
| | | | DR | CR | BAL |
| April | Balance | | | | XXX |
| 3 | Dash Ltd. Debt collected | | 2,200 | | |
| 4 | Dash Ltd. On deposit | | | 2,200 | |
| May | | | | | |
| 9 | Dash Ltd. Off deposit | | 2,218 | | |
| 9 | Dash Ltd. Returned | | | 2,218 | |

**Combined designated deposit cash account**

| Date | Details | Office | Client | | |
|---|---|---|---|---|---|
| | | | DR | CR | BAL |
| April | Balance | | | | XXX |
| 4 | Dash Ltd. On deposit | | 2,200 | | XXX |
| May | | | | | |
| 9 | Dash Ltd. Interest | | 18 | | XXX |
| 9 | Dash Ltd. Off deposit | | | 2,218 | – |

## 16.3 Rule 24(2) – payment in lieu of interest

### 16.3.1 What is involved?

The solicitor must bear in mind the table set out in Rule 24 which shows when the obligation to account arises.

Assume that as a solicitor you hold £1,600 of client money for nine weeks on behalf of your client, Smith. Rule 24 applies and you must account to Smith, out of office money, for an amount equal to the interest that would have been earned if the money had been put on deposit.

The disadvantage of this method is that the solicitor has to calculate how much would have been earned in respect of each individual client to whom the rules apply. Also, at first sight, it appears that the solicitor will be out of pocket. However, consider the following.

As a solicitor you are likely to hold a large sum of client money made up of relatively small amounts from each individual client. The Solicitors Act 1974 allows solicitors to put client money on deposit to earn interest for themselves. You will probably be able to earn a relatively high rate of interest. You must still comply with your obligation to the clients, but not every client will be entitled to interest and, for those who are, interest is paid at a rate applicable to that which would have been earned had the money been deposited separately; this is likely to be a relatively low rate.

### 16.3.2 Accounting entries

Using this method, the payment is an expense of the business and will be recorded on an interest payable account. It is equivalent to the firm paying any other business expense, such as electricity or wages.

To comply with Rule 32(4), the office money dealing must be recorded in the office section of the client ledger account. If the money is transferred from the office bank account to the client bank account and held for the client, entries must be made on the client ledger and cash account.

**Example**

To enable you to make a direct comparison, we will use the same basic facts as in the previous example, except that the money is not put into a separate designated deposit bank account.

*Notes:*

April

3 You receive the £2,200 on behalf of Dash Ltd and pay it into the current client bank account. Entries as before:

*Entries:*

| | |
|---|---|
| CR Dash Ltd ledger account<br>DR Cash account | } Client section |

May

9 You have to allow Dash Ltd £18 interest and, therefore, have to account to Dash Ltd for £2,218. You can do this in either of two ways.

**Method 1** Send two cheques: one drawn on the office bank account for the £18 in lieu of interest, and the other drawn on the client bank account for the £2,200.

Entries must be made on the client ledger office section to record the dealing with office money.

*Entries:*

To record £18 owed to client in lieu of interest

| | |
|---|---|
| DR Interest payable ledger account<br>CR Dash Ltd ledger account | } Office section |

To record £18 office cash sent to client

| | |
|---|---|
| DR Dash Ltd ledger account<br>CR Cash account | } Office section |

To record £2,200 client cash sent to client

| | |
|---|---|
| DR Dash Ltd ledger account<br>CR Cash account | } Client section |

The accounts will look like this:

| **Client:** Dash Ltd<br>**Matter:** Debt collection | | | | | | | |
|---|---|---|---|---|---|---|---|
| **Date** | **Details** | **Office account** | | | **Client account** | | |
| | | **DR** | **CR** | **BAL** | **DR** | **CR** | **BAL** |
| April | | | | | | | |
| 3 | Cash. Bingley | | | | | 2,200 | 2,200CR |
| May | | | | | | | |
| 9 | Interest payable | | 18 | 18CR | | | |
| 9 | Cash in lieu of interest | 18 | | – | | | |
| 9 | Cash. Returned | | | | 2,200 | | – |

| **Cash account** | | | | | | | |
|---|---|---|---|---|---|---|---|
| **Date** | **Details** | **Office account** | | | **Client account** | | |
| | | | **CR** | **BAL** | **DR** | **CR** | **BAL** |
| April | | | | | | | |
| 3 | Dash Ltd. Bingley | | | | 2,200 | | |
| May | | | | | | | |
| 9 | Dash Ltd. In lieu of interest | | 18 | | | | |
| 9 | Dash Ltd. Returned | | | | | 2,200 | |

| **Interest payable account** | | | | |
|---|---|---|---|---|
| **Date** | **Details** | **Office account** | | |
| | | **DR** | **CR** | **BAL** |
| May | | | | |
| 9 | Dash Ltd. | 18 | | 18DR |

**Method 2** Transfer the £18 from the office bank account to the client bank account, and then send Dash Ltd one cheque drawn on the client bank account for £2,218. In this case, additional entries must be made on the client section of the client ledger and on the client section of the cash account to show that money has been held for the client in the client bank account.

*Entries:*

To record £18 owed to client in lieu of interest

DR Interest payable ledger account
CR Dash Ltd ledger account } Office section

To record £18 office cash paid out of office bank account

DR Dash Ltd
CR Cash } Office section

To record £18 received into client bank account

CR Dash Ltd ledger account
DR Cash account } Client section

Payment to Dash Ltd of £2,218 from client bank account

DR Dash Ltd ledger account
CR Cash account } Client section

The accounts will look like this:

**Client:** Dash Ltd
**Matter:** Debt collection

| Date | Details | Office account | | | Client account | | |
|---|---|---|---|---|---|---|---|
| | | DR | CR | BAL | DR | CR | BAL |
| April | | | | | | | |
| 3 | Cash | | | | | 2,200 | 2,200CR |
| May | | | | | | | |
| 9 | Interest payable | | 18 | 18CR | | | |
| 9 | Cash. In lieu of interest | 18 | | – | | | |
| 9 | Cash. In lieu of interest | | | | | 18 | 2,218 |
| 9 | Cash. Returned | | | | 2,218 | | – |

**Cash account**

| Date | Details | Office account | | | Client account | | |
|---|---|---|---|---|---|---|---|
| | | DR | CR | BAL | DR | CR | BAL |
| April | | | | xxx | | | xxx |
| 3 | Dash Ltd. Bingley | | | | 2,200 | | |
| May | | | | | | | |
| 9 | Dash Ltd. In lieu of interest | | 18 | xxx | | | |
| | Dash Ltd. In lieu of interest | | | | 18 | | xxx |
| 9 | Dash Ltd. Returned | | | | | 2,218 | xxx |

**Interest payable account**

| Date | Details | Office account | | |
|---|---|---|---|---|
| | | DR | CR | BAL |
| May | | | | |
| 9 | Dash Ltd. | 18 | | 18DR |

Looking at this example, you may observe that, by using this method of paying interest, the solicitor is out of pocket by £18 as compared with using a separate designated deposit bank account. You are perfectly correct *if* the solicitor does nothing more. However, as we said earlier, a well-organised firm will always put a proportion of its client money on deposit in a general deposit bank account. It will then be entitled to keep the interest earned on that general deposit bank account. Provided the firm will organises its bank accounts sensibly, it should earn more interest on its general deposit bank account than it has to pay to individual clients. A firm can never put all of its client money on deposit since it must ensure that it has sufficient client money readily available to meet all day-to-day expenses for clients.

If a firm puts client money into a general deposit bank account, the entries will be:

CR Cash account
DR General client deposit cash account } Client section

Any interest earned will belong to the firm and will be office money. The bank must be instructed to pay all interest into the office cash account.

*Entries:*

DR Cash account – office section
CR Interest received account

### 16.3.3 Trust money

Trustees must be careful not to profit from their trust directly or indirectly. If a solicitor puts controlled trust money into a separate designated account, there is no problem. If it is a deposit account, the solicitor accounts to the trust for all interest allowed by the bank. If it is not a deposit account, the solicitor calculates how much interest the bank would have allowed and pays the trust that amount in lieu of interest.

If the solicitor puts controlled trust money into the general client bank account, there are problems for the solicitor.

Any interest earned on the general client bank account is office money. To avoid profiting from the trust, the solicitor must allocate the appropriate amount of interest to the controlled trust without delay.

In addition, the solicitor must avoid obtaining an indirect benefit from the controlled trust money. For example, the bank may pay a higher rate of interest because the general client bank account has a higher balance than it would without the controlled trust money.

Where a solicitor does not wish to put all controlled trust money into a separate designated bank account, it may be desirable to have a general client bank account reserved for only money of controlled trusts. All interest earned can be allocated amongst the trusts and the solicitor will not derive any benefit.

Exercise 16A

You act for the executor of Swan, deceased, and for Cygnet, the residuary beneficiary of Swan's estate. You complete the administration and ask Cygnet for instructions on what to do with the money due to him. Cygnet tells you to hold the money pending his instructions as he is hoping to buy a house in the near future.

March

20 You transfer Cygnet's residuary entitlement of £200,000 from the executor's ledger account to Cygnet's ledger account.

April

15 You realise that Cygnet will be entitled to interest on the money held for him. You calculate that he is entitled to £100 for the period from 20 March. You pay the sum from the office bank account into the client bank account.

16 You tell the bank to open a separate deposit bank account designated with Cygnet's name and to pay all the money held for Cygnet into that deposit bank account.

30 Cygnet tells you to send him the amount to which he is entitled. The bank credits £120 interest. You close the deposit bank account, transfer the money to the current client bank account and send Cygnet a cheque for the whole amount.

May

6 Cygnet tells you he thinks he is entitled to more interest for the period 20 March–15 April.

You agree and send him an office bank account cheque for £30.

Show relevant cash accounts and client ledger entries for Cygnet.

## 16.4 Solution

Exercise 16A

*Notes:*

March

20 This is an inter-client transfer from the ledger account of the executor to the ledger account of Cygnet. No entries will be made on the cash account as the money remains in the client bank account. A note would be made in the transfer journal.

April

15 To record the payment of interest from the office bank account:

DR Interest payable
CR Cygnet (conveyancing) – Office section

CR Cash
DR Cygnet (conveyancing) } Office section

Since the interest is going to be held by the solicitor for Cygnet, it must be received into the client bank account:

DR Cash
CR Cygnet (conveyancing) } Client section

16 To record the transfer of the money into a separate designated deposit bank account:

CR Cash
DR Cygnet (conveyancing) } Client section

DR Deposit cash
CR Cygnet (money held on deposit)

30 To record the bank's payment of £120 interest:

DR Deposit cash
CR Cygnet (money held on deposit)

To record the transfer of £200,220 back to the current client bank account:

CR Deposit cash
DR Cygnet (money held on deposit)

DR Cash
CR Cygnet (conveyancing) } Client section

To record the payment of £200,220 to Cygnet:

CR Cash
DR Cygnet (conveyancing) } Client section

May

6 To record the payment of £30 office money in lieu of interest:

DR Interest payable
CR Cygnet (conveyancing) – Office section

CR Cash
DR Cygnet (conveyancing) } Office section

As the £30 is paid out to Cygnet directly and is not held by the solicitor in the client bank account, no entries need be made on the client section of Cygnet's ledger account or on the client section of the cash account.

**Client:** Cygnet
**Matter:** Conveyancing

| Date | Details | Office account | | | Client account | | |
|---|---|---|---|---|---|---|---|
| | | DR | CR | BAL | DR | CR | BAL |
| March | | | | | | | |
| 20 | Executor of Swan Residuary entitlement (TJ) | | | | | 200,000 | 200,000CR |
| April | | | | | | | |
| 15 | Interest payable | | 100 | 100CR | | | |
| 15 | Cash. In lieu of interest | 100 | | – | | | |
| 15 | Cash. In lieu of interest | | | | | 100 | 200,100 |
| 16 | Cash. On deposit | | | | 200,100 | | – |
| 30 | Cash. Off deposit | | | | | 200,220 | 200,220 |
| 30 | Cash. Returned | | | | 200,220 | | – |
| May | | | | | | | |
| 6 | Interest payable | | 30 | 30CR | | | |
| 6 | Cash. In lieu of interest | 30 | | – | | | |

**Client:** Cygnet
**Matter:** Money held on deposit

| Date | Details | Office account | | | Client account | | |
|---|---|---|---|---|---|---|---|
| | | DR | CR | BAL | DR | CR | BAL |
| April | | | | | | | |
| 16 | Deposit cash | | | | | 200,100 | 200,100CR |
| 30 | Deposit cash. Interest | | | | | 120 | 200,220 |
| 30 | Deposit cash | | | | 200,220 | | – |

**Cash**

| Date | Details | Office account | | | Client account | | |
|---|---|---|---|---|---|---|---|
| | | DR | CR | BAL | DR | CR | BAL |
| April | Balance | | | xxx | | | xxx |
| 15 | Cygnet. In lieu of interest | | 100 | | | | |
| 15 | Cygnet | | | | 100 | | |
| 16 | Cygnet deposit. On deposit | | | | | 200,100 | |
| 30 | Cygnet deposit. Off deposit | | | | 200,220 | | |
| 30 | Cygnet. Conveyancing. Returned | | | | | 200,220 | |
| May | | | | | | | |
| 6 | Cygnet. In lieu of interest | | 30 | | | | |

**Deposit Cash**

| Date | Details | Office account | | | Client account | | |
|---|---|---|---|---|---|---|---|
| | | DR | CR | BAL | DR | CR | BAL |
| April | | | | | | | |
| 16 | Cygnet deposit | | | | 200,100 | | 200,100DR |
| 30 | Cygnet deposit. Interest | | | | 120 | | 200,220 |
| 30 | Cygnet deposit | | | | | 200,220 | — |

| Interest payable | | | | |
|---|---|---|---|---|
| **Date** | **Details** | **Office account** | | |
| | | **DR** | **CR** | **BAL** |
| Apr 15 | Cygnet | 100 | | 100DR |
| May 6 | Cygnet | 30 | | 130 |

# Chapter 17
# Financial Statements



## 17.1 Purpose

A solicitor who has handled money for a client should always prepare a written statement explaining how the client's money held has been dealt with.

The statement is particularly important in property transactions where it is likely to be sent to the client part-way through the transaction to inform the client how much he will have to provide or how much will be available to the client at the end of the transaction.

The *Law Society Gazette* recently included an item on solicitors' negligence which referred to the unacceptable numbers of errors made by solicitors in such statements.

## 17.2 Layout

There is no set layout but the statement must be clear and easy for the client to follow. It can be presented in two columns.

Example

**FINANCIAL STATEMENT [date]**
**TO: MR AND MRS BOUNDS**
**PURCHASE OF 3 WICKET STREET**

| | **Receipts** | | **Payments** |
|---|---|---|---|
| | £ | | £ |
| From you. On account of costs | 400 | Search | 20 |
| Mortgage advance net of legal fees | 222,340 | Stamp duty land tax | 9,000 |
| From you. For deposit | 30,000 | Land Registry fees | 100 |
| | | Deposit | 30,000 |
| | | Balance purchase price | 270,000 |
| | | Our professional charges | 400 |
| | | VAT | 70 |
| Balance required from you to complete transaction | 56,850 | | |
| | 309,590 | | 309,590 |

Another common layout is to show the statement in the form of a sum, starting with the purchase price, adding expenses and deducting receipts (or in the case of a sale, starting with the sale price, deducting expenses and adding receipts).

*Note:* Items to be deducted are frequently shown in brackets.

Example

**FINANCIAL STATEMENT [date]**
**TO: MR AND MRS BOUNDS**
**PURCHASE OF 3 WICKET STREET**

| | | £ | £ |
|---|---|---|---|
| Purchase price | | | 300,000 |
| *less:* | Prepaid deposit | (30,000) | |
| | Mortgage advance net of legal fees | (222,340) | |
| | | | (252,340) |
| | | | 47,660 |
| *add:* | Search | 20 | |
| | Stamp duty land tax | 9,000 | |
| | Land Registry fees | 100 | |
| | Professional charges | 400 | |
| | VAT | 70 | |
| | | | 9,590 |
| *less:* | Received on account of costs | | (400) |
| **DUE FROM YOU** | | | 56,850 |

Where a simultaneous sale and purchase is involved, it is good practice to show separate subtotals for the sale and for the purchase so that the client can see how much the purchase cost and how much is available from the sale. The statement will then show in a summary the total amount due to or from the client in respect of both transactions.

Exercise 17A

You act for Clara, who is selling 6 High Street for £65,000 to Priscilla and buying 'The Cedars' for £80,000 from Viola.

The Bayswater and District Building Society, for whom you act, is granting a mortgage on 'The Cedars' of £45,000, and there is a mortgage to redeem on 6 High Street of £40,000.

June

1 Clara gives you £200 on account of costs.

3 You pay search fees of £10 by cheque on 'The Cedars'.

5 You receive a cheque from Clara for £8,000 (the deposit on 'The Cedars') made out to Viola's solicitors.

7 You send the cheque for £8,000 to Viola's solicitors to hold as stakeholders. You receive a cheque for £6,000 from Priscilla's solicitors which you are to hold as stakeholders.

16 You deliver a financial statement to Clara which shows the total required from her to complete both transactions. You also present your bill which includes £200 costs on sale and £300 costs on purchase plus VAT. Your charges to the building society, which Clara is to pay by way of indemnity, are £40 on the mortgage advance and £20 on the mortgage redemption, plus VAT in each case.

18 You receive from Clara the amount requested on 16 June and you receive the mortgage advance from the building society.

20 You complete the sale and purchase.

21 You pay land registry fees of £100 and stamp duty land tax £650 on 'The Cedars' and transfer the amount due to you for costs, etc.

Prepare the financial statement sent to Clara on 16 June.

## 17.3 Solution

Exercise 17A

**FINANCIAL STATEMENT 16 JUNE**
**TO: CLARA**
**PURCHASE OF 'THE CEDARS'**

| | | £ | £ |
|---|---|---|---|
| Purchase price | | | 80,000.00 |
| *less* | Prepaid deposit | (8,000.00) | |
| | Mortgage advance | (45,000.00) | |
| | | | (53,000.00) |
| | | | 27,000.00 |
| *add* | Our professional charges | 300.00 | |
| | VAT | 52.50 | |
| | Professional charges to building society and VAT | 47.00 | |
| | Land Registry fees | 100.00[1] | |
| | Stamp duty land tax | 800.00[1] | |
| | Search fees | 10.00 | |
| | | | 1,309.50 |
| **Required for purchase** | | | 28,309.50 |

**SALE OF 6 HIGH STREET**

| | | £ | £ |
|---|---|---|---|
| Sale price | | | 65,000.00 |
| *less* | Mortgage redemption | (40,000.00) | |
| | Our professional charges | (200.00) | |
| | VAT | (35.00) | |
| | Professional charges to building society costs and VAT | (23.50) | |
| | | | (40,258.50) |
| **Available on sale** | | | 24,741.50 |
| **SUMMARY** | | | |
| | Required for purchase | | 28,309.50 |
| *less* | Available on sale | | (24,741.50) |
| | | | 3,568.00 |
| *less* | Received on account | | (200.00) |
| **DUE FROM YOU** | | | 3,368.00 |

[1] Although you have not paid these on 16 June, you know that they will be required and will, therefore, include them on the financial statement.

# Chapter 18
# Accounting Problems for Solicitors



## 18.1 How many ledger accounts?

### 18.1.1 The problem

A solicitor must show the amount of client money held for each client. This requires a separate ledger account for each client for whom money is held. (There is one exception contained in Rule 32(6) – see **18.1.6.**) A solicitor must consider carefully which client the firm is holding money for and whether money ceases to be held for one client and becomes held for someone else.

### 18.1.2 Funds originally held for one client being held for another

This can happen in a number of different types of transaction.

Example

You act for the executors of a deceased person. You complete the administration of the estate and inform the residuary beneficiary of the amount of his entitlement. The residuary beneficiary asks you to hold the money for him pending completion of a transaction on his behalf.

The money will stay in your client bank account, so no entries are made on your cash account. However, you must mark the fact that the money is no longer held for the executors, but is now held for the residuary beneficiary. You do this by an inter-client transfer.

*Entries:*

DR executors' ledger
CR residuary beneficiary's ledger } Client section

You must make a note in a Transfer Journal.

Exercise 18A

You act for George and for George & Co Ltd. George is a director of George & Co. George is selling land to George & Co for £120,000. The sale is to be completed on 5 June.

On 1 June, George tells you that he will be investing in a venture capital trust and asks you to hold the proceeds of sale of the land until he gives you further instructions.

On 4 June, the company gives you the funds to complete the purchase. On 5 June, you complete the sale. On 7 June, George tells you to pay the sale proceeds to the Gallymead Venture Capital Trust.

How will you deal with the sale proceeds of the land?

### 18.1.3 One party paying the legal costs of another

Sometimes, one party to a transaction will agree to pay the legal costs of another. The solicitor must consider which client received the legal services and which client the bill (and VAT invoice if the client is entitled to receive one) should be addressed to.

The bill (and VAT invoice if required) will be addressed to the client for whom the services were provided, A, even if another person, B, is paying.

#### 18.1.3.1 VAT

If A is a registered fully taxable person, and the supply of legal services is obtained for the purpose of the client's business, A will be entitled to an input tax credit. In that case, B need pay only the amount required for the costs exclusive of VAT.

If A is not a registered taxable person and cannot obtain an input tax credit, B is liable to pay the costs and VAT as well. However, B cannot recover the VAT. This point was decided by the High Court in *Turner (t/a Turner Agricultural) v Customs and Excise Commissioners* [1992] STC 621.

In no circumstances may a VAT invoice be issued by the solicitor or the solicitor's client to B. B is not entitled to receive an input tax credit as the services have not been rendered to him. B should therefore receive a note of the other party's costs in such terms that the note cannot be mistaken for a VAT invoice issued to the paying party (eg, a photocopy of the invoice, stamped 'copy').

#### 18.1.3.2 Entries

Costs and VAT are debited to the ledger account of A.

When cash is received, whether from client A or from the other party, the solicitor will make the following entries.

*Entries:*

| | |
|---|---|
| DR Cash<br>CR Client A's ledger account | } Office section |

Alternatively, if the solicitor is acting for both parties, the amount of costs and VAT of the first party can be transferred as a debt to the ledger account of the second party.

*Entries:*

| | |
|---|---|
| CR A's ledger account<br>DR B's ledger account | } Office section |

Then when the cash is received, it is credited to the ledger account of the second party in the normal way.

*Entries:*

| | |
|---|---|
| CR B's ledger account<br>DR Cash | } Office section |

**Example**

A solicitor acts for Schiller. On 20 January, he delivers a bill showing profit costs as £200 plus £35 VAT. Goethe has agreed to pay them. The solicitor does not act for Goethe. On 30 January, Goethe pays.

**Client:** Schiller
**Matter:**

| Date | Details | Office account | | | Client account | | |
|---|---|---|---|---|---|---|---|
| | | DR | CR | BAL | DR | CR | BAL |
| Jan | | | | | | | |
| 20 | Costs | 200 | | 200DR | | | |
| | C&E: VAT | 35 | | 235 | | | |
| 30 | Cash. From Goethe | | 235 | – | | | |

**Cash**

| Date | Details | Office account | | | Client account | | |
|---|---|---|---|---|---|---|---|
| | | DR | CR | BAL | DR | CR | BAL |
| Jan | | | | | | | |
| 30 | Schiller. From Goethe in payment of costs | 235 | | XXX | | | XXX |

See **18.1.6.5** for an example showing the alternative of transferring the debt.

### 18.1.4 Stakeholder money

A solicitor may receive a deposit to hold as stakeholder. This is clearly a receipt of client money and so must be held in the client bank account. Who is it held for?

The solicitor is holding it jointly for the buyer and the seller. It will not become the property of the seller unless and until completion takes place. Therefore, the solicitor cannot record the money as held for the seller.

The solicitor must have a separate stakeholder ledger account to which the money is credited when it is received.

*Entries:*

DR Cash
CR Stakeholder
} Client section

As soon as the completion takes place, the solicitor starts to hold the money for the seller alone. The solicitor must record this by making an inter-client transfer from the stakeholder ledger account to the seller's ledger account.

*Entries:*
On the day of completion:

DR Stakeholder ledger
CR Seller's ledger
} Client section

*Note:* Had the money been received as agent for the seller, it would have been held for the seller from the moment of receipt. It would, therefore, have been credited to the seller's ledger account.

*Entries:*

DR Cash
CR Seller's ledger } Client section

### 18.1.5 Bridging finance

A deposit received as stakeholder is not available to the seller until completion. A seller who is also purchasing a property may have insufficient cash available to pay the deposit on the purchase. It is fairly common to take a bridging loan from a bank to cover the period from exchange of contracts on the purchase to completion of the sale, when cash will become available.

A bridging loan is a personal loan to the borrower and, once received, belongs to the borrower and not the bank. Hence, when the solicitor receives the cash (whether direct from the bank or via the borrower), it will be held to the order of the borrower and must be credited to the borrower's ledger account, not to a ledger account in the name of the lending bank.

On completion of the sale, the loan, together with interest, must be repaid to the bank.

### 18.1.6 Mortgages

#### 18.1.6.1 Introduction

Many clients who buy property need to borrow money on mortgage. A client who sells property which is subject to a mortgage will have to redeem, ie, repay, that mortgage after completion.

A solicitor who acts for a conveyancing client can also act for the lender, provided that there is no conflict of interest and that the solicitor complies with Rules 3.07–3.15 of The Law Society's Code of Conduct. The Rules prohibit the solicitor from acting for lender and borrower in a private mortgage at arm's length, except in very limited circumstances.

Where a solicitor is instructed to act for both the borrower and the lender, the solicitor must bear in mind that there are two separate clients. The solicitor must consider carefully for which client the solicitor is holding client money.

#### 18.1.6.2 Mortgage advances – solicitor acting for buyer and lender

When solicitors receive a mortgage advance, they hold it for the lender until the day of completion, when it becomes available to the borrower. A solicitor's ledger accounts must clearly distinguish money held for one client from money held for every other client. This normally requires a separate ledger account for each client, so that there would have to be a separate ledger account for the lender. However, Rule 32(6) provides a limited exception to the rule that money held for each separate client must be shown on a separate ledger account.

The exception in Rule 32(6) applies only to institutional lenders which provide mortgages on standard terms in the normal course of their activities. Banks and building societies are examples of such lenders.

Where a mortgage advance is provided by an *institutional lender* which provides mortgages in the normal course of business, the solicitor need not have a separate ledger account for the lender. Instead, the advance can be credited to the ledger account of the borrower. However, it is important that the funds belonging to each client are 'clearly identifiable'. This is done by including the name of the lender in the details column of the borrower's ledger account and describing the funds as 'mortgage advance'.

**Example**

The Southern Cross Building Society advances £50,000 to Brown on 6 June for his house purchase.

**Client:** Brown
**Matter:** House Purchase

| Date | Details | Office account | | | Client account | | |
|---|---|---|---|---|---|---|---|
| | | DR | CR | BAL | DR | CR | BAL |
| June 6 | Cash. Mortgage advance held for Southern Cross Building Society | | | | | 50,000 | 50,000DR |

It is important to remember that Rule 32(6) applies only to loans from institutional lenders. A loan from a private lender must be dealt with in the ordinary way. A separate client ledger account is required in the name of the lender.

### 18.1.6.3 Costs on mortgage advance

The solicitor is entitled to charge the lender for work done in connection with the mortgage advance as well as to charge the buyer for the work done in connection with the purchase. The buyer will frequently have agreed with the lender to pay the costs charged to the lender. As we have already seen, the normal rule is that costs and VAT *must* be debited to the ledger account of person A to whom the legal services were supplied. If another person, B, is discharging the debt by way of indemnity, the debt can be transferred from A's ledger account to B's ledger account.

In the case of a mortgage advance from an institutional lender, the normal rule has to be varied because the solicitor will probably not have a ledger account for the lender. Thus, the mortgage costs will have to be debited from the beginning to the ledger account of the buyer/borrower. The conveyancing costs and the mortgage costs with appropriate VAT will be shown separately in the ledger account kept for the buyer/borrower.

*Entries:*

DR Buyer's ledger account, office section, with purchase costs and VAT
CR Costs account and HM Revenue & Customs account, with costs and VAT

DR Buyer's ledger account, office section, with mortgage costs and VAT
CR Costs account and HM Revenue & Customs account, with mortgage costs and VAT

### 18.1.6.4 Mortgage redemption – solicitor acting for both lender and seller

Rule 32(6) applies only to mortgage advances, not to mortgage redemptions. This means that, on a redemption, the solicitor will need one ledger account to show dealings with the seller's money and a separate ledger account to show dealings with the lender's money.

When the solicitor receives the balance of the price from the buyer, it is client money and must be paid into the client bank account. The whole receipt is initially credited to the seller's ledger account to give a full picture of amounts handled for the seller.

*Entries:*

| | |
|---|---|
| CR Seller's ledger account<br>DR Cash account | Client section |

However, part of the receipt is required to redeem the mortgage. That money belongs to the lender, and it must be shown as such in the lender's ledger account. It must be immediately transferred from the seller's ledger account to the lender's ledger account.

*Entries:*

| | |
|---|---|
| DR Seller's ledger account<br>CR Lender's ledger account | Client section |

The solicitor will then send the lender a cheque for the mortgage redemption money out of the client bank account.

*Entries:*

| | |
|---|---|
| DR Lender's ledger account<br>CR Cash account | Client section |

*Note 1:* It is permissible to argue that the solicitor receives part of the proceeds for the seller and part for the lender, so that it is correct to split the credit entries at the time of receipt. If this is done, the solicitor will credit part of the proceeds to the seller's ledger account and part to the lender's ledger account. The whole amount is debited to the cash account client section.

*Note 2:* Frequently, the money due for the mortgage redemption will be paid direct to the lender's solicitor. In such a case, as the seller's solicitor does not handle that money, there will be no entries relating to the money in the solicitor's accounts.

#### 18.1.6.5 Costs on mortgage redemption

The seller may have agreed to pay the profit costs of the lender. The solicitor will address a bill to the lender. As there is a separate ledger account for the lender, the mortgage redemption costs must initially be debited to the lender's ledger account. The debt will then be transferred to the seller's ledger account to show that the seller will discharge it, not the lender.

*Entries:*

DR Seller's ledger account, office section, with sale costs and VAT
CR Costs account and HM Revenue & Customs account with sale costs and VAT

DR Lender's ledger account, office section, with mortgage costs and VAT
CR Costs account and HM Revenue & Customs account with mortgage costs and VAT

Transfer debt from Lender's ledger account to Seller's ledger account as follows:

CR Lender's ledger account with mortgage costs and VAT
DR Seller's ledger account with mortgage costs and VAT

### 18.1.6.6 Private lenders

Rule 32(6) states that the solicitor must open a separate ledger account for each client.

(a) *Costs.* The mortgage costs will be charged to the lender; the purchase/sale costs will be charged to the buyer/seller. The buyer/seller is likely to be responsible for the lender's costs, which may be transferred as a debt from the lender's ledger account to the buyer/seller's.

(b) *Receipt of mortgage advance for purchase.* The solicitor receives this on behalf of the lender. It is shown in the lender's ledger account. It is transferred to the buyer's ledger account immediately before completion of the purchase to show that it is now available to the buyer.

(c) *Redemption of mortgage on sale.* The solicitor receives the proceeds of sale on behalf of the seller and then deals with the redemption in the same way as for the institutional lender.

Below are examples of transactions involving two clients.

Example 1

*Purchase – with mortgage advance*

Your firm is instructed by Eliot, who is purchasing 'The Willows' for £127,000 with the aid of an £85,000 mortgage from Gravesend Building Society for whom you also act. The following events occur:

August

4 Eliot tells you that he has paid £500 preliminary deposit to the estate agents, Coomb & Co.

5 You pay local search fee of £25.

12 You receive £12,200 from Eliot being the balance of the 10% deposit required.

15 You receive and pay surveyor's invoice in Eliot's name of £161 including VAT.

20 You exchange contracts and pay the balance of the deposit.

27 You send financial statement and bill of costs to Eliot. (Costs on purchase amount to £400 plus VAT and on mortgage to £80 plus VAT.)

September

2 You pay bankruptcy search fee of £10.

4 You receive mortgage advance from Gravesend Building Society.

5 You receive sum due for completion from Eliot.

7 You complete purchase of 'The Willows'.

8 You pay Land Registry fees of £200 and stamp duty land tax of £1,270. Transfer all sums due to the firm to close the account.

**Show the entries necessary to record the above transaction in the client ledger and cash account, together with the financial statement sent on 27 August.**

*Notes:*

August

4 You do not need to make any entries – but remember that, when contracts are exchanged and the 10% deposit is payable, £500 of the deposit has already been paid.

5 There is no money held in the client bank account for Eliot. The payment cannot be made from the client bank account. The money is paid from the office bank account.

*Entries:*

DR Eliot ledger account
CR Cash account
} Office section

12 The money is client money and is paid into the client bank account.

*Entries:*

CR Eliot ledger account
DR Cash account
} Client section

Remember that £500 has already been received. This money makes up the balance of £12,700.

You cannot reimburse yourself for the search fee out of this money. You have received it for a particular purpose, and you can use it only for that purpose.

15 The invoice is addressed to Eliot, and so you must pay it using the agency method. The money in the client bank account is specifically for payment of the deposit. It cannot therefore be used for payment of this bill. The bill must be paid out of office money as you have no client money available.

*Entries:*

DR Eliot ledger account
CR Cash account
} Office section

20 The payment can be made out of the client bank account as you have client money available.

*Entries:*

DR Eliot ledger account
CR Cash account
} Client section

27 Sending the financial statement does not require any entries in the accounts. The statement simply shows the client how much is required. A suitable financial statement is shown at the end of this example.

**Costs and VAT:** A bill is sent so the usual entries are made for profit costs and VAT. Remember to charge the costs on the mortgage advance as well as those on the purchase to Eliot. They should, however, be shown on separate lines.

*Entries:*

Profit costs DR Eliot ledger account
CR Profit costs account
} Office section

VAT DR Eliot ledger account
CR HM Revenue & Customs ledger account
} Office section

(Costs and Revenue & Customs accounts are not shown.)

September

2 There is no money in the client bank account. The money is paid out of the office bank account.

*Entries:*

DR Eliot ledger account
CR Cash
} Office section

4 The money is client money. It is paid into client bank account. You are receiving the money on behalf of your client, Gravesend Building Society. However, Rule 32(6) allows you to credit the money to Eliot's ledger account provided it is labelled as held for the Gravesend Building Society and described as a mortgage advance.

*Entries:*

CR Eliot ledger account
DR Cash account
} Client section

5 This is the amount shown in the Financial Statement. The money is a mixture of office and client money. We have not split the cheque but have paid it all into the client bank account (Rule 20).

*Entries:*

CR Eliot ledger account
DR Cash account
} Client section

7 On completion, the balance of the purchase price owing is paid out of the client bank account.

*Entries:*

DR Eliot ledger account
CR Cash account
} Client section

8 The financial statement took into account the amount which would be payable for Land Registry fees and stamp duty land tax. There is therefore enough money in the client bank account to cover them so the payment can be made from the client bank account.

*Entries:*

DR Eliot ledger account
CR Cash account
} Client section

The transfer from the client to office bank account is recorded in the usual way.

*Entries:*
Withdrawal from client bank account

DR Eliot ledger account
CR Cash account
} Client section

Receipt into office bank account

CR Eliot ledger account
DR Cash account
} Office section

The *completed* accounts look like this:

**Client:** Mr Eliot
**Matter:** Purchase of 'The Willows'

| Date | Details | Office account | | | Client account | | |
|---|---|---|---|---|---|---|---|
| | | DR | CR | BAL | DR | CR | BAL |
| Aug | | | | | | | |
| 5 | Cash. Local search fee | 25 | | 25DR | | | |
| 12 | Cash. From Eliot. Balance of deposit | | | | | 12,200 | 12,200CR |
| 15 | Cash. Surveyor's fee | 161 | | 186 | | | |
| 20 | Cash. Vendor's solicitor. Balance of deposit | | | | 12,200 | | – |
| 27 | Costs on purchase | 400 | | 586 | | | |
| | VAT | 70 | | 656 | | | |
| | Costs on mortgage | 80 | | 736 | | | |
| | VAT | 14 | | 750 | | | |
| Sep | | | | | | | |
| 2 | Cash. Bankruptcy search fee | 10 | | 760 | | | |
| 4 | Cash. From Gravesend Building Society. For mortgage advance | | | | | 85,000 | 85,000 |
| 5 | Cash. From Eliot | | | | | 31,350 | 116,530 |
| 7 | Cash. Vendor's solicitor. Completion | | | | 114,300 | | 2,230 |
| 8 | Cash. Land Registry fee | | | | 200 | | 2,030 |
| | Cash. Stamp duty land tax | | | | 1,270 | | 760 |
| | Cash. Transfer costs and disbursements | | 760 | – | 760 | | – |

**Cash account**

| Date | Details | Office account | | | Client account | | |
|---|---|---|---|---|---|---|---|
| | | DR | CR | BAL | DR | CR | BAL |
| | **Balances** | | | xxx | | | xxx |
| Aug | | | | | | | |
| 5 | Eliot. Local search fee | | 25 | | | | |
| 12 | Eliot. Balance of deposit | | | | 12,200 | | |
| 15 | Eliot. Surveyor | | 161 | | | | |
| 20 | Eliot. Payment of deposit | | | | | 12,200 | |
| Sep | | | | | | | |
| 2 | Eliot. Bankruptcy search | | 10 | | | | |
| 4 | Eliot. Mortgage advance. Gravesend B Society | | | | 85,000 | | |
| 5 | Eliot. Balance purchase price | | | | 31,530 | | |
| 7 | Eliot. Payment purchase price | | | | | 114,300 | |
| 8 | Eliot. Land Registry fee | | | | | 200 | |
| | Eliot. Stamp duty land tax | | | | | 1,270 | |
| | Eliot. Costs and disbursements | 760 | | | | 760 | |

**FINANCIAL STATEMENT 27 AUGUST**

**TO: ELIOT**
**PURCHASE OF 'THE WILLOWS'**

| | | £ | £ |
|---|---|---|---|
| | Purchase price | | 127,000 |
| *less:* | Prepaid deposit | | (12,700) |
| | | | 114,300 |
| *less:* | Mortgage advance | | (85,000) |
| | | | 29,300 |
| *add:* | Profit costs on purchase (inc VAT) | 470 | |
| | Profit costs on mortgage (inc VAT) | 94 | |
| | Local search fee | 25 | |
| | Bankruptcy search fee | 10 | |
| | Surveyor's fee (inc VAT) | 161 | |
| | Land Registry fee | 200 | |
| | Stamp duty land tax | 1,270 | |
| | | | 2,230 |
| | **DUE FROM YOU** | | 31,530 |

Example 2

*Sale and purchase – mortgage redemption and advance*

You are acting for Laura, who is selling 'Obrion' for £40,000 and buying 'The Towers' for £100,000. There is an existing mortgage of £20,000 on 'Obrion' in favour of Brighton Building Society. This is to be redeemed following completion of the sale. Brighton Building Society has also agreed to a new mortgage to Laura of £50,000 for the purchase of 'The Towers'. You have been instructed to act for Brighton Building Society in connection with the redemption and the new advance. Laura has agreed to pay the building society's legal costs in connection with the advance and redemption.

The following events occur:

May

17 You obtain official copy entries relating to 'Obrion' (pay £12 by cheque). You pay £25 by cheque for local land charges search in respect of 'The Towers'.

24 You receive £10,000 from Laura to use as the deposit on 'The Towers'.

28 You exchange contracts on sale and purchase. Receive a £4,000 deposit on 'Obrion' as stakeholder. You pay deposit on 'The Towers'.

31 You send a completion statement in respect of 'Obrion' showing the balance due (£36,000).

June

1 You receive a completion statement in respect of 'The Towers' showing the balance due (£90,000).

3 You send a bill of costs and a financial statement to Laura. Costs on sale are £400 plus VAT; on purchase £600 plus VAT; on mortgage redemption £40 plus VAT; and on the new mortgage advance £80 plus VAT.

5 You pay a bankruptcy search fee (£5) by cheque.

8 You receive £23,548 from Laura, being the amount shown due in the financial statement.

9 You receive the mortgage advance of £50,000 from the building society.

10 You complete the sale and purchase.

11 You send the building society a cheque to redeem the mortgage. You pay stamp duty land tax (£1,000) and Land Registry fee (£250) in respect of 'The Towers'.

12 You pay the estate agent's commission of £800 plus VAT. The invoice was addressed to Laura. You transfer all costs and disbursements owing to you.

Show the entries necessary to record the above transaction in the client ledger and the cash account, together with the financial statement sent on 3 June.

*Notes:*

May

17 These payments must be made from the office bank account as we have no client money.

*Entries:*

DR Laura ledger account
CR Cash account
} Office section

24 Client money must be paid into client bank account.

*Entries:*

CR Laura ledger account
DR Cash account
} Client section

28 The £4,000 deposit received is client money so is paid into the client bank account, but CR stakeholder ledger account, not Laura ledger account.

*Entries:*

CR Stakeholder account
DR Cash account
} Client section

The £10,000 due for the deposit will be paid out of client money.

*Entries:*

DR Laura ledger account
CR Cash account
} Client section

31 No entries are required. There are no apportionments referred to, so at completion only the balance of the sale price (£36,000) will be received.

June

1 This confirms that only the balance of the purchase price (£90,000) will be payable at completion.

3 The usual entries for profit costs and VAT are made.

Remember that Laura is responsible for your charges to her and for your charges to the Brighton Building Society. You must debit the mortgage redemption costs and VAT to the building society's ledger account and then transfer the debt to Laura's ledger account. The mortgage advance costs and VAT will be debited directly to Laura's ledger account.

A financial statement is given at the end of this example.

| | |
|---|---|
| 5 | There is no client money available, so payment must be from the office bank account. |
| 8 | The cheque is a combination of office and client money. We have not split it but have paid it into the client bank account (Rule 20).<br>*Entries:*<br>CR Laura ledger account<br>DR Cash account } Client section |
| 9 | The money is received on behalf of your client, Brighton Building Society, but Rule 32(6) applies and the mortgage advance can be shown immediately as a CR in Laura's ledger account. |
| 10 | **Completion of sale:**<br>£36,000 is received from the purchaser's solicitor. It is client money and paid into the client bank account.<br>*Entries:*<br>CR Laura ledger account<br>DR Cash account } Client section<br>Then transfer the deposit, which now belongs to Laura, from stakeholder account.<br>*Entries:*<br>DR Stakeholder ledger account<br>CR Laura ledger account } Client section<br>There will be a record of the transfer made in the transfer journal (Rule 32(2)).<br>**Redemption of mortgage:**<br>Part of the sale proceeds (the portion required to redeem the mortgage) is held for the building society. Transfer the redemption money from Laura to Brighton Building Society. Keep a record in the transfer journal.<br>*Entries:*<br>DR Laura ledger account<br>CR Brighton Building Society ledger account } Client section<br>**Completion of purchase:**<br>Send the vendor's solicitor the balance required of £90,000 from the client bank account.<br>*Entries:*<br>DR Laura ledger account<br>CR Cash account } Client section |
| 11 | Send Brighton Building Society a cheque for £20,000 from the client bank account.<br>*Entries:*<br>DR Brighton Building Society ledger account<br>CR Cash account } Client section<br>The Land Registry fees and stamp duty land tax can be paid from the client bank account. |

| | | |
|---|---|---|
| | DR Laura ledger account<br>CR Cash account | Client section |
| 12 | The estate agent's bill is paid from the client bank account using the agency method. | |
| | *Entries:* | |
| | DR Laura ledger account<br>CR Cash account | Client section |
| | Transfer money from the client to the office bank account in the usual way. | |
| | *Entries:*<br>Withdrawal from the client bank account | |
| | DR Laura ledger account<br>CR Cash account | Client section |
| | Receipt into the office bank account | |
| | CR Laura ledger account<br>CR Cash account | Office section |

The *completed* accounts look like this:

**Client:** Laura
**Matter:** Sale of 'Obrion'; Purchase of 'The Towers'

| Date | Details | Office account | | | Client account | | |
|---|---|---|---|---|---|---|---|
| | | DR | CR | BAL | DR | CR | BAL |
| May | | | | | | | |
| 17 | Cash. Official copies. 'Obrion' | 12 | | 12DR | | | |
| | Cash. Local search. 'The Towers' | 25 | | 37 | | | |
| 24 | Cash. From Laura. For deposit on 'The Towers' | | | | | 10,000 | 10,000CR |
| 28 | Cash. To Vendor's solicitor. Deposit on 'The Towers' | | | | 10,000 | | – |
| June | | | | | | | |
| 3 | Costs. Sale | 400 | | 437 | | | |
| | Purchase | 600 | | 1,037 | | | |
| | VAT | 175 | | 1,212 | | | |
| | Costs. Mortgage advance | 80 | | 1,292 | | | |
| | VAT | 14 | | 1,306 | | | |
| | Brighton BS. Transfer mortgage redemption costs and VAT | 47 | | 1,353 | | | |
| 5 | Cash. Bankruptcy search | 5 | | 1,358 | | | |
| 8 | Cash. From Laura | | | | | 23,548 | 23,548CR |
| 9 | Cash. From Brighton Building Society. For mortgage advance | | | | | 50,000 | 73,548 |
| 10 | Cash. Purchaser's solicitor. Complete sale | | | | | 36,000 | 109,548 |
| | Stakeholder, Transfer deposit (TJ) | | | | | 4,000 | 113,548 |
| | Cash. Vendor's solicitor. Complete purchase | | | | 90,000 | | 23,548 |
| | Brighton Building Society. Transfer mortgage redemption (TJ) | | | | 20,000 | | 3,548 |
| 11 | Cash. Stamp duty land tax. 'The Towers' | | | | 1,000 | | 2,548 |
| | Cash. Land registry fee. 'The Towers' | | | | 250 | | 2,298 |
| 12 | Cash. Estate agent. 'Obrion' | | | | 940 | | 1,358 |
| | Cash. Transfer costs and disbursements from client to office account | | 1,358 | – | 1,358 | | – |

**Client:** Brighton Building Society
**Matter:** Mortgage redemption re Laura

| Date | Details | Office account | | | Client account | | |
|---|---|---|---|---|---|---|---|
| | | DR | CR | BAL | DR | CR | BAL |
| June | | | | | | | |
| 3 | Costs | 40 | | | | | |
| | VAT | 7 | | 47DR | | | |
| | Laura. Transfer mortgage redemption costs and VAT | | 47 | – | | | |
| 10 | Laura. Transfer mortgage redemption (TJ) | | | | | 20,000 | 20,000CR |
| 11 | Cash. To Brighton Building Society | | | | 20,000 | | – |

| Cash account | | | | | | | |
|---|---|---|---|---|---|---|---|
| Date | Details | Office account | | | Client account | | |
| | | DR | CR | BAL | DR | CR | BAL |
| May | | | | xxx | | | xxx |
| 17 | Laura. Official copies | | 12 | | | | |
| | Laura. Local search | | 25 | | | | |
| 24 | Laura. For deposit | | | | 10,000 | | |
| 28 | Stakeholder | | | | 4,000 | | |
| | Laura. Deposit to vendors | | | | | 10,000 | |
| June | | | | | | | |
| 5 | Laura. Bankruptcy search | | 5 | | | | |
| 8 | Laura. Balance for purchase | | | | 23,548 | | |
| 9 | Laura. Mortgage advance. Brighton Building Society | | | | 50,000 | | |
| 10 | Laura. Purchaser's solicitors | | | | 36,000 | | |
| | Laura. Complete purchase | | | | | 90,000 | |
| 11 | Brighton Building Society. Mortgage redemption | | | | | 20,000 | |
| | Laura. Stamp duty land tax | | | | | 1,000 | |
| | Laura. Land Registry fee | | | | | 250 | |
| 12 | Laura. Estate agent | | | | | 940 | |
| | Laura. Professional charges and disbursements | 1,358 | | | | 1,358 | |

| Stakeholder account | | | | | | | |
|---|---|---|---|---|---|---|---|
| Date | Details | Office account | | | Client account | | |
| | | DR | CR | BAL | DR | CR | BAL |
| May | | | | | | | xxx |
| 28 | Cash. Deposit on 'Obrion' re Laura | | | | | 4,000 | |
| June | | | | | | | |
| 10 | Laura. Transfer deposit (TJ) | | | | 4,000 | | |

**FINANCIAL STATEMENT 3 JUNE**

**TO: LAURA**
**SALE OF 'OBRION'**

| | | £ | £ |
|---|---|---|---|
| | Sale price | | 40,000 |
| *less:* | Mortgage redemption | | (20,000) |
| | | | 20,000 |
| | Profit costs on sale (inc VAT) | 470 | |
| | Profit costs on mortgage redemption (inc VAT) | 47 | |
| | Estate agent's commission (inc VAT) | 940 | |
| | Official copy entries | 12 | (1,469) |
| | **Available on sale** | | 18,531 |
| | **PURCHASE OF 'THE TOWERS'** | | |
| | Purchase price | | 100,000 |
| *less:* | Prepaid deposit | | (10,000) |
| | | | 90,000 |
| | Mortgage advance | | (50,000) |
| | | | 40,000 |
| *add:* | Profit costs on purchase (inc VAT) | 705 | |
| | Profit costs on mortgage advance (inc VAT) | 94 | |
| | Stamp duty land tax | 1,000 | |
| | Land Registry fees | 250 | |
| | Local land charge search | 25 | |
| | Bankruptcy | 5 | 2,079 |
| | **Required for purchase** | | 42,079 |
| | **SUMMARY** | | |
| | Required for purchase | | 42,079 |
| *less:* | Available from sale | | (18,531) |
| | **DUE FROM YOU** | | 23,548 |

## 18.2 Agency transactions

A firm of solicitors may decide to use another firm as its agent. This can occur in any type of transaction but probably happens most often in the context of a litigation matter.

### 18.2.1 The agent solicitor

The agent solicitor treats the instructing solicitor like any other client. There will be a client ledger account in the name of the instructing solicitor, and the normal entries will be made to deal with any client money and the delivery of the bill.

### 18.2.2 The instructing solicitor

The fees of the agent solicitor are not a disbursement paid by the solicitor on behalf of the client. The instructing solicitor is providing legal services to the client using an agent. The cost of the agent is, therefore, an expense of the instructing solicitor's firm. The firm will charge more for its legal services in order to cover the expense of using an agent. Any true disbursements will be charged to the client as usual, and it is irrelevant whether the agent or the instructing solicitor pays them.

When the instructing solicitor pays the agent solicitor's bill, he sends one office bank account cheque for the total amount. There can be three different elements of that total: the agent's profit costs, VAT on those costs and any disbursements paid by the agent. The different elements will be recorded separately in the instructing solicitor's accounts.

*Entries:*

| | | |
|---|---|---|
| Agent's profit costs | CR Cash account<br>DR Agency expenses account | Office section |
| Agent's VAT | CR Cash account<br>DR HM Revenue & Customs account | Office section |
| Agent's disbursements | CR Cash account<br>DR Client's ledger account | Office section |

When the instructing solicitor sends his own client a bill, he adds the agent's profit costs to his own solicitor's profit costs and passes on the agent's disbursements to the client.

**Example**

You act for Williams. You instruct Gibson, Weldon & Co, Solicitors, as your agents. On 17 May, you receive their bill showing their profit costs of £200 plus VAT and a court fee of £70. You pay their bill on the same day. On 18 May, you send Williams a bill. Your own profit costs are £400 plus VAT.

*Notes:*

May

17 When you pay the agent's bill, you will pay a total of costs £200 plus £35 VAT and the court fee of £70, ie, a total of £305. However, you will make three separate pairs of DR and CR entries to record the three separate elements of the bill.

The accounts will look like this:

**Cash account**

| Date | Details | Office account | | | Client account | | |
|---|---|---|---|---|---|---|---|
| | | DR | CR | BAL | DR | CR | BAL |
| May | | | | XXX | | | XXX |
| 17 | Agency expenses | | 200 | | | | |
| | VAT | | 35 | | | | |
| | Williams | | 70 | | | | |

**Client:** Williams
**Matter:** Miscellaneous

| Date | Details | Office account | | | Client account | | |
|---|---|---|---|---|---|---|---|
| | | DR | CR | BAL | DR | CR | BAL |
| May | | | | | | | |
| 17 | Cash, Gibson, Weldon & Co. Court fee | 70 | | 70DR | | | |

| Agency expenses account | | | | |
|---|---|---|---|---|
| Date | Details | Office account | | |
| | | DR | CR | BAL |
| May 17 | Cash. Williams | 200 | | 200DR |

| HM Revenue & Customs account | | | | |
|---|---|---|---|---|
| Date | Details | Office account | | |
| | | DR | CR | BAL |
| May 17 | Cash | 35 | | 35DR |

18 When you issue your bill, you add the agent's profit costs to your own and make the usual entries for costs and VAT.

The accounts will look like this:

| Cash account | | | | | | | |
|---|---|---|---|---|---|---|---|
| Date | Details | Office account | | | Client account | | |
| | | DR | CR | BAL | DR | CR | BAL |
| | | | | xxx | | | xxx |
| May 17 | Agency expenses | | 200 | | | | |
| | Customs & Excise | | 35 | | | | |
| | Williams | | 70 | | | | |

| **Client:** Williams<br>**Matter:** Miscellaneous | | | | | | | |
|---|---|---|---|---|---|---|---|
| Date | Details | Office account | | | Client account | | |
| | | DR | CR | BAL | DR | CR | BAL |
| May 17 | Cash, Gibson, Weldon & Co. Court fee | 70 | | 70DR | | | |
| 18 | Costs (400 + 200) | 600 | | 670 | | | |
| | VAT (70 + 35) | 105 | | 775 | | | |

| Profit costs account | | | | |
|---|---|---|---|---|
| Date | Details | Office account | | |
| | | DR | CR | BAL |
| May 17 | Williams | | 600 | 600CR |

| Agency Expenses account | | | | |
|---|---|---|---|---|
| Date | Details | Office account | | |
| | | DR | CR | BAL |
| May 17 | Cash. Williams | 200 | | 200DR |

| HM Revenue & Customs account | | | | |
|---|---|---|---|---|
| Date | Details | Office account | | |
| | | DR | CR | BAL |
| May 17 | Cash. Williams | 35 | | 35DR |
| 18 | Williams | | 105 | 70CR |

## 18.3 Circumstances in which client money need not be paid into the client bank account

### 18.3.1 Rule 16 and Rule 17 exceptions from the need to pay money into client bank account

As we saw in **Chapter 10**, there are situations where client money does not have to be paid into a client bank account.

Under Rule 16, client money can be held outside the client bank account, for example, in the solicitor's safe or in a different bank account.

However, the client must have instructed the solicitor to this effect and the instructions must either have been given in writing or confirmed by the solicitor in writing.

Under Rule 17, the solicitor can withhold money from the client bank account without written instructions or written confirmation of instructions in six situations, for example, where cash is received and is without delay paid in the ordinary course of business to the client or on the client's behalf.

### 18.3.2 Rule 32(2) – the need to record dealings

Whenever the solicitor is dealing with client money, the dealing must be recorded on the cash account and on the client ledger account.

### 18.3.3 Non-recording

The only receipts which will not be recorded are those which are not regarded as 'money' in the solicitor's hands, for example, a post-dated cheque (until the post date arrives) and a cheque which is made out not to the firm but to someone else. Such cheques could not be paid into the firm's bank account and are not regarded as 'money' for this purpose.

Exercise 18B

Which of the following receipts must be paid into the client bank account? Which must be recorded as a receipt of client's money?

(1) You act for the executor of Alan. The executor gives you £250 cash which he found in Alan's house. You authorise the executor to take back the cash in partial payment of a debt due from Alan to the executor.

(2) You act for Brian in a debt collection. You receive a cheque for £5,000 from the debtor. The cheque is in part payment of the debt due to Brian and the cheque is made out to Brian.

(3) You act for Clay. Clay gives you a cheque for £500 on account of costs. He is unsure whether or not he has sufficient funds to cover the cheque and, in his accompanying letter, asks you not to pay the cheque in until he instructs you to do so.

(4) You act for the executors for Diana. You have negotiated a loan from Diana's bank of £3,841 to cover the inheritance tax due on application for a grant of probate. The bank sends you a cheque made out to the Inland Revenue.

## 18.4 Solutions

Exercise 18A

When the company gives you funds on 4 June, you must record a receipt of the company's money.

*Entries:*

| | |
|---|---|
| DR Cash<br>CR George & Co Ltd | } Client section |

When the sale is completed on 5 June, you must show that the money is now held for George. You show this by doing an inter-client transfer.

*Entries:*

| | |
|---|---|
| DR George & Co Ltd<br>CR George | } Client section |

When you complete the investment for George on 7 June, you must record a payment of George's money.

*Entries:*

| | |
|---|---|
| DR George<br>CR Cash | } Client section |

Exercise 18B

(1) This is a receipt of client money. It need not be paid into the client bank account under Rule 17(a). However, you are dealing with client money and must *record* the receipt (and payment) on your client ledger for the executor and on your cash account.

(2) This is not a receipt of money so the question of 'office or client' does not arise. No entries need be made to record the receipt. The cheque could not be paid into the firm's client bank account.

(3) This is a receipt of client money. You will not pay this cheque in as the client has given you written instructions not to (Rule 16). However, as in (1) above, you must record the receipt on your client ledger for Clay and on your cash account.

(4) As in (2) above, this is not a receipt of money so no entries need be made. The cheque could not be paid into the firm's client bank account.

# Chapter 19
# Compliance



## 19.1 Investigative powers

The Law Society, through its Monitoring and Investigation Unit, has extensive investigative powers. Any solicitor must, at a time and place fixed by the Society, produce any papers, files, records, documents and other information requested in writing by the Society. The Society's powers override any solicitor/client confidentiality or privilege.

A solicitor must be prepared to explain and justify any departures from the guidelines for accounting procedures and systems published as Appendix 3 to the 1998 Rules.

Any report produced by the Society may be sent to the Crown Prosecution Service or the Serious Fraud Office and/or used in proceedings before the Solicitor's Disciplinary Tribunal.

## 19.2 Delivery of accountants' reports

Every firm which has handled client money must deliver an Accountants' Report to the Society within six months of the end of the accounting period (Rule 35). The rules relating to Accountants' Reports were amended in 1995 and are now incorporated into the Solicitors' Accounts Rules.

The amendments stem from The Law Society's attempts to reduce the costs of default. It became apparent from the reports of the Monitoring Unit and from its inspections that some reporting accountants were not carrying out their duties effectively and that serious breaches of the Rules (and in some cases fraud) had not been identified.

The 1998 Rules require that reporting accountants must have registered auditor status, together with membership of one of the major accountancy bodies. So that The Law Society can maintain accurate records, solicitors must inform the Society of any change in the reporting accountant. Frequent changes will alert the Society to the possibility that a firm is trying to conceal matters.

Solicitors have to produce a letter of engagement for accountants, incorporating the terms set out in the Rules. These cannot be amended. The letter (and a copy) has to be signed by the solicitor (or a partner or director) and by the accountant. The letter has to be kept for three years and produced to The Law Society on request (Rule 39).

Reporting accountants have to complete and sign a Law Society checklist which the solicitor must keep for three years and produce to The Law Society on request (Rule 46 and Appendix 4). The checklist is intended to be an assurance to the solicitor and to The Law Society that the work required to be done has indeed been done.

The reporting accountant has to check that records, statements and passbooks are being kept as required by liquidators, Court of Protection receivers, etc. Accountants are also required to report on any substantial departure from the guidelines for procedures and systems.

# Appendix

## Solicitors' Accounts Rules 1998

### [last amended October 2004]

[Appendices not reproduced]

### PART A – GENERAL

#### Rule 1 – Principles

The following principles must be observed. A solicitor must:

(a) comply with the requirements of practice rule 1 as to the solicitor's integrity, the duty to act in the client's best interests, and the good repute of the solicitor and the solicitor's profession;

(b) keep other people's money separate from money belonging to the solicitor or the practice;

(c) keep other people's money safely in a bank or building society account identifiable as a client account (except when the rules specifically provide otherwise);

(d) use each client's money for that client's matters only;

(e) use controlled trust money for the purposes of that trust only;

(f) establish and maintain proper accounting systems, and proper internal controls over those systems, to ensure compliance with the rules;

(g) keep proper accounting records to show accurately the position with regard to the money held for each client and each controlled trust;

(h) account for interest on other people's money in accordance with the rules;

(i) co-operate with the Society in checking compliance with the rules; and

(j) deliver annual accountant's reports as required by the rules.

#### Rule 2 – Interpretation

(1) The rules are to be interpreted in the light of the notes.

(2) In the rules, unless the context otherwise requires:

  (a) 'accounting period' has the meaning given in rule 36;

  (b) 'agreed fee' has the meaning given in rule 19(5);

  (c) 'bank' means an institution authorised under the Banking Act 1987 (which includes a European authorised institution), the Post Office in the exercise of its powers to provide banking services, or the Bank of England;

  (d) 'building society' means a building society within the meaning of the Building Societies Act 1986;

  (e) 'client' means the person for whom a solicitor acts;

  (f) 'client account' has the meaning given in rule 14(2);

  (g) 'client money' has the meaning given in rule 13;

  (h) a 'controlled trust' arises when:

    (i) a solicitor of the Supreme Court or registered European lawyer is the sole trustee of a trust, or co-trustee only with one or more of his or her partners or employees;

(ii) a registered foreign lawyer who practises in partnership with a solicitor of the Supreme Court or registered European lawyer is, by virtue of being a partner in that partnership, the sole trustee of a trust, or co-trustee only with one or more of the other partners or employees of that partnership;

(iii) a recognised body which is a company is the sole trustee of a trust, or co-trustee only with one or more of the recognised body's officers or employees; or

(iv) a recognised body which is a limited liability partnership is the sole trustee of a trust, or co-trustee only with one or more of the recognised body's members or employees;

and 'controlled trustee' means a trustee of a controlled trust; (see also paragraph (y) below on the meaning of 'trustee' and 'trust');

(i) 'controlled trust money' has the meaning given in rule 13;

(j) 'costs' means a solicitor's fees and disbursements;

(k) 'disbursement' means any sum spent or to be spent by a solicitor on behalf of the client or controlled trust (including any VAT element);

(l) 'fees' of a solicitor means the solicitor's own charges or profit costs (including any VAT element);

(m) 'general client account' has the meaning given in rule 14(5)(b);

(n) 'mixed payment' has the meaning given in rule 20(1);

(o) 'non-solicitor employer' means an employer who or which is not a solicitor;

(p) 'office account' means an account of the solicitor or the practice for holding office money, or other means of holding office money (for example, the office cash box);

(q) 'office money' has the meaning given in rule 13;

(qa) 'partnership' means an unincorporated partnership and does not include a limited liability partnership, and 'partner' is to be construed accordingly;

(r) 'principal' means:

(i) a sole practitioner;

(ii) a partner or a person held out as a partner (including a 'salaried' or 'associate' partner);

(iii) the principal solicitor (or any one of the principal solicitors) in an in-house practice (for example, in a law centre or in commerce and industry);

(s) 'professional disbursement' means the fees of counsel or other lawyer, or of a professional or other agent or expert instructed by the solicitor;

(t) 'recognised body' means a company or limited liability partnership recognised by the Society under section 9 of the Administration of Justice Act 1985;

(ta) 'registered European lawyer' means a person registered by the Society under regulation 17 of the European Communities (Lawyer's Practice) Regulations 2000;

(u) 'registered foreign lawyer' means a person registered by the Society under section 89 of the Courts and Legal Services Act 1990;

(ua) 'regular payment' has the meaning given in rule 21;

(v) 'separate designated client account' has the meaning given in rule 14(5)(a);

(w) 'Society' means the Law Society of England and Wales;

(x) 'solicitor' means a solicitor of the Supreme Court; and for the purposes of these rules also includes: a registered European lawyer; a registered foreign lawyer practising in partnership with a solicitor of the Supreme Court or registered European lawyer or as the director of a recognised body which is a company or as a member of a recognised body which is a limited liability partnership; a recognised body; and a partnership including at least one solicitor of the Supreme Court, registered European lawyer or recognised body;

(xa) 'solicitor of the Supreme Court' means an individual who is a solicitor of the Supreme Court of England and Wales;

(y) 'trustee' includes a personal representative (i.e. an executor or an administrator), and 'trust' includes the duties of a personal representative; and

(z) 'without delay' means, in normal circumstances, either on the day of receipt or on the next working day.

**Notes**

(i) Although many of the rules are expressed as applying to an individual solicitor, the effect of the definition of 'solicitor' in rule 2(2)(x) is that the rules apply equally to all those who carry on a practice and to the practice itself. See also rule 4(1)(a) (persons governed by the rules) and rule 5 (persons exempt from the rules).

(ii) A client account must be at a bank or building society's branch in England and Wales - see rule 14(4).

(iii) For the full definition of a 'European authorised institution' (rule 2(2)(c)), see the Banking Co-ordination (Second Council Directive) Regulations 1992 (S.I. 1992 no. 3218).

(iv) The definition of a controlled trust (rule 2(2)(h)), which derives from statute, gives rise to some anomalies. For example, a partner, assistant solicitor or consultant acting as sole trustee will be a controlled trustee. So will a sole solicitor trustee who is a director of a recognised body which is a company, or a member of a recognised body which is a limited liability partnership. Two or more partners acting as trustees will be controlled trustees. However two or more assistant solicitors or consultants acting as trustees will fall outside the definition, as will two or more directors of a recognised body which is a company, or two or more members of a recognised body which is a limited liability partnership. In these cases, if the matter is dealt with through the practice, the partners (or the recognised body) will hold any money as client money.

(iva) Exceptionally, where a trust is handled by registered European lawyers, the trustees might be two partners at the firm's head office in the home state who are not directly subject to the rules. Money in the trust should be held by the firm as client money. However it should be treated as if it were controlled trust money in relation to choice of account, accounting for interest, etc., to ensure that there is no breach of duty by the trustees.

(v) The fees of interpreters, translators, process servers, surveyors, estate agents, etc., instructed by the solicitor are professional disbursements (see rule 2(2)(s)). Travel agents' charges are not professional disbursements.

(vi) The general definition of 'office account' is wide (see rule 2(2)(p)). However, rule 19(1)(b) (receipt and transfer of costs) and rule 21(1)(b) and 21(2)(b) (payments from the Legal Services Commission) specify that certain money is to be placed in an office account at a bank or building society.

(vii) An index is attached to the rules but it does not form part of the rules. For the status of the flowchart (Appendix 1) and the chart dealing with special situations (Appendix 2), see note (xiii) to rule 13.

### Rule 3 – Geographical scope

The rules apply to practice carried on from an office in England and Wales.

#### Note

Practice carried on from an office outside England and Wales is governed by the Solicitors' Overseas Practice Rules.

### Rule 4 – Persons governed by the rules

(1) The rules apply to:

- (a) solicitors of the Supreme Court who are:
  - (i) sole practitioners;
  - (ii) partners in a practice, or held out as partners (including 'salaried' and 'associate' partners);
  - (iii) assistants, associates, consultants or locums in a private practice;
  - (iv) employed as in-house solicitors (for example, in a law centre or in commerce and industry);
  - (v) directors of recognised bodies which are companies; or
  - (vi) members of recognised bodies which are limited liability partnerships;
- (aa) registered European lawyers who are:
  - (i) sole practitioners;
  - (ii) partners in a practice, or held out as partners (including 'salaried' and 'associate' partners);
  - (iii) assistants, associates, consultants or locums in a private practice;
  - (iv) employed as in-house lawyers (for example, in a law centre or in commerce and industry);
  - (v) directors of recognised bodies which are companies; or
  - (vi) members of recognised bodies which are limited liability partnerships;
- (b) registered foreign lawyers who are:
  - (i) practising in partnership with solicitors of the Supreme Court or registered European lawyers, or held out as partners (including 'salaried' and 'associate' partners) of solicitors of the Supreme Court or registered European lawyers;
  - (ii) directors of recognised bodies which are companies; or
  - (iii) members of recognised bodies which are limited liability partnerships; and
- (c) recognised bodies.

(2) Part F of the rules (accountants' reports) also applies to reporting accountants.

**Notes**

(i) In practical terms, the rules also bind anyone else working in a practice, such as cashiers and non-lawyer fee earners. Non-compliance by any member of staff will lead to the principals being in breach of the rules – see rule 6. Misconduct by an employee can also lead to an order of the Solicitors' Disciplinary Tribunal under section 43 of the Solicitors Act 1974 imposing restrictions on his or her employment.

(ii) Solicitors who have held or received client money or controlled trust money, but no longer do so, whether or not they continue in practice, continue to be bound by some of the rules – for instance:

- rule 7 (duty to remedy breaches);
- rule 19(2), and note (xi) to rule 19, rule 32(8) to (15) and rule 33 (retention of records);
- rule 34 (production of records);
- Part F (accountants' reports), and in particular rule 35(1) and rule 36(5) (delivery of final report), and rule 38(2) and rule 46 (retention of records).

(iii) The rules do not cover a solicitor's trusteeships carried on in a purely personal capacity outside any legal practice. It will normally be clear from the terms of the appointment whether the solicitor is being appointed trustee in a purely personal capacity or in his or her professional capacity. If a solicitor is charging for the work, it is clearly being done as solicitor. Use of professional stationery may also indicate that the work is being done in a professional capacity.

(iv) A solicitor who wishes to retire from private practice must make a decision about any professional trusteeship. There are three possibilities:

(a) continue to act as a professional trustee (as evidenced by, for instance, charging for work done, or by continuing to use the title 'solicitor' in connection with the trust). In this case, the solicitor must continue to hold a practising certificate, and money subject to the trust must continue to be dealt with in accordance with the rules.

(b) continue to act as trustee, but in a purely personal capacity. In this case, the solicitor must stop charging for the work, and must not be held out as a solicitor (unless this is qualified by words such as 'non-practising' or 'retired') in connection with the trust.

(c) cease to be a trustee.

### Rule 5 – Persons exempt from the rules

The rules do not apply to:

(a) a solicitor when practising as an employee of:

(i) a local authority;

(ii) statutory undertakers;

(iii) a body whose accounts are audited by the Comptroller and Auditor General;

(iv) the Duchy of Lancaster;

(v) the Duchy of Cornwall; or

(vi) the Church Commissioners; or

(b) a solicitor who practises as the Solicitor of the City of London; or

(c) a solicitor when carrying out the functions of:

(i) a coroner or other judicial office; or

(ii) a sheriff or under-sheriff.

**Notes**

(i) 'Statutory undertakers' means:

(a) any persons authorised by any enactment to carry on any railway, light railway, tramway, road transport, water transport, canal, inland navigation, dock, harbour, pier or lighthouse undertaking or any undertaking for the supply of hydraulic power; and

(b) any licence holder within the meaning of the Electricity Act 1989, any public gas supplier, any water or sewerage undertaker, the Environment Agency, any public telecommunications operator, the Post Office, the Civil Aviation Authority and any relevant airport operator within the meaning of Part V of the Airports Act 1986.

(ii) 'Local authority' means any of those bodies which are listed in section 270 of the Local Government Act 1972 or in section 21(1) of the Local Government and Housing Act 1989.

### Rule 6 – Principals' responsibility for compliance

All the principals in a practice must ensure compliance with the rules by the principals themselves and by everyone else working in the practice. This duty also extends to the directors of a recognised body which is a company, or to the members of a recognised body which is a limited liability partnership, and to the recognised body itself.

### Rule 7 – Duty to remedy breaches

(1) Any breach of the rules must be remedied promptly upon discovery. This includes the replacement of any money improperly withheld or withdrawn from a client account.

(2) In a private practice, the duty to remedy breaches rests not only on the person causing the breach, but also on all the principals in the practice. This duty extends to replacing missing client money or controlled trust money from the principals' own resources, even if the money has been misappropriated by an employee or fellow principal, and whether or not a claim is subsequently made on the Solicitors' Indemnity or Compensation Funds or on the firm's insurance.

(3) In the case of a recognised body, this duty falls on the recognised body itself.

**Note**

For payment of interest when money should have been held in a client account but was not, see rule 24(2).

### Rule 8 – Controlled trustees

A solicitor who in the course of practice acts as a controlled trustee must treat the controlled trust money as if it were client money, except when the rules provide to the contrary.

**Note**

The following are examples of controlled trust money being treated differently from client money:

- rule 18 (controlled trust money withheld from a client account) – special provisions for controlled trusts, in place of rules 16 and 17 (which apply to client money);

- rule 19(2), and note (xi) to rule 19 – original bill etc., to be kept on file, in addition to central record or file of copy bills;
- rule 23, note (v) and rule 32, note (ii)(d) – controlled trustees may delegate to an outside manager the day to day keeping of accounts of the business or property portfolio of an estate or trust;
- rule 24(7), and note (x) to rule 24 – interest;
- rule 32(7) – quarterly reconciliations.

### Rule 9 – Liquidators, trustees in bankruptcy, Court of Protection receivers and trustees of occupational pension schemes

(1) A solicitor who in the course of practice acts as

- a liquidator
- a trustee in bankruptcy,
- a Court of Protection receiver, or
- a trustee of an occupational pension scheme which is subject to section 47(1)(a) of the Pensions Act 1995 (appointment of an auditor) and section 49(1) (separate bank account) and regulations under section 49(2)(b) (books and records),

must comply with:

(a) the appropriate statutory rules or regulations;

(b) the principles set out in rule 1; and

(c) the requirements of paragraphs (2) to (4) below;

and will then be deemed to have satisfactorily complied with the Solicitors' Accounts Rules.

(2) In respect of any records kept under the appropriate statutory rules, there must also be compliance with:

(a) rule 32(8) – bills and notifications of costs;

(b) rule 32(9)(c) – retention of records;

(c) rule 32(12) – centrally kept records;

(d) rule 34 – production of records; and

(e) rule 42(1)(l) and (p) – reporting accountant to check compliance.

(3) If a liquidator or trustee in bankruptcy uses any of the practice's client accounts for holding money pending transfer to the Insolvency Services Account or to a local bank account authorised by the Secretary of State, he or she must comply with the Solicitors' Accounts Rules in all respects whilst the money is held in the client account.

(4) If the appropriate statutory rules or regulations do not govern the holding or receipt of client money in a particular situation (for example, money below a certain limit), the solicitor must comply with the Solicitors' Accounts Rules in all respects in relation to that money.

**Notes**

(i) The Insolvency Regulations 1986 (S.I. 1986 no. 994) regulate liquidators and trustees in bankruptcy.

(ii) The Court of Protection Rules 1994 (S.I. 1994 no. 3046) regulate Court of Protection receivers.

(iii) Money held or received by solicitor liquidators, trustees in bankruptcy and Court of Protection receivers is client money but, because of the statutory rules and rule 9(1), it will not normally be kept in a client account. If for any reason it is held in a client account, the Solicitors' Accounts Rules apply to that money for the time it is so held (see rule 9(3) and (4)).

(iv) Money held or received by solicitor trustees of occupational pension schemes is either client money or controlled trust money but, because of the statutory rules and rule 9(1), it will not normally be kept in a client account. If for any reason it is held in a client account, the Solicitors' Accounts Rules apply to that money for the time it is so held (see rule 9(4)).

### Rule 10 – Joint accounts

(1) If a solicitor acting in a client's matter holds or receives money jointly with the client, another solicitors' practice or another third party, the rules in general do not apply, but the following must be complied with:
   (a) rule 32(8) – bills and notifications of costs;
   (b) rule 32(9)(b)(ii) – retention of statements and passbooks;
   (c) rule 32(13) – centrally kept records;
   (d) rule 34 – production of records; and
   (e) rule 42(1)(m) and (p) – reporting accountant to check compliance.

**Operation of the joint account by the solicitor only**

(2) If the joint account is operated only by the solicitor, the solicitor must ensure that he or she receives the statements from the bank, building society or other financial institution, and has possession of any passbooks.

**Shared operation of the joint account**

(3) If the solicitor shares the operation of the joint account with the client, another solicitor's practice or another third party, the solicitor must:
   (a) ensure that he or she receives the statements or duplicate statements from the bank, building society or other financial institution and retains them in accordance with rule 32(9)(b) (ii); and
   (b) ensure that he or she either has possession of any passbooks, or takes copies of the passbook entries before handing any passbook to the other signatory, and retains them in accordance with rule 32(9)(b)(ii).

**Operation of the joint account by the other account holder**

(4) If the joint account is operated solely by the other account holder, the solicitor must ensure that he or she receives the statements or duplicate statements from the bank, building society or other financial institution and retains them in accordance with rule 32(9)(b)(ii).

**Note**

Although a joint account is not a client account, money held in a joint account is client money.

### Rule 11 – Operation of a client's own account

(1) If a solicitor in the course of practice operates a client's own account as signatory (for example, as donee under a power of attorney), the rules in general do not apply, but the following must be complied with:
   (a) rule 33(1) to (3) – accounting records for clients' own accounts;
   (b) rule 34 – production of records; and
   (c) rule 42(1)(n) and (p) – reporting accountant to check compliance.

**Operation by the solicitor only**

(2) If the account is operated by the solicitor only, the solicitor must ensure that he or she receives the statements from the bank, building society or other financial institution, and has possession of any passbooks.

**Shared operation of the account**

(3) If the solicitor shares the operation of the account with the client or a co-attorney outside the solicitor's practice, the solicitor must:

(a) ensure that he or she receives the statements or duplicate statements from the bank, building society or other financial institution and retains them in accordance with rule 33(1) to (3); and

(b) ensure that he or she either has possession of any passbooks, or takes copies of the passbook entries before handing any passbook to the client or co-attorney, and retains them in accordance with rule 33(1) to (3).

**Operation of the account for a limited purpose**

(4) If the solicitor is given authority (whether as attorney or otherwise) to operate the account for a limited purpose only, such as the taking up of a share rights issue during the client's temporary absence, the solicitor need not receive statements or possess passbooks, provided that he or she retains details of all cheques drawn or paid in, and retains copies of all passbook entries, relating to the transaction, and retains them in accordance with rule 33(1) and (2).

**Application**

(5) This rule applies only to solicitors in private practice.

**Notes**

(i) Money held in a client's own account (under a power of attorney or otherwise) is not 'client money' for the purpose of the rules because it is not 'held or received' by the solicitor. If the solicitor closes the account and receives the closing balance, this becomes client money and must be paid into a client account, unless the client instructs to the contrary in accordance with rule 16(1)(a).

(ii) A solicitor who merely pays money into a client's own account, or helps the client to complete forms in relation to such an account, is not 'operating' the account.

(iii) A solicitor executor who operates the deceased's account (whether before or after the grant of probate) will be subject to the limited requirements of rule 11. If the account is subsequently transferred into the solicitor's name, or a new account is opened in the solicitor's name, the solicitor will have 'held or received' controlled trust money (or client money) and is then subject to all the rules.

(iv) The rules do not cover money held or received by a solicitor attorney acting in a purely personal capacity outside any legal practice. If a solicitor is charging for the work, it is clearly being done in the course of legal practice. See rule 4, note (iv) for the choices which can be made on retirement from private practice.

(v) 'A client's own account' covers all accounts in a client's own name, whether opened by the client himself or herself, or by the solicitor on the client's instructions under rule 16(1)(b).

(vi) 'A client's own account' also includes an account opened in the name of a person designated by the client under rule 16(1)(b).

(vii) Solicitors should also remember the requirements of rule 32(8) - bills and notifications of costs.

(viii) For payment of interest, see rule 24, note (iii).

### Rule 12 – Solicitor's rights not affected

Nothing in these rules deprives a solicitor of any recourse or right, whether by way of lien, set off, counterclaim, charge or otherwise, against money standing to the credit of a client account.

### Rule 13 – Categories of money

All money held or received in the course of practice falls into one of the following categories:

(a) 'client money' - money held or received for a client, and all other money which is not controlled trust money or office money;

(b) 'controlled trust money' - money held or received for a controlled trust; or

(c) 'office money' - money which belongs to the solicitor or the practice.

**Notes**

(i) 'Client money' includes money held or received:

  (a) as agent, bailee, stakeholder, or as the donee of a power of attorney, or as a liquidator, trustee in bankruptcy or Court of Protection receiver;

  (b) for payment of unpaid professional disbursements (for definition of 'professional disbursement' see rule 2(2)(s));

  (c) for payment of stamp duty land tax, Land Registry registration fees, telegraphic transfer fees and court fees; this is not office money because the solicitor has not incurred an obligation to the Inland Revenue, the Land Registry, the bank or the court to pay the duty or fee (contrast with note (xi)(c)(C) below); (on the other hand, if the solicitor has already paid the duty or fee out of his or her own resources, or has received the service on credit, payment subsequently received from the client will be office money - see note (xi)(c)(B) below);

  (d) as a payment on account of costs generally;

  (e) as commission paid in respect of a solicitor's client, unless the client has given the solicitor prior authority to retain it in accordance with practice rule 10, or unless it falls within the £20 de minimis figure specified in that rule.

(ii) A solicitor to whom a cheque or draft is made out, and who in the course of practice endorses it over to a client or employer, has received client money. Even if no other client money is held or received, the solicitor will be subject to some provisions of the rules, eg:

- rule 7 (duty to remedy breaches);
- rule 32 (accounting records for client money);
- rule 34 (production of records);
- rule 35 (delivery of accountants' reports).

(iii) Money held by solicitors who are trustees of occupational pension schemes will either be client money or controlled trust money, according to the circumstances.

(iv) Money held jointly with another person outside the practice (for example, with a lay trustee, or with another firm of solicitors) is client money subject to a limited application of the rules – see rule 10.

(v) Money held to the sender's order is client money.

  (a) If money is accepted on such terms, it must be held in a client account.

  (b) However, a cheque or draft sent to a solicitor on terms that the cheque or draft (as opposed to the money) is held to the sender's order must not be presented for payment without the sender's consent.

  (c) The recipient is always subject to a professional obligation to return the money, or the cheque or draft, to the sender on demand.

(vi) An advance to a client from the solicitor which is paid into a client account under rule 15 (2)(b) becomes client money. For interest, see rule 24(3)(e).

(vii) Money subject to a trust will be either:

  (a) controlled trust money (basically if members of the practice are the only trustees, but see the detailed definition of 'controlled trust' in rule 2(2)(h)); or

  (b) client money (if the trust is not a controlled trust; typically the solicitor will be co-trustee with a lay person, or is acting for lay trustees).

(viii) If the Law Society intervenes in a practice, money from the practice is held or received by the Society's intervention agent subject to a trust under Schedule 1 paragraph 7(1) of the Solicitors Act 1974, and is therefore controlled trust money. The same provision requires the agent to pay the money into a client account.

(ix) A solicitor who, as the donee of a power of attorney, operates the donor's own account is subject to a limited application of these rules – see rule 11. Money kept in the donor's own account is not 'client money', because it is not 'held or received' by the solicitor.

(x) Money held or received by a solicitor in the course of his or her employment when practising in one of the capacities listed in rule 5 (persons exempt from the rules) is not 'client money' for the purpose of the rules, because the rules do not apply at all.

(xi) Office money includes:

  (a) money held or received in connection with running the practice; for example, PAYE, or VAT on the firm's fees;

  (b) interest on general client accounts; the bank or building society should be instructed to credit such interest to the office account – but see also rule 15(2)(d), and note (vi) to rule 15 for interest on controlled trust money; and

  (c) payments received in respect of:

    (A) fees due to the practice against a bill or written notification of costs incurred, which has been given or sent in accordance with rule 19(2);

    (B) disbursements already paid by the practice (for definition of 'disbursement' see rule 2(2)(k));

    (C) disbursements incurred but not yet paid by the practice, but excluding unpaid professional disbursements (for definition of 'professional disbursement' see rule 2(2)(s), and note (v) to rule 2);

(D) money paid for or towards an agreed fee – see rule 19(5); and

(d) money held in a client account and earmarked for costs under rule 19(3) (transfer of costs from client account to office account); and

(e) money held or received from the Legal Services Commission as a regular payment (see rule 21(2)).

(xii) A solicitor cannot be his or her own client for the purpose of the rules, so that if a practice conducts a personal or office transaction – for instance, conveyancing – for a principal (or for a number of principals), money held or received on behalf of the principal(s) is office money. However, other circumstances may mean that the money is client money, for example:

(a) If the practice also acts for a lender, money held or received on behalf of the lender is client money.

(b) If the practice acts for a principal and, for example, his or her spouse jointly (assuming the spouse is not a partner in the practice), money received on their joint behalf is client money.

(c) If the practice acts for an assistant solicitor, consultant or non-solicitor employee, or (if it is a company) a director, or (if it is a limited liability partnership) a member, he or she is regarded as a client of the practice, and money received for him or her is client money – even if he or she conducts the matter personally.

(d) See also note (iva) to rule 2 (money held on behalf of trustees who are head office partners of a registered European lawyer is client money).

(xiii) For a flowchart summarising the effect of the rules, see Appendix 1. For more details of the treatment of different types of money, see the chart 'Special situations – what applies' at Appendix 2. These two appendices are included to help solicitors and their staff find their way about the rules. Unlike the notes, they are not intended to affect the meaning of the rules.

## PART B – CLIENT MONEY, CONTROLLED TRUST MONEY AND OPERATION OF A CLIENT ACCOUNT

### Rule 14 – Client accounts

(1) A solicitor who holds or receives client money and/or controlled trust money must keep one or more client accounts (unless all the client money and controlled trust money is always dealt with outside any client account in accordance with rule 9, rule 10 or rules 16 to 18).

(2) A 'client account' is an account of a practice kept at a bank or building society for holding client money and/or controlled trust money, in accordance with the requirements of this part of the rules.

(3) The client account(s) of:

(a) a sole practitioner must be either in the solicitor's own name or in the practice name;

(b) a partnership must be in the firm name;

(c) a recognised body must be in the company name, or the name of the limited liability partnership;

(d) in-house solicitors must be in the name of the current principal solicitor or solicitors;

(e) executors or trustees who are controlled trustees must be either in the name of the firm or in the name of the controlled trustee(s);

and the name of the account must also include the word 'client'.

(4) A client account must be:

(a) a bank account at a branch (or a bank's head office) in England and Wales; or

(b) a building society deposit or share account at a branch (or a society's head office) in England and Wales.

(5) There are two types of client account:

(a) a 'separate designated client account', which is a deposit or share account for money relating to a single client, or a current, deposit or share account for money held for a single controlled trust; and which includes in its title, in addition to the requirements of rule 14(3) above, a reference to the identity of the client or controlled trust; and

(b) a 'general client account', which is any other client account.

### Notes

(i) For the client accounts of an executor, trustee or nominee company owned by a solicitors' practice, see rule 31.

(ii) In the case of in-house solicitors, any client account should be in the names of all solicitors held out on the notepaper as principals. The names of other solicitor employees may also be included if so desired. Any solicitor whose name is included will be subject to the full Compensation Fund contribution and his or her name will have to be included on the accountant's report.

(iii) 'Bank' and 'building society' are defined in rule 2(2)(c) and (d) respectively.

(iv) A practice may have any number of separate designated client accounts and general client accounts.

(v) The word 'client' must appear in full; an abbreviation is not acceptable.

(vi) Compliance with rule 14(1) to (4) ensures that clients, as well as the bank or building society, have the protection afforded by section 85 of the Solicitors Act 1974.

(vii) Money held in a client account must be immediately available, even at the sacrifice of interest, unless the client otherwise instructs, or the circumstances clearly indicate otherwise.

### Rule 15 – Use of a client account

(1) Client money and controlled trust money must without delay be paid into a client account, and must be held in a client account, except when the rules provide to the contrary (see rules 16 to 18).

(2) Only client money or controlled trust money may be paid into or held in a client account, except:

(a) an amount of the solicitor's own money required to open or maintain the account;

(b) an advance from the solicitor to fund a payment on behalf of a client or controlled trust in excess of funds held for that client or controlled trust; the sum becomes client money or controlled trust money on payment into the account (for interest on client money, see rule 24 (3)(e); for interest on controlled trust money, see rule 24(7) and note (x) to rule 24);

(c) money to replace any sum which for any reason has been drawn from the account in breach of rule 22; the replacement money becomes client money or controlled trust money on payment into the account; and

(d) a sum in lieu of interest which is paid into a client account for the purpose of complying with rule 24(2) as an alternative to paying it to the client direct; (for interest on controlled trust money, see note (vi) below);

and except when the rules provide to the contrary (see note (iv) below).

**Notes**

(i) See rule 13 and notes for the definition and examples of client money and controlled trust money.

(ii) 'Without delay' is defined in rule 2(2)(z).

(iii) Exceptions to rule 15(1)(client money and controlled trust money must be paid into a client account) can be found in:

- rule 9 – liquidators, trustees in bankruptcy, Court of Protection receivers and trustees of occupational pension schemes;
- rule 10 – joint accounts;
- rule 16 – client's instructions;
- rules 17 and 18
  - cash paid straight to client, beneficiary or third party;
  - cheque endorsed to client, beneficiary or third party;
  - money withheld from client account on the Society's authority;
  - controlled trust money paid into an account which is not a client account;
- rule 19(1)(b) – receipt and transfer of costs;
- rule 21(1) – payments by the Legal Services Commission.

(iv) Rule 15(2)(a) to (d) provides for exceptions to the principle that only client money and controlled trust money may be paid into a client account. Additional exceptions can be found in:

- rule 19(1)(c) – receipt and transfer of costs;
- rule 20(2)(b) – receipt of mixed payments;
- rule 21(2)(c)(ii) – transfer to client account of a sum for unpaid professional disbursements, where the solicitor receives regular payments from the Legal Services Commission.

(v) Only a nominal sum will be required to open or maintain an account. In practice, banks will usually open (and, if instructed, keep open) accounts with nil balances.

(vi) Rule 15 allows controlled trust money to be mixed with client money in a general client account. However, the general law requires a solicitor to act in the best interests of a controlled trust and not to benefit from it. The interest rules in Part C do not apply to controlled trust money. A solicitor's legal duty means that the solicitor must obtain the best reasonably obtainable rate of interest, and must account to the relevant controlled trust for all the interest earned, whether the controlled trust money is held in a separate designated client account or in a general client account. To ensure that all interest is accounted for, one option might be to set up a general client account just for controlled trust money. When controlled trust money is held in a general client account, interest will be credited to the office account in the normal way, but all interest must be promptly allocated to each controlled trust - either by transfer to the general client account, or to separate designated client account(s) for the particular trust(s), or by payment to each trust in some other way.

Solicitors should also consider whether they have received any indirect benefit from controlled trust money at the expense of the controlled trust(s). For example, the bank might charge a reduced overdraft rate by reference to the total funds (including controlled trust money) held, in return for paying a lower rate of interest on those funds. In this type of case, the law may require the solicitor to do more than simply account for any interest earned.

(vii) If controlled trust money is invested in the purchase of assets other than money - such as stocks or shares - it ceases to be controlled trust money, because it is no longer money held by the solicitor. If the investment is subsequently sold, the money received is, again, controlled trust money. The records kept under rule 32 must include entries to show the purchase or sale of investments.

(viii) Some schemes proposed by banks would aggregate the sums held in a number of client accounts in order to maximise the interest payable. It is not acceptable to aggregate money held in separate designated client accounts with money held in general client accounts (see note (i) to rule 24).

(ix) In the case of Wood and Burdett (case number 8669/2002 filed on 13 January 2004), the Solicitors' Disciplinary Tribunal said that it is not a proper part of a solicitor's everyday business or practice to operate a banking facility for third parties, whether they are clients of the firm or not. Solicitors should not, therefore, provide banking facilities through a client account. Further, solicitors are likely to lose the exemption under the Financial Services and Markets Act 2000 if a deposit is taken in circumstances which do not form part of a solicitor's practice. It should also be borne in mind that there are criminal sanctions against assisting money launderers.

### Rule 16 – Client money withheld from client account on client's instructions

(1) Client money may be:

- (a) held by the solicitor outside a client account by, for example, retaining it in the solicitor's safe in the form of cash, or placing it in an account in the solicitor's name which is not a client account, such as an account outside England and Wales; or
- (b) paid into an account at a bank, building society or other financial institution opened in the name of the client or of a person designated by the client;

but only if the client instructs the solicitor to that effect for the client's own convenience, and only if the instructions are given in writing, or are given by other means and confirmed by the solicitor to the client in writing.

(2) It is improper to seek blanket agreements, through standard terms of business or otherwise, to hold client money outside a client account.

#### Notes

(i) For advance payments from the Legal Services Commission, withheld from a client account on the Commission's instructions, see rule 21(1)(a).

(ii) If a client instructs the solicitor to hold part only of a payment in accordance with rule 16(1)(a) or (b), the entire payment must first be placed in a client account. The relevant part can then be transferred out and dealt with in accordance with the client's instructions.

(iii) Money withheld from a client account under rule 16(1)(a) remains client money, and the record-keeping provisions of rule 32 must be complied with.

(iv) Once money has been paid into an account set up under rule 16(1)(b), it ceases to be client money. Until that time, the money is client money and a record must therefore be kept of the solicitor's receipt of the money, and its payment into the account in the name of the client or designated person, in accordance with rule 32. If the solicitor can operate the account, the solicitor must comply with rule 11 (operating a client's own account) and rule 33 (accounting records for clients' own accounts). In the absence of instructions to the contrary, any money withdrawn must be paid into a client account - see rule 15(1).

(v) Clients' instructions under rule 16(1) must be kept for at least six years - see rule 32(9)(d).

(vi) A payment on account of costs received from a person who is funding all or part of the solicitor's fees may be withheld from a client account on the instructions of that person given in accordance with rule 16(1) and (2).

(vii) For payment of interest, see rule 24(6) and notes (ii) and (iii) to rule 24.

### Rule 17 – Other client money withheld from a client account

The following categories of client money may be withheld from a client account:

(a) cash received and without delay paid in cash in the ordinary course of business to the client or, on the client's behalf, to a third party;

(b) a cheque or draft received and endorsed over in the ordinary course of business to the client or, on the client's behalf, to a third party;

(c) money withheld from a client account on instructions under rule 16;

(d) unpaid professional disbursements included in a payment of costs dealt with under rule 19(1)(b);

(e) (i) advance payments from the Legal Services Commission withheld from client account (see rule 21(1)(a)); and

(ii) unpaid professional disbursements included in a payment of costs from the Legal Services Commission (see rule 21(1)(b)); and

(f) money withheld from a client account on the written authorisation of the Society. The Society may impose a condition that the solicitor pay the money to a charity which gives an indemnity against any legitimate claim subsequently made for the sum received.

**Notes**

(i) 'Without delay' is defined in rule 2(2)(z).

(ii) If money is withheld from a client account under rule 17(a) or (b), rule 32 requires records to be kept of the receipt of the money and the payment out.

(iii) It makes no difference, for the purpose of the rules, whether an endorsement is effected by signature in the normal way or by some other arrangement with the bank.

(iv) The circumstances in which authorisation would be given under rule 17(f) must be extremely rare. Applications for authorisation should be made to the Professional Ethics Division.

### Rule 18 – Controlled trust money withheld from a client account

The following categories of controlled trust money may be withheld from a client account:

(a) cash received and without delay paid in cash in the execution of the trust to a beneficiary or third party;
(b) a cheque or draft received and without delay endorsed over in the execution of the trust to a beneficiary or third party;
(c) money which, in accordance with the trustee's powers, is paid into or retained in an account of the trustee which is not a client account (for example, an account outside England and Wales), or properly retained in cash in the performance of the trustee's duties;
(d) money withheld from a client account on the written authorisation of the Society. The Society may impose a condition that the solicitor pay the money to a charity which gives an indemnity against any legitimate claim subsequently made for the sum received.

**Notes**

(i) 'Without delay' is defined in rule 2(2)(z).
(ii) If money is withheld from a client account under rule 18(a) or (b), rule 32 requires records to be kept of the receipt of the money and the payment out – see also rule 15, note (vii). If money is withheld from a client account under rule 18 (c), rule 32 requires a record to be kept of the receipt of the money.
(iii) It makes no difference, for the purpose of the rules, whether an endorsement is effected by signature in the normal way or by some other arrangement with the bank.
(iv) The circumstances in which authorisation would be given under rule 18(d) must be extremely rare. Applications for authorisation should be made to the Professional Ethics Division.

## Rule 19 – Receipt and transfer of costs

(1) A solicitor who receives money paid in full or part settlement of the solicitor's bill (or other notification of costs) must follow one of the following four options:
  (a) determine the composition of the payment without delay, and deal with the money accordingly:
    (i) if the sum comprises office money only, it must be placed in an office account;
    (ii) if the sum comprises only client money (for example an unpaid professional disbursement – see rule 2(2)(s), and note (v) to rule 2), the entire sum must be placed in a client account;
    (iii) if the sum includes both office money and client money (such as unpaid professional disbursements; purchase money; or payments in advance for court fees, stamp duty land tax, Land Registry registration fees or telegraphic transfer fees), the solicitor must follow rule 20 (receipt of mixed payments); or
  (b) ascertain that the payment comprises only office money, and/or client money in the form of professional disbursements incurred but not yet paid, and deal with the payment as follows:
    (i) place the entire sum in an office account at a bank or building society branch (or head office) in England and Wales; and
    (ii) by the end of the second working day following receipt, either pay any unpaid professional disbursement, or transfer a sum for its settlement to a client account; or

(c) pay the entire sum into a client account (regardless of its composition), and transfer any office money out of the client account within 14 days of receipt; or

(d) on receipt of costs from the Legal Services Commission, follow the option in rule 21(1)(b).

(2) A solicitor who properly requires payment of his or her fees from money held for the client or controlled trust in a client account must first give or send a bill of costs, or other written notification of the costs incurred, to the client or the paying party.

(3) Once the solicitor has complied with paragraph (2) above, the money earmarked for costs becomes office money and must be transferred out of the client account within 14 days.

(4) A payment on account of costs generally is client money, and must be held in a client account until the solicitor has complied with paragraph (2) above. (For an exception in the case of legal aid payments, see rule 21(1)(a).)

(5) A payment for an agreed fee must be paid into an office account. An 'agreed fee' is one that is fixed not a fee that can be varied upwards, nor a fee that is dependent on the transaction being completed. An agreed fee must be evidenced in writing.

**Notes**

(i) For the definition and further examples of office and client money, see rule 13 and notes.

(ii)
- Money received for paid disbursements is office money.
- Money received for unpaid professional disbursements is client money.
- Money received for other unpaid disbursements for which the solicitor has incurred a liability to the payee (for example, travel agents' charges, taxi fares, courier charges or Land Registry search fees, payable on credit) is office money.
- Money received for disbursements anticipated but not yet incurred is a payment on account, and is therefore client money.

(iii) The option in rule 19(1)(a) allows a solicitor to place all payments in the correct account in the first instance. The option in rule 19(1)(b) allows the prompt banking into an office account of an invoice payment when the only uncertainty is whether or not the payment includes some client money in the form of unpaid professional disbursements. The option in rule 19(1)(c) allows the prompt banking into a client account of any invoice payment in advance of determining whether the payment is a mixture of office and client money (of whatever description) or is only office money.

(iv) A solicitor who is not in a position to comply with the requirements of rule 19 (1)(b) cannot take advantage of that option.

(v) The option in rule 19(1)(b) cannot be used if the money received includes a payment on account – for example, a payment for a professional disbursement anticipated but not yet incurred.

(vi) In order to be able to use the option in rule 19(1)(b) for electronic payments or other direct transfers from clients, a solicitor may choose to establish a system whereby clients are given an office account number for payment of costs. The system must be capable of ensuring that, when invoices are sent to the client, no request is made for any client money, with the sole exception of money for professional disbursements already incurred but not yet paid.

(vii) Rule 19(1)(c) allows clients to be given a single account number for making direct payments by electronic or other means – under this option, it has to be a client account.

(viii) A solicitor will not be in breach of rule 19 as a result of a misdirected electronic payment or other direct transfer, provided:

(A) appropriate systems are in place to ensure compliance;

(B) appropriate instructions were given to the client;

(C) the client's mistake is remedied promptly upon discovery; and

(D) appropriate steps are taken to avoid future errors by the client.

(ix) 'Properly' in rule 19(2) implies that the work has actually been done, whether at the end of the matter or at an interim stage, and that the solicitor is entitled to appropriate the money for costs.

(x) Costs transferred out of a client account in accordance with rule 19(2) and (3) must be specific sums relating to the bill or other written notification of costs, and covered by the amount held for the particular client or controlled trust. Round sum withdrawals on account of costs will be a breach of the rules.

(xi) In the case of a controlled trust, the paying party will be the controlled trustee(s) themselves. The solicitor must keep the original bill or notification of costs on the file, in addition to complying with rule 32(8) (central record or file of copy bills, etc.).

(xii) Undrawn costs must not remain in a client account as a 'cushion' against any future errors which could result in a shortage on that account, and cannot be regarded as available to set off against any general shortage on client account.

(xiii) The rules do not require a bill of costs for an agreed fee, although a solicitor's VAT position may mean that in practice a bill is needed. If there is no bill, the written evidence of the agreement must be filed as a written notification of costs under rule 32(8)(b).

### Rule 20 – Receipt of mixed payments

(1) A 'mixed payment' is one which includes client money or controlled trust money as well as office money.

(2) A mixed payment must either:

(a) be split between a client account and office account as appropriate; or

(b) be placed without delay in a client account.

(3) If the entire payment is placed in a client account, all office money must be transferred out of the client account within 14 days of receipt.

(4) See rule 19(1)(b) and (c) for additional ways of dealing with (among other things) mixed payments received in response to a bill or other notification of costs.

(5) See rule 21(1)(b) for (among other things) mixed payments received from the Legal Services Commission.

**Note**

'Without delay' is defined in rule 2(2)(z).

## Rule 21 – Treatment of payments to legal aid practitioners

**Payments from the Legal Services Commission**

(1) Two special dispensations apply to payments (other than regular payments) from the Legal Services Commission:

(a) An advance payment in anticipation of work to be carried out, although client money, may be placed in an office account, provided the Commission instructs in writing that this may be done.

(b) A payment for costs (interim and/or final) may be paid into an office account at a bank or building society branch (or head office) in England and Wales, regardless of whether it consists wholly of office money, or is mixed with client money in the form of:

(i) advance payments for fees or disbursements; or

(ii) money for unpaid professional disbursements;

provided all money for payment of disbursements is transferred to a client account (or the disbursements paid) within 14 days of receipt.

(2) The following provisions apply to regular payments from the Legal Services Commission:

(a) 'Regular payments' (which are office money) are:

(i) standard monthly payments paid by the Commission under the civil legal aid contracting arrangements;

(ii) monthly payments paid by the Commission under the criminal legal aid contracting arrangements; and

(iii) any other payments for work done or to be done received from the Commission under an arrangement for payments on a regular basis.

(b) Regular payments must be paid into an office account at a bank or building society branch (or head office) in England and Wales.

(c) A solicitor must within 28 days of submitting a report to the Commission, notifying completion of a matter, either:

(i) pay any unpaid professional disbursement(s), or

(ii) transfer to a client account a sum equivalent to the amount of any unpaid professional disbursement(s),

relating to that matter.

(d) In cases where the Commission permits solicitors to submit reports at various stages during a matter rather than only at the end of a matter, the requirement in paragraph (c) above applies to any unpaid professional disbursement(s) included in each report so submitted.

**Payments from a third party**

(3) If the Legal Services Commission has paid any costs to a solicitor or a previously nominated solicitor in a matter (advice and assistance or legal help costs, advance payments or interim costs), or has paid professional disbursements direct, and costs are subsequently settled by a third party:

(a) The entire third party payment must be paid into a client account.

(b) A sum representing the payments made by the Commission must be retained in the client account.

(c) Any balance belonging to the solicitor must be transferred to an office account within 14 days of the solicitor sending a report to the Commission containing details of the third party payment.

(d) The sum retained in the client account as representing payments made by the Commission must be:

(i) either recorded in the individual client's ledger account, and identified as the Commission's money;

(ii) or recorded in a ledger account in the Commission's name, and identified by reference to the client or matter;

and kept in the client account until notification from the Commission that it has recouped an equivalent sum from subsequent payments due to the solicitor. The retained sum must be transferred to an office account within 14 days of notification.

**Notes**

(i) This rule deals with matters which specifically affect legal aid practitioners. It should not be read in isolation from the remainder of the rules which apply to all solicitors, including legal aid practitioners.

(ii) Franchised firms can apply for advance payments on the issue of a certificate. The Legal Services Commission has issued instructions that these payments may be placed in office account. For regular payments, see notes (vii)-(x) below.

(iii) Rule 21(1)(b) deals with the specific problems of legal aid practitioners by allowing a mixed or indeterminate payment of costs (or even a payment consisting entirely of unpaid professional disbursements) to be paid into an office account, which for the purpose of rule 21(1)(b) must be an account at a bank or building society. However, it is always open to the solicitor to comply with rule 19(1)(a) to (c), which are the options for all solicitors for the receipt of costs. For regular payments, see notes (vii) – (x) below.

(iv) Solicitors are required by the Legal Services Commission to report promptly to the Commission on receipt of costs from a third party. It is advisable to keep a copy of the report on the file as proof of compliance with the Commission's requirements, as well as to demonstrate compliance with the rule.

(v) A third party payment may also include unpaid professional disbursements or outstanding costs of the client's previous solicitor. This part of the payment is client money and must be kept in a client account until the solicitor pays the professional disbursement or outstanding costs.

(vi) In rule 21, and elsewhere in the rules, references to the Legal Services Commission are to be read, where appropriate, as including the Legal Aid Board.

(vii) Regular payments are office money and are defined as such in the rules (rule 13, note (xi)(e)). They are neither advance payments nor payments of costs for the purposes of the rules. Regular payments must be paid into an office account which for the purpose of rule 21(2)(b) must be an account at a bank or building society.

(viii) Firms in receipt of regular payments must deal with unpaid professional disbursements in the way prescribed by rule 21(2)(c). The rule permits a solicitor who is required to transfer an amount to cover unpaid professional disbursements into a client account to make the transfer from his or her own resources if the regular payments are insufficient.

(ix) The 28 day time limit for paying, or transferring an amount to a client account for, unpaid professional disbursements is for the purposes of these rules only. An earlier deadline may be imposed by contract with the

Commission or with counsel, agents or experts. On the other hand, a solicitor may have agreed to pay later than 28 days from the submission of the report notifying completion of a matter, in which case rule 21(2)(c) will require a transfer of the appropriate amount to a client account (but not payment) within 28 days. Solicitors are reminded of their professional obligation to pay the fees of counsel, agents and experts.

(x) For the appropriate accounting records for regular payments, see note (v) to rule 32.

### Rule 22 – Withdrawals from a client account

(1) Client money may only be withdrawn from a client account when it is:

- (a) properly required for a payment to or on behalf of the client (or other person on whose behalf the money is being held);
- (b) properly required for payment of a disbursement on behalf of the client;
- (c) properly required in full or partial reimbursement of money spent by the solicitor on behalf of the client;
- (d) transferred to another client account;
- (e) withdrawn on the client's instructions, provided the instructions are for the client's convenience and are given in writing, or are given by other means and confirmed by the solicitor to the client in writing;
- (f) a refund to the solicitor of an advance no longer required to fund a payment on behalf of a client (see rule 15(2)(b));
- (g) money which has been paid into the account in breach of the rules (for example, money paid into the wrong separate designated client account) – see paragraph (4) below; or
- (h) money not covered by (a) to (g) above, withdrawn from the account on the written authorisation of the Society. The Society may impose a condition that the solicitor pay the money to a charity which gives an indemnity against any legitimate claim subsequently made for the sum received.

(2) Controlled trust money may only be withdrawn from a client account when it is:

- (a) properly required for a payment in the execution of the particular trust, including the purchase of an investment (other than money) in accordance with the trustee's powers;
- (b) properly required for payment of a disbursement for the particular trust;
- (c) properly required in full or partial reimbursement of money spent by the solicitor on behalf of the particular trust;
- (d) transferred to another client account;
- (e) transferred to an account other than a client account (such as an account outside England and Wales), but only if the trustee's powers permit, or to be properly retained in cash in the performance of the trustee's duties;
- (f) a refund to the solicitor of an advance no longer required to fund a payment on behalf of a controlled trust (see rule 15(2)(b));
- (g) money which has been paid into the account in breach of the rules (for example, money paid into the wrong separate designated client account) – see paragraph (4) below; or

(h) money not covered by (a) to (g) above, withdrawn from the account on the written authorisation of the Society. The Society may impose a condition that the solicitor pay the money to a charity which gives an indemnity against any legitimate claim subsequently made for the sum received.

(3) Office money may only be withdrawn from a client account when it is:

(a) money properly paid into the account to open or maintain it under rule 15(2)(a);

(b) properly required for payment of the solicitor's costs under rule 19(2) and (3);

(c) the whole or part of a payment into a client account under rule 19(1)(c);

(d) part of a mixed payment placed in a client account under rule 20(2)(b); or

(e) money which has been paid into a client account in breach of the rules (for example, interest wrongly credited to a general client account) – see paragraph (4) below.

(4) Money which has been paid into a client account in breach of the rules must be withdrawn from the client account promptly upon discovery.

(5) Money withdrawn in relation to a particular client or controlled trust from a general client account must not exceed the money held on behalf of that client or controlled trust in all the solicitor's general client accounts (except as provided in paragraph (6) below).

(6) A solicitor may make a payment in respect of a particular client or controlled trust out of a general client account, even if no money (or insufficient money) is held for that client or controlled trust in the solicitor's general client account(s), provided:

(a) sufficient money is held for that client or controlled trust in a separate designated client account; and

(b) the appropriate transfer from the separate designated client account to a general client account is made immediately.

(7) Money held for a client or controlled trust in a separate designated client account must not be used for payments for another client or controlled trust.

(8) A client account must not be overdrawn, except in the following circumstances:

(a) A separate designated client account for a controlled trust can be overdrawn if the controlled trustee makes payments on behalf of the trust (for example, inheritance tax) before realising sufficient assets to cover the payments.

(b) If a sole practitioner dies and his or her client accounts are frozen, the solicitor-manager can operate client accounts which are overdrawn to the extent of the money held in the frozen accounts.

### Notes

### Withdrawals in favour of solicitor, and for payment of disbursements

(i) Disbursements to be paid direct from a client account, or already paid out of the solicitor's own money, can be withdrawn under rule 22(1)(b) or (c) (or rule 22(2)(b) or (c)) in advance of preparing a bill of costs. Money to be withdrawn from a client account for the payment of costs (fees and disbursements) under rule 19(2) and (3) becomes office money and is dealt with under rule 22(3)(b).

(ii) Money is 'spent' under rule 22(1)(c) (or rule 22(2)(c)) at the time when the solicitor despatches a cheque, unless the cheque is to be held to the solicitor's order. Money is also regarded as 'spent' by the use of a credit account, so that, for example, search fees, taxi fares and courier charges incurred in this way may be transferred to the solicitor's office account.

(iii) See rule 23(3) for the way in which a withdrawal from a client account in favour of the solicitor must be effected.

**Cheques payable to banks, building societies, etc.**

(iv) In order to protect clients' funds (or controlled trust funds) against misappropriation when cheques are made payable to banks, building societies or other large institutions, it is strongly recommended that solicitors add the name and number of the account after the payee's name.

**Drawing against uncleared cheques**

(v) A solicitor should use discretion in drawing against a cheque received from or on behalf of a client before it has been cleared. If the cheque is not met, other clients' money will have been used to make the payment in breach of the rules. See rule 7 (duty to remedy breaches). A solicitor may be able to avoid a breach of the rules by instructing the bank or building society to charge all unpaid credits to the solicitor's office or personal account.

**Non-receipt of telegraphic transfer**

(vi) If a solicitor acting for a client withdraws money from a general client account on the strength of information that a telegraphic transfer is on its way, but the telegraphic transfer does not arrive, the solicitor will have used other clients' money in breach of the rules. See also rule 7 (duty to remedy breaches).

**Withdrawals on instructions**

(vii) One of the reasons why a client might authorise a withdrawal under rule 22 (1)(e) might be to have the money transferred to a type of account other than a client account. If so, the requirements of rule 16 must be complied with.

**Withdrawals on the Society's authorisation**

(viii) Applications for authorisation under rule 22(1)(h) or 22(2)(h) should be made to the Professional Ethics Division, who can advise on the criteria which must normally be met for authorisation to be given.

(ix) After a practice has been wound up, banks sometimes discover unclaimed balances in an old client account. This money remains subject to rule 22 and rule 23. An application can be made to the Society under rule 22(1)(h) or 22(2) (h).

## Rule 23 – Method of and authority for withdrawals from client account

(1) A withdrawal from a client account may be made only after a specific authority in respect of that withdrawal has been signed by at least one of the following:

(a) a solicitor who holds a current practising certificate or a registered European lawyer;

(b) a Fellow of the Institute of Legal Executives of at least three years standing who is employed by such a solicitor, a registered European lawyer or a recognised body;

(c) in the case of an office dealing solely with conveyancing, a licensed conveyancer who is employed by such a solicitor, a registered European lawyer or a recognised body; or

(d) a registered foreign lawyer who is a partner in the practice, or who is a director of the practice (if it is a company), or who is a member of the practice (if it is a limited liability partnership).

(2) There is no need to comply with paragraph (1) above when transferring money from one general client account to another general client account at the same bank or building society.

(3) A withdrawal from a client account in favour of the solicitor or the practice must be either by way of a cheque to the solicitor or practice, or by way of a transfer to the office account or to the solicitor's personal account. The withdrawal must not be made in cash.

**Notes**

(i) Instructions to the bank or building society to withdraw money from a client account (rule 23(1)) may be given over the telephone, provided a specific authority has been signed in accordance with this rule before the instructions are given. If a solicitor decides to take advantage of this arrangement, it is of paramount importance that the scheme has appropriate in-built safeguards, such as passwords, to give the greatest protection possible for client money (or controlled trust money). Suitable safeguards will also be needed for practices which operate a CHAPS terminal.

(ii) In the case of a withdrawal by cheque, the specific authority (rule 23(1)) is usually a signature on the cheque itself. Signing a blank cheque is not a specific authority.

(iii) A withdrawal from a client account by way of a private loan from one client to another can only be made if the provisions of rule 30(2) are complied with.

(iv) It is advisable that a withdrawal for payment to or on behalf of a client (or on behalf of a controlled trust) be made by way of a crossed cheque whenever possible.

(v) Controlled trustees who instruct an outside manager to run, or continue to run, on a day to day basis, the business or property portfolio of an estate or trust will not need to comply with rule 23(1), provided all cheques are retained in accordance with rule 32(10). (See also rule 32, note (ii)(d).)

(vi) Where the sum due to the client is sufficiently large, the solicitor should consider whether it should not appropriately be transferred to the client by direct bank transfer. For doing this, the solicitor would be entitled to make a modest administrative charge in addition to any charge made by the bank in connection with the transfer.

## PART C – INTEREST

### Rule 24 – When interest must be paid

(1) When a solicitor holds money in a separate designated client account for a client, or for a person funding all or part of the solicitor's fees, the solicitor

must account to the client or that person for all interest earned on the account.

(2) When a solicitor holds money in a general client account for a client, or for a person funding all or part of the solicitor's fees (or if money should have been held for a client or such other person in a client account but was not), the solicitor must account to the client or that person for a sum in lieu of interest calculated in accordance with rule 25.

(3) A solicitor is not required to pay a sum in lieu of interest under paragraph (2) above:

(a) if the amount calculated is £20 or less;

(b) (i) if the solicitor holds a sum of money not exceeding the amount shown in the left hand column below for a time not exceeding the period indicated in the right hand column:

| Amount | Time |
| --- | --- |
| £1,000 | 8 weeks |
| £2,000 | 4 weeks |
| £10,000 | 2 weeks |
| £20,000 | 1 week |

(ii) if the solicitor holds a sum of money exceeding £20,000 for one week or less, unless it is fair and reasonable to account for a sum in lieu of interest having regard to all the circumstances;

(c) on money held for the payment of counsel's fees, once counsel has requested a delay in settlement;

(d) on money held for the Legal Services Commission;

(e) on an advance from the solicitor under rule 15(2)(b) to fund a payment on behalf of the client in excess of funds held for that client; or

(f) if there is an agreement to contract out of the provisions of this rule under rule 27.

(4) If sums of money are held intermittently during the course of acting, and the sum in lieu of interest calculated under rule 25 for any period is £20 or less, a sum in lieu of interest should still be paid if it is fair and reasonable in the circumstances to aggregate the sums in respect of the individual periods.

(5) If money is held for a continuous period, and for part of that period it is held in a separate designated client account, the sum in lieu of interest for the rest of the period when the money was held in a general client account may as a result be £20 or less. A sum in lieu of interest should, however, be paid if it is fair and reasonable in the circumstances to do so.

(6) (a) If a solicitor holds money for a client (or person funding all or part of the solicitor's fees) in an account opened on the instructions of the client (or that person) under rule 16(1)(a), the solicitor must account to the client (or that person) for all interest earned on the account.

(b) If a solicitor has failed to comply with instructions to open an account under rule 16(1)(a), the solicitor must account to the client (or the person funding all or part of the solicitor's fees) for a sum in lieu of any net loss of interest suffered by the client (or that person) as a result.

(7) This rule does not apply to controlled trust money.

## Notes

### Requirement to pay interest

(i) The whole of the interest earned on a separate designated client account must be credited to the account. However, the obligation to pay a sum in lieu of interest for amounts held in a general client account is subject to the de minimis provisions in rule 24(3)(a) and (b). Section 33(3) of the Solicitors Act 1974 permits solicitors to retain any interest earned on client money held in a general client account over and above that which they have to pay under these rules. (See also note (viii) to rule 15 on aggregation of accounts.)

(ii) There is no requirement to pay a sum in lieu of interest on money held on instructions under rule 16(1)(a) in a manner which attracts no interest.

(iii) Accounts opened in the client's name under rule 16(1)(b) (whether operated by the solicitor or not) are not subject to rule 24, as the money is not held by the solicitor. All interest earned belongs to the client. The same applies to any account in the client's own name operated by the solicitor as signatory under rule 11.

(iv) Money subject to a trust which is not a controlled trust is client money (see rule 13, note (vii)), and rule 24 therefore applies to it.

### De minimis provisions (rule 24(3)(a) and (b))

(v) The sum in lieu of interest is calculated over the whole period for which money is held (see rule 25(2)); if this sum is £20 or less, the solicitor need not account to the client. If sums of money are held in relation to separate matters for the same client, it is normally appropriate to treat the money relating to the different matters separately, so that, if any of the sums calculated is £20 or less, no sum in lieu of interest is payable. There will, however, be cases when the matters are so closely related that they ought to be considered together – for example, when a solicitor is acting for a client in connection with numerous debt collection matters.

### Administrative charges

(vi) It is not improper to charge a reasonable fee for the handling of client money when the service provided is out of the ordinary.

### Unpresented cheques

(vii) A client may fail to present a cheque to his or her bank for payment. Whether or not it is reasonable to recalculate the amount due will depend on all the circumstances of the case. A reasonable charge may be made for any extra work carried out if the solicitor is legally entitled to make such a charge.

### Liquidators, trustees in bankruptcy, Court of Protection receivers and trustees of occupational pension schemes

(viii) Under rule 9, Part C of the rules does not normally apply to solicitors who are liquidators, etc. Solicitors must comply with the appropriate statutory rules and regulations, and rules 9(3) and (4) as appropriate.

### Joint accounts

(ix) Under rule 10, Part C of the rules does not apply to joint accounts. If a solicitor holds money jointly with a client, interest earned on the account will be for the benefit of the client unless otherwise agreed. If money is held jointly with another solicitors' practice, the allocation of interest earned will depend on the agreement reached.

**Requirements for controlled trust money (rule 24(7))**

(x) Part C does not apply to controlled trust money. Under the general law, trustees of a controlled trust must account for all interest earned. For the treatment of interest on controlled trust money in a general client account, see rule 13, note (xi)(b), rule 15(2)(d) and note (vi) to rule 15. (See also note (viii) to rule 15 on aggregation of accounts.)

### Rule 25 – Amount of interest

(1) Solicitors must aim to obtain a reasonable rate of interest on money held in a separate designated client account, and must account for a fair sum in lieu of interest on money held in a general client account (or on money which should have been held in a client account but was not). The sum in lieu of interest need not necessarily reflect the highest rate of interest obtainable but it is not acceptable to look only at the lowest rate of interest obtainable.

(2) The sum in lieu of interest for money held in a general client account (or on money which should have been held in a client account but was not) must be calculated

- on the balance or balances held over the whole period for which cleared funds are held
- at a rate not less than (whichever is the higher of) the following
  - (i) the rate of interest payable on a separate designated client account for the amount or amounts held, or
  - (ii) the rate of interest payable on the relevant amount or amounts if placed on deposit on similar terms by a member of the business community
- at the bank or building society where the money is held.

(3) If the money, or part of it, is held successively or concurrently in accounts at different banks or building societies, the relevant bank or building society for the purpose of paragraph (2) will be whichever of those banks or building societies offered the best rate on the date when the money was first held.

(4) If, contrary to the rules, the money is not held in a client account, the relevant bank or building society for the purpose of paragraph (2) will be a clearing bank or building society nominated by the client (or other person on whose behalf client money is held).

**Notes**

(i) The sum in lieu of interest has to be calculated over the whole period for which money is held – see rule 25(2). The solicitor will usually account to the client at the conclusion of the client's matter, but might in some cases consider it appropriate to account to the client at intervals throughout.

(ii) When looking at the period over which the sum in lieu of interest must be calculated, it will usually be unnecessary to check on actual clearance dates. When money is received by cheque and paid out by cheque, the normal clearance periods will usually cancel each other out, so that it will be satisfactory to look at the period between the dates when the incoming cheque is banked and the outgoing cheque is drawn.

(iii) Different considerations apply when payments in and out are not both made by cheque. So, for example, the relevant periods would normally be:
- from the date when a solicitor receives incoming money in cash until the date when the outgoing cheque is sent;
- from the date when an incoming telegraphic transfer begins to earn interest until the date when the outgoing cheque is sent;
- from the date when an incoming cheque or banker's draft is or would normally be cleared until the date when the outgoing telegraphic transfer is made or banker's draft is obtained.

(iv) The sum in lieu of interest is calculated by reference to the rates paid by the appropriate bank or building society (see rule 25(2) to (4)). Solicitors will therefore follow the practice of that bank or building society in determining how often interest is compounded over the period for which the cleared funds are held.

(v) Money held in a client account must be immediately available, even at the sacrifice of interest, unless the client otherwise instructs, or the circumstances clearly indicate otherwise. The need for access can be taken into account in assessing the appropriate rate for calculating the sum to be paid in lieu of interest, or in assessing whether a reasonable rate of interest has been obtained for a separate designated client account.

### Rule 26 – Interest on stakeholder money

When a solicitor holds money as stakeholder, the solicitor must pay interest, or a sum in lieu of interest, on the basis set out in rule 24 to the person to whom the stake is paid.

**Note**

For contracting out of this provision, see rule 27(2) and the notes to rule 27.

### Rule 27 – Contracting out

(1) In appropriate circumstances a client and his or her solicitor may by a written agreement come to a different arrangement as to the matters dealt with in rule 24 (payment of interest).

(2) A solicitor acting as stakeholder may, by a written agreement with his or her own client and the other party to the transaction, come to a different arrangement as to the matters dealt with in rule 24.

**Notes**

(i) Solicitors should act fairly towards their clients and provide sufficient information to enable them to give informed consent if it is felt appropriate to depart from the interest provisions. Whether it is appropriate to contract out depends on all the circumstances, for example, the size of the sum involved or the nature or status or bargaining position of the client. It might, for instance, be appropriate to contract out by standard terms of business if the client is a substantial commercial entity and the interest involved is modest in relation to the size of the transaction. The larger the sum of interest involved, the more there would be an onus on the solicitor to show that a client who had accepted a contracting out provision was properly informed and had been treated fairly. Contracting out is never appropriate if it is against the client's interests.

(ii) In principle, a solicitor-stakeholder is entitled to make a reasonable charge to the client for acting as stakeholder in the client's matter.

(iii) Alternatively, it may be appropriate to include a special provision in the contract that the solicitor-stakeholder retains the interest on the deposit to cover his or her charges for acting as stakeholder. This is only acceptable if it will provide a fair and reasonable payment for the work and risk involved in holding a stake. The contract could stipulate a maximum charge, with any interest earned above that figure being paid to the recipient of the stake.

(iv) Any right to charge the client, or to stipulate for a charge which may fall on the client, would be excluded by, for instance, a prior agreement with the client for a fixed fee for the client's matter, or for an estimated fee which cannot be varied upwards in the absence of special circumstances. It is therefore not normal practice for a stakeholder in conveyancing transactions to receive a separate payment for holding the stake.

(v) A solicitor-stakeholder who seeks an agreement to exclude the operation of rule 26 should be particularly careful not to take unfair advantage either of the client, or of the other party if unrepresented.

### Rule 28 – Interest certificates

**Without prejudice to any other remedy:**

(a) any client, including one of joint clients, or a person funding all or part of a solicitor's fees, may apply to the Society for a certificate as to whether or not interest, or a sum in lieu of interest, should have been paid and, if so, the amount; and

(b) if the Society certifies that interest, or a sum in lieu of interest, should have been paid, the solicitor must pay the certified sum.

**Notes**

(i) Applications for an interest certificate should be made to the Law Society's Consumer Complaints Service. It is advisable for the client (or other person) to try to resolve the matter with the solicitor before approaching the Consumer Complaints Service.

(ii) If appropriate, the Law Society will require the solicitor to obtain an interest calculation from the relevant bank or building society.

## PART D – ACCOUNTING SYSTEMS AND RECORDS

### Rule 29 – Guidelines for accounting procedures and systems

The Council of the Law Society, with the concurrence of the Master of the Rolls, may from time to time publish guidelines for accounting procedures and systems to assist solicitors to comply with Parts A to D of the rules, and solicitors may be required to justify any departure from the guidelines.

**Notes**

(i) The current guidelines appear at Appendix 3.

(ii) The reporting accountant does not carry out a detailed check for compliance, but has a duty to report on any substantial departures from the guidelines discovered whilst carrying out work in preparation of his or her report (see rules 43 and 44(e)).

### Rule 30 – Restrictions on transfers between clients

(1) A paper transfer of money held in a general client account from the ledger of one client to the ledger of another client may only be made if:

(a) it would have been permissible to withdraw that sum from the account under rule 22(1); and

(b) it would have been permissible to pay that sum into the account under rule 15;

(but there is no requirement in the case of a paper transfer for the written authority of a solicitor, etc., under rule 23(1)).

(2) No sum in respect of a private loan from one client to another can be paid out of funds held for the lender either:

(a) by a payment from one client account to another;

(b) by a paper transfer from the ledger of the lender to that of the borrower; or

(c) to the borrower directly,

except with the prior written authority of both clients.

**Notes**

(i) 'Private loan' means a loan other than one provided by an institution which provides loans on standard terms in the normal course of its activities – rule 30(2) does not apply to loans made by an institutional lender. See also practice rule 6, which prohibits a solicitor from acting for both lender and borrower in a private mortgage at arm's length.

(ii) If the loan is to be made by (or to) joint clients, the consent of each client must be obtained.

## Rule 31 – Recognised bodies

(1) If a solicitors' practice owns all the shares in a recognised body which is an executor, trustee or nominee company, the practice and the recognised body must not operate shared client accounts, but may:

(a) use one set of accounting records for money held, received or paid by the practice and the recognised body; and/or

(b) deliver a single accountant's report for both the practice and the recognised body.

(2) If a recognised body as nominee receives a dividend cheque made out to the recognised body, and forwards the cheque, either endorsed or subject to equivalent instructions, to the share-owner's bank or building society, etc., the recognised body will have received (and paid) controlled trust money. One way of complying with rule 32 (accounting records) is to keep a copy of the letter to the share-owner's bank or building society, etc., on the file, and, in accordance with rule 32(14), to keep another copy in a central book of such letters. (See also rule 32(9)(f) (retention of records for six years).)

**Notes**

(i) Rule 31(1) applies equally to a recognised body owned by a sole practitioner, or by a multi-national partnership, or indeed by another recognised body.

(ii) If a recognised body holds or receives money as executor, trustee or nominee, it is a controlled trustee.

## Rule 32 – Accounting records for client accounts, etc.

### Accounting records which must be kept

(1) A solicitor must at all times keep accounting records properly written up to show the solicitor's dealings with:

(a) client money received, held or paid by the solicitor; including client money held outside a client account under rule 16(1)(a);

(b) controlled trust money received, held or paid by the solicitor; including controlled trust money held under rule 18(c) in accordance with the trustee's powers in an account which is not a client account; and

(c) any office money relating to any client matter, or to any controlled trust matter.

(2) All dealings with client money (whether for a client or other person), and with any controlled trust money, must be appropriately recorded:

(a) in a client cash account or in a record of sums transferred from one client ledger account to another; and

(b) on the client side of a separate client ledger account for each client (or other person, or controlled trust).

No other entries may be made in these records.

(3) If separate designated client accounts are used:

(a) a combined cash account must be kept in order to show the total amount held in separate designated client accounts; and

(b) a record of the amount held for each client (or other person, or controlled trust) must be made either in a deposit column of a client ledger account, or on the client side of a client ledger account kept specifically for a separate designated client account, for each client (or other person, or controlled trust).

(4) All dealings with office money relating to any client matter, or to any controlled trust matter, must be appropriately recorded in an office cash account and on the office side of the appropriate client ledger account.

**Current balance**

(5) The current balance on each client ledger account must always be shown, or be readily ascertainable, from the records kept in accordance with paragraphs (2) and (3) above.

**Acting for both lender and borrower**

(6) When acting for both lender and borrower on a mortgage advance, separate client ledger accounts for both clients need not be opened, provided that:

(a) the funds belonging to each client are clearly identifiable; and

(b) the lender is an institutional lender which provides mortgages on standard terms in the normal course of its activities.

**Reconciliations**

(7) The solicitor must, at least once every fourteen weeks for controlled trust money held in passbook-operated separate designated client accounts, and at least once every five weeks in all other cases:

(a) compare the balance on the client cash account(s) with the balances shown on the statements and passbooks (after allowing for all unpresented items) of all general client accounts and separate designated client accounts, and of any account which is not a client account but in which the solicitor holds client money under rule 16(1)(a) (or controlled trust money under rule 18(c)), and any client money (or controlled trust money) held by the solicitor in cash; and

(b) as at the same date prepare a listing of all the balances shown by the client ledger accounts of the liabilities to clients (and other persons, and controlled trusts) and compare the total of those balances with the balance on the client cash account; and also

(c) prepare a reconciliation statement; this statement must show the cause of the difference, if any, shown by each of the above comparisons.

**Bills and notifications of costs**

(8) The solicitor must keep readily accessible a central record or file of copies of:

(a) all bills given or sent by the solicitor; and

(b) all other written notifications of costs given or sent by the solicitor;

in both cases distinguishing between fees, disbursements not yet paid at the date of the bill, and paid disbursements.

**Retention of records**

(9) The solicitor must retain for at least six years from the date of the last entry:

(a) all documents or other records required by paragraphs (1) to (8) above;

(b) all statements and passbooks, as printed and issued by the bank, building society or other financial institution, and/or all duplicate statements and copies of passbook entries permitted in lieu of the originals by rule 10(3) or (4), for:

(i) any general client account or separate designated client account;

(ii) any joint account held under rule 10;

(iii) any account which is not a client account but in which the solicitor holds client money under rule 16(1)(a);

(iv) any account which is not a client account but in which controlled trust money is held under rule 18(c); and

(v) any office account maintained in relation to the practice;

(c) any records kept under rule 9 (liquidators, trustees in bankruptcy, Court of Protection receivers and trustees of occupational pension schemes) including, as printed or otherwise issued, any statements, passbooks and other accounting records originating outside the solicitor's office;

(d) any written instructions to withhold client money from a client account (or a copy of the solicitor's confirmation of oral instructions) in accordance with rule 16;

(e) any central registers kept under paragraphs (11) to (13) below; and

(f) any copy letters kept centrally under rule 31(2) (dividend cheques endorsed over by recognised body).

(10) The solicitor must retain for at least two years:

(a) originals or copies of all authorities, other than cheques, for the withdrawal of money from a client account; and

(b) all original paid cheques (or digital images of the front and back of all original paid cheques), unless there is a written arrangement with the bank, building society or other financial institution that:

(i) it will retain the original cheques on the solicitor's behalf for that period; or

(ii) in the event of destruction of any original cheques, it will retain digital images of the front and back of those cheques on the solicitor's behalf for that period and will, on demand by the solicitor, the solicitor's reporting accountant or the Society, produce copies of the digital images accompanied, when requested, by a certificate of verification signed by an authorised officer.

**Centrally kept records for certain accounts, etc.**

(11) Statements and passbooks for client money or controlled trust money held outside a client account under rule 16(1)(a) or rule 18(c) must be kept together centrally, or the solicitor must maintain a central register of these accounts.

(12) Any records kept under rule 9 (liquidators, trustees in bankruptcy, Court of Protection receivers and trustees of occupational pension schemes) must be kept together centrally, or the solicitor must maintain a central register of the appointments.

(13) The statements, passbooks, duplicate statements and copies of passbook entries relating to any joint account held under rule 10 must be kept together centrally, or the solicitor must maintain a central register of all joint accounts.

(14) If a recognised body as nominee follows the option in rule 31(2) (keeping instruction letters for dividend payments), a central book must be kept of all instruction letters to the share-owner's bank or building society, etc.

**Computerisation**

(15) Records required by this rule may be kept on a computerised system, apart from the following documents, which must be retained as printed or otherwise issued:

(a) original statements and passbooks retained under paragraph (9)(b) above;

(b) original statements, passbooks and other accounting records retained under paragraph (9)(c) above; and

(c) original cheques and copy authorities retained under paragraph (10) above.

There is no obligation to keep a hard copy of computerised records. However, if no hard copy is kept, the information recorded must be capable of being reproduced reasonably quickly in printed form for at least six years, or for at least two years in the case of digital images of paid cheques retained under paragraph (10) above.

**Suspense ledger accounts**

(16) Suspense client ledger accounts may be used only when the solicitor can justify their use; for instance, for temporary use on receipt of an unidentified payment, if time is needed to establish the nature of the payment or the identity of the client.

**Notes**

(i) It is strongly recommended that accounting records are written up at least weekly, even in the smallest practice, and daily in the case of larger firms.

(ii) Rule 32(1) to (6) (general record-keeping requirements) and rule 32(7) (reconciliations) do not apply to:

(a) solicitor liquidators, trustees in bankruptcy, Court of Protection receivers and trustees of occupational pension schemes operating in accordance with statutory rules or regulations under rule 9(1)(a);

(b) joint accounts operated under rule 10;

(c) a client's own account operated under rule 11, the record-keeping requirements for this type of account are set out in rule 33;

(d) controlled trustees who instruct an outside manager to run, or continue to run, on a day to day basis, the business or property portfolio of an estate or trust, provided the manager keeps and retains appropriate accounting records, which are available for inspection by the Society in accordance with rule 34. (See also note (v) to rule 23.)

(iii) When a cheque or draft is received on behalf of a client and is endorsed over, not passing through a client account, it must be recorded in the books of account as a receipt and payment on behalf of the client. The same applies to cash received and not deposited in a client account but paid out to or on behalf of a client. A cheque made payable to a client, which is forwarded to the client by the solicitor, is not client money and falls outside the rules, although it is advisable to record the action taken.

(iv) For the purpose of rule 32, money which has been paid into a client account under rule 19(1)(c) (receipt of costs), or under rule 20(2)(b) (mixed money), and for the time being remains in a client account, is to be treated as client money; it should be recorded on the client side of the client ledger account, but must be appropriately identified.

(v) For the purpose of rule 32, money which has been paid into an office account under rule 19(1)(b) (receipt of costs), rule 21(1)(a) (advance payments from the Legal Services Commission), or under rule 21(1)(b) (payment of costs from the Legal Services Commission), and for the time being remains in an office account without breaching the rules, is to be treated as office money. Money paid into an office account under rule 21(2)(b) (regular payments) is office money. All these payments should be recorded on the office side of the client ledger account (for the individual client or for the Legal Services Commission), and must be appropriately identified.

(vi) Some accounting systems do not retain a record of past daily balances. This does not put the solicitor in breach of rule 32(5).

(vii) 'Clearly identifiable' in rule 32(6) means that by looking at the ledger account the nature and owner of the mortgage advance are unambiguously stated. For example, if a mortgage advance of £100,000 is received from the ABC Building Society, the entry should be recorded as '£100,000, mortgage advance, ABC Building Society'. It is not enough to state that the money was received from the ABC Building Society without specifying the nature of the payment, or vice versa.

(viii) Although the solicitor does not open a separate ledger account for the lender, the mortgage advance credited to that account belongs to the lender, not to the borrower, until completion takes place. Improper removal of these mortgage funds from a client account would be a breach of rule 22.

(ix) Reconciliations should be carried out as they fall due, and in any event no later than the due date for the next reconciliation. In the case of a separate designated client account operated with a passbook, there is no need to ask the bank, building society or other financial institution for confirmation of the balance held. In the case of other separate designated client accounts, the solicitor should either obtain statements at least monthly, or should obtain written confirmation of the balance direct from the bank, building society or other financial institution. There is no requirement to check that interest has been credited since the last statement, or the last entry in the passbook.

(x) In making the comparisons under rule 32(7)(a) and (b), some solicitors use credits of one client against debits of another when checking total client liabilities. This is improper because it fails to show up the shortage.

(xi) The effect of rule 32(9)(b) is that the solicitor must ensure that the bank issues hard copy statements. Statements sent from the bank to its solicitor customer by means of electronic mail, even if capable of being printed off as hard copies, will not suffice.

(xii) Rule 32(9)(d) – retention of client's instructions to withhold money from a client account – does not require records to be kept centrally; however this may be prudent, to avoid losing the instructions if the file is passed to the client.

(xiii) A solicitor who holds client money (or controlled trust money) in a currency other than sterling should hold that money in a separate account for the appropriate currency. Separate books of account should be kept for that currency.

(xiv) The requirement to keep paid cheques under rule 32(10)(b) extends to all cheques drawn on a client account, or on an account in which client money is held outside a client account under rule 16(1)(a), or on an account in which controlled trust money is held outside a client account under rule 18(c).

(xv) Solicitors may enter into an arrangement whereby the bank keeps digital images of paid cheques in place of the originals. The bank should take an electronic image of the front and back of each cheque in black and white and agree to hold such images, and to make printed copies available on request, for at least two years. Alternatively, solicitors may take and keep their own digital images of paid cheques.

(xvi) Microfilmed copies of paid cheques are not acceptable for the purposes of rule 32(10)(b). If a bank is able to provide microfilmed copies only, the solicitor must obtain the original paid cheques from the bank and retain them for at least two years.

(xvii) Certificates of verification in relation to digital images of cheques may on occasion be required by the Society when exercising its investigative and enforcement powers. The reporting accountant will not need to ask for a certificate of verification but will be able to rely on the printed copy of the digital image as if it were the original.

### Rule 33 – Accounting records for clients' own accounts

(1) When a solicitor operates a client's own account as signatory under rule 11, the solicitor must retain, for at least six years from the date of the last entry, the statements or passbooks as printed and issued by the bank, building society or other financial institution, and/or the duplicate statements, copies of passbook entries and cheque details permitted in lieu of the originals by rule 11(3) or (4); and any central register kept under paragraph (2) below.

(2) The solicitor must either keep these records together centrally, or maintain a central register of the accounts operated under rule 11.

(3) If, when the solicitor ceases to operate the account, the client requests the original statements or passbooks, the solicitor must take photocopies and keep them in lieu of the originals.

(4) This rule applies only to solicitors in private practice.

**Note**

Solicitors should remember the requirements of rule 32(8) (central record of bills, etc.).

## PART E – MONITORING AND INVESTIGATION BY THE SOCIETY

### Rule 34 – Production of records

(1) Any solicitor must at the time and place fixed by the Society produce to any person appointed by the Society any records, papers, client and controlled trust matter files, financial accounts and other documents, and any other information, necessary to enable preparation of a report on compliance with the rules.

(2) A requirement for production under paragraph (1) above must be in writing, and left at or sent by registered post or recorded delivery to the most recent address held by the Society's Registration Department, or delivered by the Society's appointee. If sent through the post, receipt will be deemed 48 hours (excluding Saturdays, Sundays and Bank Holidays) after posting.

(3) Material kept electronically must be produced in the form required by the Society's appointee.

(4) The Society's appointee is entitled to seek verification from clients and staff, and from the banks, building societies and other financial institutions used by the solicitor. The solicitor must, if necessary, provide written permission for the information to be given.

(5) The Society's appointee is not entitled to take original documents away but must be provided with photocopies on request.

(6) A solicitor must be prepared to explain and justify any departures from the guidelines for accounting procedures and systems published by the Society (see rule 29).

(7) Any report made by the Society's appointee may, if appropriate, be sent to the Crown Prosecution Service or the Serious Fraud Office and/or used in proceedings before the Solicitors' Disciplinary Tribunal. In the case of a registered European lawyer or registered foreign lawyer, the report may also be sent to the competent authority in that lawyer's home state or states. In the case of a solicitor of the Supreme Court who is established in another state under the Establishment of Lawyers Directive 98/5/EC, the report may also be sent to the competent authority in the host state. The report may also be sent to any of the accountancy bodies set out in rule 37(1)(a) and/or taken into account by the Society in relation to a possible disqualification of a reporting accountant under rule 37(3).

(8) Without prejudice to paragraph (1) above, any solicitor must produce documents relating to any account kept by the solicitor at a bank or with a building society:

 (a) in connection with the solicitor's practice; or

 (b) in connection with any trust of which the solicitor is or formerly was a trustee,

 for inspection by a person appointed by the Society for the purpose of preparing a report on compliance with the rules or on whether the account has been used for or in connection with a breach of any other rules, codes or guidance made or issued by the Council of the Society. Paragraphs (2)-(7) above apply in relation to this paragraph in the same way as to paragraph (1).

**Notes**

(i) 'Solicitor' in rule 34 (as elsewhere in the rules) includes any person to whom the rules apply – see rule 2(2)(x), rule 4 and note (ii) to rule 4.

(ii) The Society's powers override any confidence or privilege between solicitor and client.

(iii) The Society's monitoring and investigation powers are exercised by Forensic Investigations (Compliance Directorate).

(iv) Reasons are never given for a visit by Forensic Investigations, so as:
   (a) to safeguard the Society's sources of information; and
   (b) not to alert a defaulting principal or employee to conceal or compound his or her misappropriations.

(v) Rule 34(8) does not apply to registered foreign lawyers in the absence of an order by the Lord Chancellor under section 89(5) of the Courts and Legal Services Act 1990. The Society can nevertheless exercise the powers under rule 34(8) in the case of a multi-national partnership, because the rule applies to those partners who are solicitors or registered European lawyers even though it does not apply to the registered foreign lawyers.

## PART F – ACCOUNTANTS' REPORTS

### Rule 35 – Delivery of accountants' reports

A solicitor of the Supreme Court, registered European lawyer, registered foreign lawyer or recognised body who or which has, at any time during an accounting period, held or received client money or controlled trust money, or operated a client's own account as signatory, must deliver to the Society an accountant's report for that accounting period within six months of the end of the accounting period. This duty extends to the directors of such a recognised body if it is a company, and to the members of such a recognised body if it is a limited liability partnership.

**Notes**

(i) Section 34 of the Solicitors Act 1974 requires every solicitor of the Supreme Court to deliver an accountant's report once in every twelve months ending 31st October, unless the Society is satisfied that this is unnecessary. This provision is applied to recognised bodies by the Administration of Justice Act 1985, Schedule 2, paragraph 5(1). The Courts and Legal Services Act 1990, Schedule 14, paragraph 8(1) imposes the same duty on registered foreign lawyers, and this provision is extended to registered European lawyers by the European Communities (Lawyer's Practice) Regulations 2000, Schedule 4, paragraph 5(2). In general, the Society is satisfied that no report is necessary when the rules do not require a report to be delivered, but this is without prejudice to the Society's overriding discretion. In addition, a condition imposed on a solicitor's practising certificate under section 12(4)(b) of the Solicitors Act 1974 may require the solicitor to deliver accountant's reports at more frequent intervals.

(ii) A solicitor who practises only in one or more of the ways set out in rule 5 is exempt from the rules, and therefore does not have to deliver an accountant's report.

(iii) The requirement in rule 35 for a registered foreign lawyer to deliver an accountant's report applies only to a registered foreign lawyer practising in partnership with a solicitor of the Supreme Court or registered European lawyer, or as a director of a recognised body which is a company, or as a member of a recognised body which is a limited liability partnership.

(iv) The form of report is dealt with in rule 47.

(v) When client money is held or received by a practice, the principals in the practice (including those held out as principals) will have held or received client money. A salaried partner whose name is included in the list of partners on a firm's letterhead, even if the name appears under a separate heading of 'salaried partners' or 'associate partners', has been held out as a principal.

(va) In the case of an incorporated practice, it is the company or limited liability partnership (i.e. the recognised body) which will have held or received client money. The recognised body and its directors (in the case of a company) or members (in the case of a limited liability partnership) will have the duty to deliver an accountant's report, although the directors or members will not usually have held client money.

(vi) Assistant solicitors and consultants do not normally hold client money. An assistant solicitor or consultant might be a signatory for a firm's client account, but this does not constitute holding or receiving client money. If a client or third party hands cash to an assistant solicitor or consultant, it is the sole principal or the partners (rather than the assistant solicitor or consultant) who are regarded as having received and held the money. In the case of a recognised body, whether a company or a limited liability partnership, it would be the recognised body itself which would be regarded as having held or received the money.

(vii) If, exceptionally, an assistant solicitor or consultant has a client account (for example, as a controlled trustee), or operates a client's own account as signatory, the assistant solicitor or consultant will have to deliver an accountant's report. The assistant solicitor or consultant can be included in the report of the practice, but must ensure that his or her name is added, and an explanation given.

(viii) A solicitor to whom a cheque or draft is made out, and who in the course of practice endorses it over to a client or employer, has received (and paid) client money. That solicitor will have to deliver an accountant's report, even if no other client money has been held or received.

(ix) When only a small number of transactions is undertaken or a small volume of client money is handled in an accounting period, a waiver of the obligation to deliver a report may sometimes be granted. Applications should be made to the Registration Department.

(x) If a solicitors' practice owns all the shares in a recognised body which is an executor, trustee or nominee company, the practice and the recognised body may deliver a single accountant's report (see rule 31(1)(b)).

## Rule 36 – Accounting periods

### The norm

(1) An 'accounting period' means the period for which the accounts of the solicitor are ordinarily made up, except that it must:

   (a) begin at the end of the previous accounting period; and

   (b) cover twelve months.

Paragraphs (2) to (5) below set out exceptions.

**First and resumed reports**

(2) For a solicitor who is under a duty to deliver his or her first report, the accounting period must begin on the date when the solicitor first held or received client money or controlled trust money (or operated a client's own account as signatory), and may cover less than twelve months.

(3) For a solicitor who is under a duty to deliver his or her first report after a break, the accounting period must begin on the date when the solicitor for the first time after the break held or received client money or controlled trust money (or operated a client's own account as signatory), and may cover less than twelve months.

**Change of accounting period**

(4) If a practice changes the period for which its accounts are made up (for example, on a merger, or simply for convenience), the accounting period immediately preceding the change may be shorter than twelve months, or longer than twelve months up to a maximum of 18 months, provided that the accounting period shall not be changed to a period longer than twelve months unless the Law Society receives written notice of the change before expiry of the deadline for delivery of the accountant's report which would have been expected on the basis of the firm's old accounting period.

**Final reports**

(5) A solicitor who for any reason stops holding or receiving client money or controlled trust money (and operating any client's own account as signatory) must deliver a final report. The accounting period must end on the date upon which the solicitor stopped holding or receiving client money or controlled trust money (and operating any client's own account as signatory), and may cover less than twelve months.

**Notes**

(i) In the case of solicitors joining or leaving a continuing partnership, any accountant's report for the practice as a whole will show the names and dates of the principals joining or leaving. For a solicitor who did not previously hold or receive client money, etc., and has become a principal in the firm, the report for the practice will represent, from the date of joining, the solicitor's first report for the purpose of rule 36(2). For a solicitor who was a principal in the firm and, on leaving, stops holding or receiving client money, etc., the report for the practice will represent, up to the date of leaving, the solicitor's final report for the purpose of rule 36(5) above.

(ii) When a partnership splits up, it is usually appropriate for the books to be made up as at the date of dissolution, and for an accountant's report to be delivered within six months of that date. If, however, the old partnership continues to hold or receive client money, etc., in connection with outstanding matters, accountant's reports will continue to be required for those matters; the books should then be made up on completion of the last of those matters and a report delivered within six months of that date. The same would be true for a sole practitioner winding up matters on retirement.

(iii) When a practice is being wound up, the solicitor may be left with money which is unattributable, or belongs to a client who cannot be traced. It may be appropriate to apply to the Society for authority to withdraw this money from the solicitor's client account – see rule 22(1)(h), rule 22(2)(h), and note (viii) to rule 22.

### Rule 37 – Qualifications for making a report

(1) A report must be prepared and signed by an accountant

(a) who is a member of:

(i) the Institute of Chartered Accountants in England and Wales;

(ii) the Institute of Chartered Accountants of Scotland;

(iii) the Association of Chartered Certified Accountants;

(iv) the Institute of Chartered Accountants in Ireland; or

(v) the Association of Authorised Public Accountants; and

(b) who is also:

(i) an individual who is a registered auditor within the terms of section 35(1)(a) of the Companies Act 1989; or

(ii) an employee of such an individual; or

(iii) a partner in or employee of a partnership which is a registered auditor within the terms of section 35(1)(a) of the Companies Act 1989; or

(iv) a director or employee of a company which is a registered auditor within the terms of section 35(1)(a) of the Companies Act 1989; or

(v) a member or employee of a limited liability partnership which is a registered auditor within the terms of section 35(1)(a) of the Companies Act 1989.

(2) An accountant is not qualified to make a report if:

(a) at any time between the beginning of the accounting period to which the report relates, and the completion of the report:

(i) he or she was a partner or employee, or an officer or employee (in the case of a company), or a member or employee (in the case of a limited liability partnership) in the practice to which the report relates; or

(ii) he or she was employed by the same non-solicitor employer as the solicitor for whom the report is being made; or

(b) he or she has been disqualified under paragraph (3) below and notice of disqualification has been given under paragraph (4) (and has not subsequently been withdrawn).

(3) The Society may disqualify an accountant from making any accountant's report if:

(a) the accountant has been found guilty by his or her professional body of professional misconduct or discreditable conduct; or

(b) the Society is satisfied that a solicitor has not complied with the rules in respect of matters which the accountant has negligently failed to specify in a report.

In coming to a decision, the Society will take into account any representations made by the accountant or his or her professional body.

(4) Written notice of disqualification must be left at or sent by registered post or recorded delivery to the address of the accountant shown on an accountant's report or in the records of the accountant's professional body. If sent through the post, receipt will be deemed 48 hours (excluding Saturdays, Sundays and Bank Holidays) after posting.

(5) An accountant's disqualification may be notified to any solicitor likely to be affected and may be printed in the Law Society's Gazette or other publication.

**Note**

It is not a breach of the rules for a solicitor to retain an outside accountant to write up the books of account and to instruct the same accountant to prepare the accountant's report. However, the accountant will have to disclose these circumstances in the report – see the form of report in Appendix 5.

### Rule 38 – Reporting accountant's rights and duties – letter of engagement

(1) The solicitor must ensure that the reporting accountant's rights and duties are stated in a letter of engagement incorporating the following terms:

'In accordance with rule 38 of the Solicitors' Accounts Rules 1998, you are instructed as follows:

(i) that you may, and are encouraged to, report directly to the Law Society without prior reference to me/this firm/this company/this limited liability partnership should you, during the course of carrying out work in preparation of the accountant's report, discover evidence of theft or fraud affecting client money, controlled trust money, or money in a client's own account operated by a solicitor (or registered European lawyer, or registered foreign lawyer, or recognised body) as signatory; or information which is likely to be of material significance in determining whether any solicitor (or registered European lawyer, or registered foreign lawyer, or recognised body) is a fit and proper person to hold client money or controlled trust money, or to operate a client's own account as signatory;

(ii) to report directly to the Law Society should your appointment be terminated following the issue of, or indication of intention to issue, a qualified accountant's report, or following the raising of concerns prior to the preparation of an accountant's report;

(iii) to deliver to me/this firm/this company/this limited liability partnership with your report the completed checklist required by rule 46 of the Solicitors' Accounts Rules 1998; to retain for at least three years from the date of signature a copy of the completed checklist; and to produce the copy to the Law Society on request;

(iv) to retain these terms of engagement for at least three years after the termination of the retainer and to produce them to the Law Society on request; and

(v) following any direct report made to the Law Society under (i) or (ii) above, to provide to the Law Society on request any further relevant information in your possession or in the possession of your firm.

To the extent necessary to enable you to comply with (i) to (v) above, I/we waive my/the firm's/the company's/the limited liability partnership's right of confidentiality. This waiver extends to any report made, document produced or information disclosed to the Law Society in good faith pursuant to these instructions, even though it may subsequently transpire that you were mistaken in your belief that there was cause for concern.'

(2) The letter of engagement and a copy must be signed by the solicitor (or by a partner, or in the case of a company by a director, or in the case of a limited liability partnership by a member) and by the accountant. The solicitor must keep the copy of the signed letter of engagement for at least three years after the termination of the retainer and produce it to the Society on request.

Notes

(i) Any direct report by the accountant to the Society under rule 38(1)(i) or (ii) should be made to the Fraud Intelligence Unit.

(ii) Rule 38(1) envisages that the specified terms are incorporated in a letter from the solicitor to the accountant. Instead, the specified terms may be included in a letter from the accountant to the solicitor setting out the terms of the engagement. If so, the text must be adapted appropriately. The letter must be signed in duplicate by both parties – the solicitor will keep the original, and the accountant the copy.

### Rule 39 – Change of accountant

On instructing an accountancy practice to replace that previously instructed to produce accountant's reports, the solicitor must immediately notify the Society of the change and provide the name and business address of the new accountancy practice.

### Rule 40 – Place of examination

Unless there are exceptional circumstances, the place of examination of a solicitor's accounting records, files and other relevant documents must be the solicitor's office and not the office of the accountant. This does not prevent an initial electronic transmission of data to the accountant for examination at the accountant's office with a view to reducing the time which needs to be spent at the solicitor's office.

### Rule 41 – Provision of details of bank accounts, etc.

The accountant must request, and the solicitor must provide, details of all accounts kept or operated by the solicitor in connection with the solicitor's practice at any bank, building society or other financial institution at any time during the accounting period to which the report relates. This includes client accounts, office accounts, accounts which are not client accounts but which contain client money or controlled trust money, and clients' own accounts operated by the solicitor as signatory.

### Rule 42 – Test procedures

(1) The accountant must examine the accounting records (including statements and passbooks), client and controlled trust matter files selected by the accountant as and when appropriate, and other relevant documents of the solicitor, and make the following checks and tests:

(a) confirm that the accounting system in every office of the solicitor complies with:

- rule 32 – accounting records for client accounts, etc;
- rule 33 – accounting records for clients' own accounts;

and is so designed that:

(i) an appropriate client ledger account is kept for each client (or other person for whom client money is received, held or paid) and each controlled trust;

(ii) the client ledger accounts show separately from other information details of all client money and controlled trust money received, held or paid on account of each client (or other person for whom client money is received, held or paid) and each controlled trust; and

(iii) transactions relating to client money, controlled trust money and any other money dealt with through a client account are recorded in the accounting records in a way which distinguishes them from transactions relating to any other money received, held or paid by the solicitor;

(b) make test checks of postings to the client ledger accounts from records of receipts and payments of client money and controlled trust money, and make test checks of the casts of these accounts and records;

(c) compare a sample of payments into and from the client accounts as shown in bank and building society statements or passbooks with the solicitor's records of receipts and payments of client money and controlled trust money;

(d) test check the system of recording costs and of making transfers in respect of costs from the client accounts;

(e) make a test examination of a selection of documents requested from the solicitor in order to confirm:

(i) that the financial transactions (including those giving rise to transfers from one client ledger account to another) evidenced by such documents comply with Parts A and B of the rules, rule 30 (restrictions on transfers between clients) and rule 31 (recognised bodies); and

(ii) that the entries in the accounting records reflect those transactions in a manner complying with rule 32;

(f) subject to paragraph (2) below, extract (or check extractions of) balances on the client ledger accounts during the accounting period under review at not fewer than two dates selected by the accountant (one of which may be the last day of the accounting period), and at each date:

(i) compare the total shown by the client ledger accounts of the liabilities to the clients (or other persons for whom client money is held) and controlled trusts with the cash account balance; and

(ii) reconcile that cash account balance with the balances held in the client accounts, and accounts which are not client accounts but in which client money or controlled trust money is held, as confirmed direct to the accountant by the relevant banks, building societies and other financial institutions;

(g) confirm that reconciliation statements have been made and kept in accordance with rule 32 (7)and (9)(a);

(h) make a test examination of the client ledger accounts to see whether payments from the client account have been made on any individual account in excess of money held on behalf of that client (or other person for whom client money is held) or controlled trust;

(i) check the office ledgers, office cash accounts and the statements provided by the bank, building society or other financial institution for any office account maintained by the solicitor in connection with the practice, to see whether any client money or controlled trust money has been improperly paid into an office account or, if properly paid into an office account under rule 19(1)(b) or rule 21(1), has been kept there in breach of the rules;

(j) check the accounting records kept under rule 32(9)(d) and (11) for client money held outside a client account to ascertain what transactions have been effected in respect of this money and to confirm that the client has given appropriate instructions under rule 16(1)(a);

(k) make a test examination of the client ledger accounts to see whether rule 32(6) (accounting records when acting for both lender and borrower) has been complied with;

(l) for liquidators, trustees in bankruptcy, Court of Protection receivers and trustees of occupational pension schemes, check that records are being kept in accordance with rule 32 (8), (9)(c) and (12), and cross-check transactions with client or controlled trust matter files when appropriate;

(m) check that statements and passbooks and/or duplicate statements and copies of passbook entries are being kept in accordance with rule 32(9)(b)(ii) and (13) (record-keeping requirements for joint accounts), and cross-check transactions with client matter files when appropriate;

(n) check that statements and passbooks and/or duplicate statements, copies of passbook entries and cheque details are being kept in accordance with rule 33 (record-keeping requirements for clients' own accounts), and cross-check transactions with client matter files when appropriate;

(o) check that interest earned on separate designated client accounts, and in accounts opened on clients' instructions under rule 16(1)(a), is credited in accordance with rule 24(1) and (6)(a), and note (i) to rule 24;

(p) in the case of private practice only, check that for the period which will be covered by the accountant's report (excluding any part of that period falling before 1st September 2000) the practice was covered for the purposes of the Solicitors' Indemnity Insurance Rules 2000 in respect of its offices in England and Wales by:

- certificates of qualifying insurance outside the assigned risks pool; or
- a policy issued by the assigned risks pool manager; or
- certificates of indemnity cover under the professional requirements of a registered European lawyer's home jurisdiction in accordance with paragraph 1 of Appendix 4 to those Rules; or
- certificates of additional insurance with a qualifying insurer under paragraph 2 of Appendix 4 to those Rules; and

(q) ask for any information and explanations required as a result of making the above checks and tests.

### Extracting balances

(2) For the purposes of paragraph (1)(f) above, if a solicitor uses a computerised or mechanised system of accounting which automatically produces an extraction of all client ledger balances, the accountant need not check all client ledger balances extracted on the list produced by the computer or

machine against the individual records of client ledger accounts, provided the accountant:

(a) confirms that a satisfactory system of control is in operation and the accounting records are in balance;

(b) carries out a test check of the extraction against the individual records; and

(c) states in the report that he or she has relied on this exception.

**Notes**

(i) The rules do not require a complete audit of the solicitor's accounts nor do they require the preparation of a profit and loss account or balance sheet.

(ii) In making the comparisons under rule 42(1)(f), some accountants improperly use credits of one client against debits of another when checking total client liabilities, thus failing to disclose a shortage. A debit balance on a client account when no funds are held for that client results in a shortage which must be disclosed as a result of the comparison.

(iii) The main purpose of confirming balances direct with banks, etc., under rule 42(1)(f)(ii) is to ensure that the solicitor's records accurately reflect the sums held at the bank. The accountant is not expected to conduct an active search for undisclosed accounts.

### Rule 43 – Departures from guidelines for accounting procedures and systems

The accountant should be aware of the Council's guidelines for accounting procedures and systems (see rule 29), and must note in the accountant's report any substantial departures from the guidelines discovered whilst carrying out work in preparation of the report. (See also rule 44(e).)

### Rule 44 – Matters outside the accountant's remit

The accountant is not required:

(a) to extend his or her enquiries beyond the information contained in the documents produced, supplemented by any information and explanations given by the solicitor;

(b) to enquire into the stocks, shares, other securities or documents of title held by the solicitor on behalf of the solicitor's clients;

(c) to consider whether the accounting records of the solicitor have been properly written up at any time other than the time at which his or her examination of the accounting records takes place;

(d) to check compliance with the provisions in rule 24(2) to (5) and (6)(b) on payment of sums in lieu of interest; or

(e) to make a detailed check on compliance with the guidelines for accounting procedures and systems (see rules 29 and 43).

### Rule 45 – Privileged documents

A solicitor, acting on a client's instructions, always has the right on the grounds of privilege as between solicitor and client to decline to produce any document requested by the accountant for the purposes of his or her examination. In these circumstances, the accountant must qualify the report and set out the circumstances.

## Rule 46 – Completion of checklist

The accountant should exercise his or her professional judgment in adopting a suitable 'audit' programme, but must also complete and sign a checklist in the form published from time to time by the Council of the Law Society. The solicitor must obtain the completed checklist, retain it for at least three years from the date of signature and produce it to the Society on request.

**Notes**

(i) The current checklist appears at Appendix 4. It is issued by the Society to solicitors at the appropriate time for completion by their reporting accountants.

(ii) The letter of engagement required by rule 38 imposes a duty on the accountant to hand the completed checklist to the solicitor, to keep a copy for three years and to produce the copy to the Society on request.

## Rule 47 – Form of accountant's report

The accountant must complete and sign his or her report in the form published from time to time by the Council of the Law Society.

**Notes**

(i) The current form of accountant's report appears at Appendix 5.

(ii) The form of report is prepared and issued by the Society to solicitors at the appropriate time for completion by their reporting accountants. Separate reports can be delivered for each principal in a partnership but most firms deliver one report in the name of all the principals. For assistant solicitors and consultants, see rule 35, notes (vi) and (vii).

(iia) A recognised body will deliver only one report, on behalf of the company and its directors, or on behalf of the limited liability partnership and its members – see rule 35(1).

(iii) Although it may be agreed that the accountant send the report direct to the Society, the responsibility for delivery is that of the solicitor. The form of report requires the accountant to confirm that either a copy of the report has been sent to each of the solicitors of the Supreme Court, registered European lawyers and registered foreign lawyers to whom the report relates, or a copy of the report has been sent to a named partner on behalf of all the partners in the firm. A similar confirmation is required in respect of the directors of a recognised body which is a company, or the members of a recognised body which is a limited liability partnership.

(iv) A reporting accountant is not required to report on trivial breaches due to clerical errors or mistakes in book-keeping, provided that they have been rectified on discovery and the accountant is satisfied that no client suffered any loss as a result.

(v) In many practices, clerical and book-keeping errors will arise. In the majority of cases these may be classified by the reporting accountant as trivial breaches. However, a 'trivial breach' cannot be precisely defined. The amount involved, the nature of the breach, whether the breach is deliberate or accidental, how often the same breach has occurred, and the time outstanding before correction (especially the replacement of any shortage) are all factors which should be considered by the accountant before deciding whether a breach is trivial.

(vi) The Society receives a number of reports which are qualified only by reference to trivial breaches, but which show a significant difference between liabilities to clients and client money held in client and other accounts. An explanation for this difference, from either the accountant or the solicitor, must be given.

(vii) Accountants' reports should be sent to Regulation and Information Services.

(viii) For direct reporting by the accountant to the Society in cases of concern, see rule 38 and note (i) to that rule.

### Rule 48 – Practices with two or more places of business

If a practice has two or more offices:

(a) separate reports may be delivered in respect of the different offices; and

(b) separate accounting periods may be adopted for different offices, provided that:

  (i) separate reports are delivered;

  (ii) every office is covered by a report delivered within six months of the end of its accounting period; and

  (iii) there are no gaps between the accounting periods covered by successive reports for any particular office or offices.

### Rule 49 – Waivers

The Society may waive in writing in any particular case or cases any of the provisions of Part F of the rules, and may revoke any waiver.

**Note**

Applications for waivers should be made to Regulation and Information Services. In appropriate cases, solicitors may be granted a waiver of the obligation to deliver an accountant's report (see rule 35, and note (ix) to that rule). The circumstances in which a waiver of any other provision of Part F would be given must be extremely rare.

## PART G – COMMENCEMENT

### Rule 50 – Commencement

(1) These rules must be implemented not later than 1st May 2000; until a practice implements these rules, it must continue to operate the Solicitors' Accounts Rules 1991.

(2) Practices opting to implement these rules before 1st May 2000 must implement them in their entirety, and not selectively.

(3) Part F of the rules (accountants' reports) will apply to:

  (a) reports covering any period of time after 30th April 2000; and also

  (b) reports covering any earlier period of time for which a practice has opted to operate these rules.

(4) The Accountant's Report Rules 1991 will continue to apply to:

  (a) reports covering any period of time before 22nd July 1998; and also

  (b) reports covering any period of time after 21st July 1998 and before 1st May 2000 during which a practice continued to operate the Solicitors' Accounts Rules 1991.

(5) If a practice operated the Solicitors' Accounts Rules 1991 for part of an accounting period, and these rules for the rest of the accounting period, the

practice may, in respect of that accounting period ('the transitional accounting period') either:

(a) deliver a single accountant's report covering the whole of the transitional accounting period, made partly under the Accountant's Report Rules 1991 and partly under Part F of these rules, as appropriate; or

(b) deliver a separate accountant's report for each part of the transitional accounting period, one under the Accountant's Report Rules 1991 and the other under Part F of these rules; or

(c) deliver a report under the Accountant's Report Rules 1991 to cover that part of the transitional accounting period during which the practice operated the Solicitors' Accounts Rules 1991; and subsequently a report under Part F of these rules to cover the remaining part of the transitional accounting period plus the whole of the next accounting period; or

(d) deliver a report under the Accountant's Report Rules 1991 to cover the last complete accounting period during which the practice operated the Solicitors' Accounts Rules 1991 plus that part of the transitional accounting period during which the practice continued to operate those rules; and subsequently a report under Part F of these rules to cover the remaining part of the transitional accounting period.

# Index